MW00356252

I Was a Stranger

Hope for a Hidden World

Feliberto Pereira & Chris Kelley

BROWN BOOKS
PUBLISHING GROUP

I WAS A STRANGER

Hope for a Hidden World

© 2008 Feliberto Pereira and Chris Kelley

All rights reserved. No part of this publication may be used or reproduced in any manner whatsoever without written permission except in the case of brief quotations embodied in critical articles and reviews.
Scripture taken from the HOLY BIBLE, NEW INTERNATIONAL VER-SION® Copyright © 1973,1978, 1984 by International Bible Society. Used by permission. Zondervan. All rights reserved.

Manufactured in the United States of America

For information, please contact:

Brown Books Publishing Group
16200 North Dallas Parkway, Suite 170
Dallas, Texas 75248
www.brownbooks.com
972-381-0009

A New Era in Publishing™

ISBN-13: 978-1-934812-17-4
ISBN-10: 1-934812-17-X
LCCN: 2008925650

1 2 3 4 5 6 7 8 9 10

For Sheryl

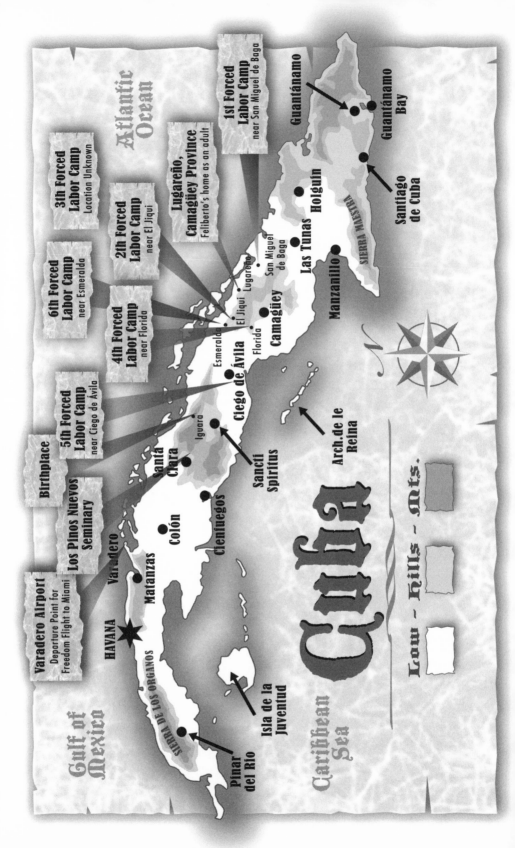

Alice

Corpus Christi

Kingsville

Gulf of Mexico

San Benito, Texas
Home of Second Christian Church
(Later Named Emmanuel Christian Church)
and La Posada Providencia Refugee Home

Bayview, Texas
Casa Compasion,
Southwest Good Samaritan Ministries

Port Isabel Processing Center
U.S. Immigration and
Customs Enforcement Detention Center

Texas

Los Fresnos, Texas
Ebenezer Christian Church
(Disciples of Christ)

Harlingen

Bayview

San Benito

Los Fresnos

South Padre Island

Port Isabel

Brownsville →
Matamoros →

U.S./Mexican Border

Matamoros, Mexico
Casa Bethel Orphanage

Mexico

Matamoros, Mexico
Derechos Humanos Colonia

Contents

Introduction

Between 1965 and 1973, twice-daily flights between Varadero, Cuba, and Miami, Florida, carried more than 261,000 Cuban refugees to freedom—the largest airlift of refugees in the history of the United States.

On board these "freedom flights" were mostly middle-class families fleeing Fidel Castro's regime.

Most arrived with little more than the clothing they wore.

The Cubans were bound by a shared experience: they had left everything familiar for a life of complete uncertainty.

On November 10, 1969, the morning flight to Miami carried a refugee named Feliberto Pereira.

Settling in Texas, he would become a servant to others.

And for thousands of people this man would embrace, strangers among us, life would never be the same.

This is his story.

Chapter One

Beneath a Mango Tree

My legs in high gear, my jet black hair slicked back, I raced up the path leading from the creek behind our family farmhouse. I headed for the back door as if a bolt of lightning were chasing me. Clutched in my right hand was a piece of cedar wood that had been whittled by my father into the shape of a microphone—his contribution to my budding career as a radio broadcaster.

I was screaming at the top of my nine-year-old lungs.

"Mommy! Mommy!"

Panting like a thirsty dog, I reached the back door and barreled into the kitchen.

"Mommy, I am feeling something all around me!"

Between gulps of air, I explained where I had been, how I had built radio antennas from tree branches for my latest imaginary "broadcast," and how I had been shouting into my wooden microphone beneath the mango tree, mimicking the voices that came from the real radio I listened to faithfully every Saturday morning.

I had played this game of "radio" many times before. But this time, something surprising had happened.

A minute or so into my broadcast, delivered to a rapt audience of four- and five-year-olds (mostly cousins), I felt a strong tug in my chest, followed immediately by a mysterious, overpowering sensation. Terrified, I sprinted for the safety of my mother's kitchen.

She looked up from washing vegetables.

"Maybe you are playing too much," she said. However, quickly reconsidering her words, she said: "*Quizas . . . Dios te quiere.*" Or *. . . maybe God wants you* (1).

And so it was that in the fall of 1947, while playing beneath a mango tree on my family's farm in central Cuba, I, Francisco Feliberto Pereira Navarro, was called by God to Christian service as a minister of the Gospel.

I had not been hit by lightning; I had been struck by awe.

Few were surprised to learn of my religious experience. Around the neighborhood of the Pereira family farm, *Finca La Lucha*, I was known from my earliest days for my spiritual curiosity and, some would say, excesses. "Why does a person have to die?" I questioned my father. "What is hell? Where is God?"

I was particularly zealous when it came to the traditions of the Roman Catholic Church, my family's longtime faith. Before I could toddle, my mother tells me, I was known to genuflect whenever I saw anything remotely resembling a cross. As a child, I always revered religious symbols and feelings. Some might say that these feelings came naturally. My ancestors fled Spain to Portugal in the early nineteenth century, eventually migrating to the Canary Islands in pursuit of freedom to worship as they wished. They were Jews who, to protect themselves from persecution, shielded their identities by changing their names. For some reason, many of the families adopted the names of fruits. Mine chose "Pereira" (pronounced puh-ray-ruh, with rolling Rs), meaning "stem of a pear."

From the Canaries, three branches of the Pereira family tree sailed to the Spanish colony of Cuba around 1850. My family settled near the historic city of Sancti Spiritus near the center of the island. Founded in 1514 by Diego Velazquez, the city is one of Cuba's seven original garrison towns; the only settlement that was truly inland, and, thus, protected from marauding invaders (2). There, my family began growing rice, beans, corn, tobacco, and sugar cane. At some point, my ancestors converted to Catholicism, the faith that European explorers from Columbus on had brought to the New World.

My family prospered. My father, Juan Francisco, was the fifth of seventeen children (3). As a tall, strapping carpenter of twenty-two, Francisco, as he was known, married the beautiful blonde girl from the farm next door, nineteen-year-old Hermenegilda Navarro—my mother. She was the sixth of eleven children. Her family had arrived in the 1880s from the Canaries, as well.

I joined the family at 4 p.m. on March 9, 1938, delivered on the family farm by my father's great aunt, a skilled mid-wife.

I grew up surrounded by family. Aunts, uncles, and cousins lived nearby in simple homes on small plots of twenty acres or so, ranchos that dotted the countryside outside our village, Iguara, in Las Villas Province. Homes there were linked by horse trails, not roads (4).

My childhood home was typical of the area's housing stock: two long wooden buildings—kitchen and dining room on one side, large living room and two bedrooms on the other—connected by a breezeway covered in thatched palm fronds. Attached to the back of the house like a big porch was a carpentry shop where my father built furniture: tables, chairs, beds, wardrobes, and dressers.

Our home was simple and unrefined. The floor was packed dirt. Light came from kerosene lamps. Water came in buckets, hauled from a well about a block away. The lavatory, seventy paces out a side door, had two rooms. One had a pit toilet; the other, a shower—a spray delivered from a pull-chain barrel.

We grew our own food. Our farmland, rich and fertile, nurtured vegetable gardens and citrus trees—grapefruits and oranges (5). We raised swine for ham and cattle for beef. And we had a plentiful egg supply, thanks to the family's self-proclaimed poultry expert—me.

I had nicknames for all my fowl—names like Coco, Pesco, Kapira, and Kretuda. At feeding times, the chickens responded to my voice the way puppies take to a nursing mother. I had as many as forty laying hens. But make no mistake: The chickens were a source of food and income, not only my friends. I sold many of them. To teach me financial responsibility, my father let me pocket the money from these poultry sales, after I'd pitched in some of the proceeds for my clothing and shoes.

Responsibility and discipline were part of the daily lessons for me and my younger brother, Eldo. My daily chores included milking cows, herding cattle, shucking corn, and, of course, feeding my chickens. Before meals, our hands had to be washed and our hair combed neatly. No shirt or no shoes meant no food. We were expected to display good manners at all times. If my parents were talking to somebody else, we could not walk in front of them. If they were speaking, we had to wait until they were finished.

A minor violation of the rules brought "the look" from my mother or father. Mid-level offenses meant serving time standing or kneeling facing a living room wall. Spankings were reserved for serious misconduct. I remember being on the receiving end of three—once for failing to kiss the hand of an arriving grandfather and twice for fighting with Eldo.

Despite our strict upbringing, there was plenty of room for mischief. At age seven, I persuaded Eldo, who was two years younger, to join me in an unauthorized visit to a nearby tobacco farm. Tempted by the weed, we rolled up a leaf, lit it, and inhaled. Woozy afterward, we hid beneath our beds until we could walk normally.

A favorite target for our mischief: uncles. Eldo and I and our cousins would set trip wires on farm footpaths, lure our uncles down the lanes, and then watch for their inevitable stumbles. Hiding in nearby brush, we'd laugh until our sides hurt. Other recreation was similarly simple: We swam in a river that threaded an uncle's pasture. I loved to ride my horse, El Dorado, a gift from my father (along with a saddle) for my sixth birthday. Of course, Eldo and I took part in the Cuban pastime—baseball. Also, reading, a passion for my father, became a pleasure for me.

In fact, it was a textbook about careers in the radio industry—a book my father had ordered from an American mail correspondence school—that led me to build my "radio station" beneath the mango tree when I was nine.

I was in love with radio—even though our family didn't own one. I would make a point to visit a neighbor and listen to his. I especially liked to stop by on Saturday mornings, when Cuban preachers were broadcasting.

Dreams of a career in radio became my favorite diversion. From the creek behind our farmhouse, I would beam my outdoor "broadcasts" to all of Cuba, clutching the carved cedar microphone that my father had made for me. I would hold my audience of young cousins spellbound—or so I hoped—with my tales of the neighborhood. When the spirit really moved me, I would hold the microphone over my head and exhort the Gospel, imitating my favorite radio preachers: "Accept Jesus as your savior and be SAVED!" I would shout.

For me, that was a familiar statement, having heard it echoed many times, and not just on the radio. When I was seven, my father converted from Catholicism to evangelical Christianity (6). His deep spiritual hunger, he would later tell me, had never been satisfied by his Catholic upbringing. He grew disillusioned by what he saw as the materialism of Catholic priests. The final straw came when a drunken priest demanded $6 in cash to baptize a godchild of my father's. One day, my father's spiritual longing led him to a local evangelist handing out religious tracts. The man urged him to read the New Testament.

As God would have it, a Bible appeared a few days later, delivered on horseback by a traveling grocer, Chi Chi, who made regular stops in our neighborhood to sell or trade for goods. My father asked the grocer if he happened to have a copy of the New Testament. "I just might," Chi Chi said, fishing inside the wooden boxes strapped to his horse. He pulled out a New Testament and traded it for some eggs and a cleaned chicken. My father opened it immediately and began reading.

As my father flipped through the pages, Chi Chi suggested that he get in touch with a minister from a nearby seminary, a man who could answer my father's theological questions. My father did so, and a few days later the minister, Amado Rodriguez, visited us at the farm.

At the end of the visit, Amado prayed with my father. Eager to experience the salvation promised in the New Testament, my father repented of his sins and asked Jesus to become his personal Lord and savior. Within a matter of days, it seemed, he became a new person. He quit smoking; previously a worrier, he now seemed calm; and where he once rarely talked about his faith, my father now spoke openly about the Bible and Jesus' love for his neighbor.

This evangelical "born again" experience created stress for my mother and my father's parents—all devout Catholics. My mother warned my father that he would suffer consequences for leaving the traditions of their fathers and mothers. His parents called him *loco*, crazy. They worried that his new beliefs would affect his business decisions.

But after several difficult months of tension, life on the farm gradually settled down. In silence, my father prayed daily for my mother to be converted to an evangelical Christian faith. And then, one day, it just happened. My mother prayed the same prayer that my father had spoken six months earlier. The Lord touched her. Soon, other relatives followed my parents' example and came to know a personal Lord and savior.

Eventually, those who thought my father was crazy came to recognize that the changes in him were real. Most accepted his new faith. Soon, my mother and father began teaching us to pray and read the Bible in the morning and before we went to bed at night. I can't recall exactly when or where I bowed my head and asked for a personal savior, but it was shortly after my father's conversion.

I prayed: "Lord Jesus, I am a sinner, and I am sorry for my sins. I repent and give my life to you. I receive you as the Christ, the son of the living God, and I take you as my Lord and savior. From now on, I want to follow you. In Jesus' name, amen."

Through prayer, God became a daily companion in my life. Sometimes, his company was overwhelming. Such was the case when, preaching to my young cousins under the mango tree, I felt the sharp tug on my heart and the warm, overwhelming sensation that started me running pell-mell for my mother's arms.

I'll never forget that moment. As I held my wooden microphone, preaching, I felt something around me that I cannot explain, something out of my control. Tears flooded my eyes but in the midst of great joy. Startled by the feeling, I ran home as fast as I could.

My mother's affirming words, God wants you, resounded in the depths of my young soul. Right then I felt the call to become a Christian worker, a minister or missionary—or both. I could not put this ambition into words until I read Matthew 9:37: *The harvest is plentiful but the workers are few* . . . . I also related deeply to the words of the Apostle Paul, who wrote (in I Corinthians 9:16): . . . *Woe to me if I do not preach the gospel!*

As I grew older, the call to serve God became greater in my heart and my life. In response, I said: 'Here I am, Lord, send me.' The Lord was preparing for me a life that began that day under the mango tree.

After his conversion, my father was determined that his children, and others from the neighborhood whose parents so desired, receive a Christian education. He organized the building of a modest one-room schoolhouse on our property and brought in three teachers—female missionary students from Amado's seminary. My father built a separate addition to the farmhouse for the three to live in.

Parents of the thirty children who enrolled pitched in to help pay the missionaries' salaries—about $15 a month for all three. Soon, the school became the community's heart and soul. We celebrated Christmas with a colorful school pageant and play. So many people came to see our dramas of the Gospel. The teachers had a strong influence on me. Their lives were a testimony to how a life of faith can be lived.

In 1948, when I was ten, my father surprised our family once more—this time by bringing home a Philco radio from the village store, a large and elaborate wooden box with big dials and even bigger speakers. You cannot imagine my joy! Strict rules were established for use of the family Philco, which had a big and expensive battery. Only news, Bible preaching, and "authorized" serials were permitted. No music.

Now, from my own home, I could listen to my favorite program, *Wings of the Dawn*, which aired at 8:30 a.m. Sundays through Thursdays (7). The hostess, Liduvina Martinez, was a schoolteacher who read Bible stories over the air. She became my hero, as the program stirred a deep feeling in me.

Meanwhile, I thrived at the small Christian school, growing in spirit and in body and developing healthy disciplines that I practice to this day. Arising each day before sunrise, I read the Bible and prayed, learning to trust God's will for my life, learning to surrender all my thoughts, feelings, attitudes, and behavior to Him.

But as I and the other children grew older, my father knew that the small school he had built wouldn't serve our needs much longer. Indeed, significant changes were sweeping through all of Cuba. Cities and towns were getting electricity, running water, and public transportation. Small businesses were becoming bigger businesses. And private industry started offering better-paying jobs to rural men with growing families—men like my father.

A man who owned a construction company, a fellow Christian, offered my father a job that he couldn't refuse: overseeing the carpentry work for all of the company's building projects. But the opportunity carried a big price. We had to leave the farm and move to the city.

In the summer of 1951, when I was thirteen, my family sold the family farm and moved to Zaza del Medio, a city of about 8,000 people twenty miles to the southeast. We bought a house and became active in a church. It was a big change, but it was a good change.

Once in the city, my father placed Eldo and me with a private teacher. But soon the church we attended opened a Christian school, and we transferred there for some classes. It was a positive environment for me. Thanks to the teachers there, I developed a strong sense of self-esteem, a confidence that with God's help, I could do anything I set my mind to do.

With our family settled in the city, I decided—as was the custom of most teen-aged boys at that time in Cuba—to turn my attention to work. Formal schooling—by then, I had the equivalent of about a fourth-grade education—would have to take a back seat. I took a part-time job at a farm on the city outskirts. Navigating an oxen-pulled plow, I planted beans and corn for the princely sum of 40 cents a day. For a boy of thirteen, it was big money. After planting season, I took another job, this one in a bakery. It paid five pesos a month, about $5, but it was hard, hot, hazardous duty. Indeed, the job nearly killed me. After six months of tending ovens, I came home one day with breathing problems and severe chest pains. At first, the doctor thought it was just a cold. But in the space of one day, I developed a bronchial infection that would not respond to medicine. Within a week, I had pneumonia.

My parents consulted doctor after doctor. The physicians told them little could be done for me. Their best advice was to expose me to the sun's warming rays. When I didn't improve after weeks, the doctors began preparing my parents for my death.

Desperate with fear, my father seemed to give up on finding an earthly cure for my illness. He prayed for God's direction. Some-how, he learned of a revival and healing service that was to take place at a church in the city of Ciego de Avila, a two-hour train ride to the west. He took me, now very ill and weak, to the service.

This was no ordinary Bible church. It belonged to Pentecostals, who believed healing came through the Holy Spirit summoned by prayer and the touch of one anointed by God. I was scared to be in the church (8). The preacher prayed for me, placing his hand on my forehead. I couldn't wait to return home by train.

Within a few days, I started feeling better. And then one day, I was healed.

The fatigue that had left me coughing and barely able to speak disappeared from my body, and I returned with a wonderful, strong voice. It was an emotional time for me. I am convinced that the Lord healed me.

I quit the bakery job and soon had a new opportunity, this one at a grocery store. I did so well that the owner asked me to oversee a second store. By the time I was sixteen, I was buying goods for the stores and paying vendors. Whenever the owner was gone, I was in charge of the other employees.

While the most popular items at the store, tobacco and liquor, would have tempted many teenagers—many Cubans smoked and drank—they were no temptation for me. I was too busy with work and with going to school part-time at night. With $15 of my earnings, I purchased a bicycle, something I'd always dreamed of owning. I painted it brilliant orange in hopes of attracting the attention of a neighborhood girl. I was in love, but of course the girl never knew it.

I worked with the grocer for three years, until I was seventeen. Had I remained in his employment, in all likelihood I would have become a wealthy young entrepreneur. The store owner was very fond of me, and he had dreams of expanding his chain. At the time, the spirit of American capitalism was sweeping through Cuba. This was good at first, but under President Fulgencio Batista, corruption became a cancer in our government and economy. A few Cuban business owners began amassing riches from a flood of American tourists pouring onto the island to enjoy gambling, prostitutes, and our sunny beaches. Batista enjoyed the support of the U.S. government, which turned a blind eye to the illegal activities poisoning our island.

Since the 1930s, Cuba—just forty-five minutes by air from Key West, Florida—had been promoted as a tropical paradise catering to pleasure-seeking Americans. It was a place that was exotic and elegant, sensual and simple. Travel literature described Havana, our capital, as "the Paris of the Caribbean" complete with magnificent hotels, art deco architecture, and exciting music.

However, the sun-drenched beaches, the palm trees swaying in tropical breezes, and the night clubs and casinos filled with cigar smoke and exotic dancers stood in stark contrast to the real Cuba. The vast majority of Cubans were poor, uneducated, and largely unemployed. They were ill-served by corrupt government officials who stole millions in tax dollars every month. By the mid-1950s, Batista's corrupt practices were sowing the seeds of revolution among the Cuban people, many of whom felt enormous resentment toward the United States for supporting the Batista regime (9).

My countrymen and I followed the news of an organized rebellion to topple Batista—a revolution led by a bearded young lawyer with a fondness for cigars: Fidel Castro. News reports said Castro and his band of rebels had fled Cuba for Mexico, promising to return soon to liberate our nation.

But in 1955, I, too, was planning a major change in my life, and my country's political turmoil took a back seat to my dreams. Turning down a bright future as a grocery executive, I decided to attend seminary and become a minister. I felt the calling strongly. While no one in my family was surprised, the decision was easier made than accomplished. There were several obstacles in my way—my young age (seventeen); my limited formal education (fourth grade); and the expense of tuition, room, and board ($15 per month), which neither I nor my parents could afford.

For guidance, I turned to a man who by now was a dear family friend: Amado Rodriguez, the man who brought my father to Christ and a graduate of the seminary I wanted to attend. I knew that getting in to seminary, and getting through it, would not be easy. But I possessed the one ingredient I needed most. I had faith—faith that had taken root in my life at the age of nine beneath a mango tree. And, I would need every ounce of it.

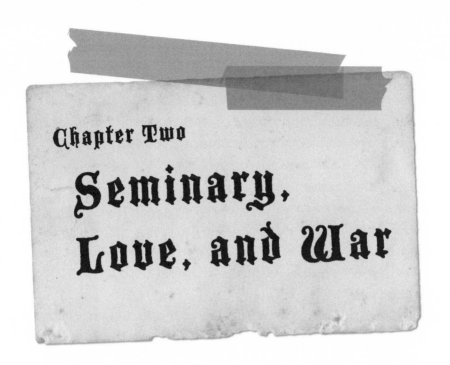

Chapter Two
Seminary, Love, and War

Amado Rodriguez persuaded the seminary to admit me on one condition: I would have to take an entrance exam to measure my existing knowledge and my future capacity to learn complex subjects. The biggest obstacle—money—was overcome when an anonymous donor agreed to sponsor my education. To help with incidental expenses, such as shoes and haircuts, my father and brother, Eldo, sent their young seminarian five pesos a month, then about $5.

At the ripe age of seventeen, barely educated but with an overwhelming desire to serve God, I entered Los Pinos Nuevos Seminary (Seminary of the New Pines) on September 15, 1955. Founded in 1928, the seminary in Placetas, Cuba, about fifty-five miles northeast from where my family and I lived, would become a "city set on a hill"—a place where I would fully embrace the light that had entered my life as a young boy (1).

Passing the entrance exam, my score confirmed what I knew in my heart: I would have a reasonable chance of success at a seminary education, which included college-level courses and, in later years, theological studies. However, I was required to take remedial classes in basic subjects, such as reading and math, until my test scores reflected the education of a high school graduate—a tall order considering my starting point.

I was enthusiastic about attending seminary. Nonetheless, leaving home was difficult. A bit of a mommy's boy—I had never been away from home before—I surprised myself, however, and quickly adjusted. In just a few days' time, I settled into a simple, disciplined routine at school.

Function, not form, ruled seminary life. My dorm room was spare and my belongings few. Because the daily uniform changed not one stitch—for males, white shirt, black tie, black or blue pants, and dress socks and shoes (for women, long dresses were required)—my entire wardrobe fit inside a small suitcase. I owned two pair of pants, two shirts, one tie, one pair of shoes, and one pair of socks that I washed nightly.

The rules were strict. No shorts for men and no short dresses for women. Male and female students could not talk to one another. Appropriate eye contact—a look akin to a nod—was all that was permitted. Good behavior was expected at all times, and a strict system of demerits enforced those expectations. Unacceptable conduct, such as speaking to a member of the opposite sex, resulted in demerits. Three demerits and you were confined to the dormitory for the weekend. Those who got more than three demerits could be suspended for up to one year. For serious infractions, such as smoking, drinking or sexual contact, there was but one consequence—expulsion.

Our time was tightly managed, but I was aided by my childhood routine of rising before the sun. After quickly shaving and brushing my teeth, I would lie on my bed or sit at my dorm room desk for thirty minutes of Bible reading before heading to the cafeteria and breakfast at 7 a.m. The bell for the first class rang at 7:30 a.m. There was little free time during the school week—about ninety minutes following supper. By 7 p.m., students were expected to be in their rooms for three hours of homework. At 10 p.m., they were to devote a half-hour to Bible reading, followed by quick showers and lights out.

My remedial education requirements took several extra hours each week. To aid my efforts, I devoured popular Spanish-language periodicals of the day: *National Geographic, Reader's Digest*, and *Popular Electronics*. I quickly developed a reputation for being well-read. In my freshman astronomy class, my well-constructed explanations about stars and solar systems earned me the nickname "scientifico"—the scientist. I was angry when my classmates called me that, and, of course, that just made them call me it more. I was also teased by a second nickname—trumpet nose. It was all in good fun.

My regular seminary classes were much more challenging: Old Testament, New Testament, homiletics (the study of preaching), hermeneutics (the study of Biblical interpretation), history, philosophy, psychology, and journalism. The curriculum was intense. The first year was very difficult for me since all the other students were much better-educated. I was the only one who had been admitted by passing an entrance exam.

The pressure of keeping up my studies—let alone earning good grades—soon overwhelmed me. At the end of the first month, I packed my suitcase to leave the seminary because my test scores were low. I did not understand what the teachers were saying. Depressed, I felt that I was good-for-nothing compared to the other students who passed their tests with flying colors.

Near despair, I sat in a corner of the seminary's chapel one day and buried my head in my hands. I was near tears when a teacher, Flora Gonzales, approached and asked why I was so sad.

"I won't make it as a preacher," I told her. "I will do other things. This is too hard for me."

Sitting beside me, the teacher said, "I know you can do this. Just have some patience. You have the capacity. Just study."

Taking her words to heart, I knuckled down on my school work, forgoing all recreation. I studied and studied and studied. My hard work soon paid off. It took me just seven months to achieve test scores that were the equivalent of a high school graduate. I praise God for this. It helped a lot that I was an avid reader. I went from the fourth grade to eighth grade to tenth grade to twelfth grade in my studies—while at the same time studying theology. By the end of my freshman year, I ranked third in my class of thirty.

Homiletics was one of my tougher classes. Preaching to my younger cousins was one thing. Preparing a sermon for a congregation of adults was another. My classmates and I practiced our preaching skills by delivering devotionals to one another. Timid and nervous during these test runs, I regularly froze up. When I attempted to speak, I was overwhelmed by insecurity. As a sophomore, I was assigned mentors—third- and fourth-year students—to coach me on preaching skills. Believing experience is the best teacher, our professors soon assigned us the task of delivering Sunday morning sermons to congregations at nearby churches.

Gradually, my confidence in the pulpit grew. I was encouraged by a special man, the founder of Los Pinos Nuevos, B.G. Lavastida. Although reserved, he was a loving person who taught us how to be faithful ministers and how to win souls. An inspiration to many, Lavastida named the seminary "The New Pines" to reflect the sturdiness of those who stick with Christ through life's storms.

My preparation for full-time ministry saw my faith practices mature and blossom. Seminary was the place where I made the transition from adolescence to adulthood. As a sophomore, I eagerly anticipated the required monthly fast—twenty-four hours without food (water only)—and the silent time spent kneeling in the chapel. In praying twelve, even sixteen, hours at a stretch, I sometimes felt that I was not even on Earth. I prepared a brief statement of my faith—a statement rooted in Bible passages and anchored by five core principles, which helped me focus my convictions (2).

By the third year of seminary, I began feeling more secure about my progress and made time to have some fun. A decent baseball and volleyball player, I was most admired for my skill at ping-pong. Agile and quick, I became a highly sought doubles player.

In my third year, I was partnered with a favorite player—my younger brother Eldo, who had decided to explore whether ministry was for him. Eldo told me that he hoped seminary would bring more purpose to his life; he also confessed that he missed his older brother. Whatever the reasons, Eldo soon became a beloved companion to my friends and me.

Monday afternoons were especially rambunctious. That's when we students were allowed two hours of recreation, from 3 p.m. to 5 p.m. Male and female students alternated Mondays swimming in a river located across a large field from the seminary, a distance of about five blocks. When the river was our domain, my friends and I would swing Tarzan-style from trees in a competition to see whose splash into the water would be biggest. As was the custom of the day, we wore no clothing. I'll never forget one Monday afternoon when Eldo swung past what was considered the river's safe drop zone, the place where the water was deepest. Eldo landed head-first in shallow water near the stream's far side. He came up dizzy and tried to swim back to us, but he couldn't make it, and he began drowning. I, along with some of my friends, rescued him. Eldo was so scared, and we, of course, were laughing our heads off.

Shaken by the experience, and probably more than a little humiliated by the laughter, Eldo ran off across the field, toward the seminary and the girl's dormitories—forgetting that he had no clothes on.

While running after him with his clothes, we laughed until our sides hurt.

Eldo, after a tough freshman year, decided that seminary life was not for him.

No laughing matter was the political turmoil engulfing Cuba. By the early spring of 1958, the region around Los Pinos Nuevos was particularly tumultuous. Once protected by the cocoon of seminary existence, our lives became inextricably linked to events unfolding in our country. By then, Batista's government had turned into a gangster-style dictatorship. He routinely ordered the murders of political opponents. His military leaders ran protection rackets, raking in hundreds of thousands of dollars each month from Havana's legal and illegal businesses. And, with the help of the U.S. Mafia, Havana—by far, the largest city in Cuba, with a population of two million—became one of the hemisphere's centers of prostitution and gambling.

Cuba's newspapers reported on these abuses, and I, along with other Cubans, was outraged by Batista's actions. We wanted him removed from power. Batista had rigged the last election so he would win, and all of us wanted the democracy that we had once enjoyed restored. Only the U.S. government's unwavering support of Cuba's army high command, along with certain well-protected U.S. business interests, kept Batista in power.

Life for rural Cubans, meantime, was wretched. Seventy percent of the rich farmland was controlled by fewer than 10 percent of the landowners. Few peasants could afford meat for the family table; only about half could read or write, and almost none had access to running water or electricity. Batista's corrupt ways had sown the seeds of revolution across Cuba. By the fall of 1958, most Cubans supported Fidel Castro, the young, charismatic rebel who had returned from Mexico in December 1956 (3).

Politically savvy, Castro welcomed foreign reporters to secret mountain hideouts to explain his "people-first" brand of politics. A flattering series of articles in *The New York Times* about his "freedom fighting" efforts appeared in February 1957. "Power does not interest me," Castro told reporter Herbert Matthews. "After victory I want to go back to my village and just be a lawyer again."

If victorious against Batista, Castro promised to hold free elections within eighteen months. *The Times'* articles were so influential that they effectively reversed the U.S. government's support of Batista. A month after their appearance, Washington announced that it was cutting off arms sales to the Batista government. Taking full advantage of the situation, Castro's forces—divided into different columns—went on the offensive, attacking Batista's troops at posts across Cuba.

My fellow Cubans and I watched these developments with keen interest. We wanted Castro to succeed in overthrowing Batista and restore democracy. Civic organizations like the Lions Club initiated fund-raising efforts to buy weapons for Castro's guerillas.

To further solidify popular support, Castro's forces established *Radio Rebelde*, a vast, clandestine broadcasting network that urged everyday Cubans to revolt against Batista. Soon, it was the most listened-to station in the nation, and thousands of Cubans, many of them poor peasants, answered the call to donate money, weapons, food, clothing, and other equipment for Castro's revolutionary movement (4). There were armed student uprisings against Batista in Havana and other cities.

By April 1958, pitched fighting between rebel and government forces reached fields surrounding Los Pinos Nuevos, forcing our school to close. All of us were sent home, and classes remained suspended until the gunfire subsided, which happened only when Batista's forces retreated. Although we deplored the violence sparked by the revolution, my seminary friends and I speculated on what Cuba's fortunes might be like under Fidel Castro. We contrasted Batista's iron-fisted, corrupt regime with Castro's promises of a kinder, gentler liberation movement. Castro promised to make Cuba a rich country, democratic and free, built on true humanistic principles.

As the fighting went on, Batista saw more and more of his troops fall to defeat, desert or change sides, and join the revolutionaries. When two key cities, Santa Clara and Santiago, fell to the rebels in late December 1958, Batista was through. On New Year's Day 1959, he, his family, and close associates boarded a plane for the Dominican Republic, where he was granted political asylum. Before fleeing, he looted the treasury, wiring $300 million in government funds—money that belonged to the Cuban people— to foreign bank accounts.

On January 7, 1959, the U.S. government recognized the provisional government led by Fidel Castro. The next day, he arrived by Jeep from Santiago to enter a jubilant Havana. I joined my fellow Cubans in celebrating Castro's victory. Church bells tolled, factory whistles blew, and ship sirens sounded.

The overthrow of Batista captivated the world. People thought Castro was the marvel of marvels. I was in favor of the revolution from the beginning, believing it would be a blessing to Cuba (5). Castro routinely invoked Christ as his role model, and he would read Bible passages at the beginning of his speeches. The revolutionaries who accompanied him were religious people who carried New Testaments in their shirt pockets, shared Christian literature, and wore medals of the Virgen de la Caridad (the Virgin of Charity), the patron saint of Cuba. In 1959, the Catholic Church in Cuba backed Castro (6).

In his victory speech, Cuba's new leader announced that government vice was a thing of the past. He promised the poor better education, better health care, and land on which to grow crops.

All of us believed that corruption in Cuban would finally be destroyed.

For me, the heady revolutionary days were extraordinary for another reason: I was in love. Jacqueline Rosales Dominguez— Jacqui—was a fellow freshman from Oriente Province, a girl with china-doll looks whom I met my first day in class. The two of us instantly bonded, though only our closest friends knew it, since we kept the news from our families. Our classes were so conservative that women had to sit on the front row and men on the back row. Talking was prohibited. Under such restrictions, one might wonder how romance could blossom. Ours did through eye contact and small signs. I always had my eyes on her, even though this was risky and logistically difficult. We communicated when the teacher wasn't looking. We also wrote letters to each other.

Jacqui was as enamored of me as I was of her. Jacqui told a friend: "I loved him, and he loved me from the first moment, in the same moment. He was the best man in the world."

On April 16, 1960, with our families looking on, Jacqui Rosales and I received our diplomas from Los Pinos Nuevos. The next day, we surprised our families by announcing our engagement. The date of our wedding would be within one year's time. While I launched my career in ministry, Jacqui would return to Oriente with her family to plan the wedding.

When the day arrived to leave Los Pinos Nuevos, I sobbed.

I had arrived at the seminary an uneducated boy of seventeen. I was leaving a young man of twenty-two, who had graduated cum laude. I was engaged to the love of my life. At the time, I wished I could have stayed in seminary. I didn't want to leave.

As I packed my belongings for the bus ride home, I had no way of knowing that my graduating class of 1960 would be the last to matriculate from Los Pinos Nuevos until 1967.

At the time, all I knew was that my first job would be as a pastor at a small church in Lugareno, Camaguey Province, a town of about 2,000 people that was a six-hour bus ride to the east. I knew that in a few weeks, I would be ordained a minister of the Evangelistic Association of Cuba, the denominational affiliation of Los Pinos Nuevos. And, of course, I knew that in a year, I would become a happily married man.

At least, these were my hopes and dreams.

Chapter Three

Castro Plunders Cuba

I tried to ignore the cynics. I neither had time nor inclination to believe what opponents of Fidel Castro were saying about the leader whom I and most of my fellow Cubans revered as a hero. I was annoyed when some of my relatives and friends began voicing their suspicions that Castro was a Communist, or at least had Communist leanings. In my mind, he was a freedom-loving, Christ-bearing populist who had his work cut out for him. Righting years of Batistas' wrongs required radical action—action that would naturally generate controversy and backlash. As for the thousands of Cubans fleeing the island for nearby Florida, fearful for their future under Castro, I truly believed that they were not giving the revolution a fair chance.

Castro's new policies did not set well with the U.S. government. For one thing, he closed the casinos, nightclubs, and brothels. Castro made it clear that Cuba was now fully independent, and the United States, once an influential overseer of the island, resented losing its dominion and its adult playgrounds.

I felt the new leader should be given an opportunity to enact long-needed reforms, especially for Cuba's poor. The changes he announced were making headlines around the world. In his first year in power, Castro did the following:

- Nationalized the Cuban telephone company.
- Announced a new law limiting land ownership to 966 acres per individual and forbidding foreign land ownership.
- Nationalized 70,000 acres owned by U.S. sugar companies.
- Signed a trade agreement with the Communist Soviet Union that included the sale of Cuban sugar to the Soviets and the sale of Soviet oil to Cuba. Within three months of the agreement, the two countries would establish diplomatic relations.
- Dismissed or accepted the resignations of twelve of twenty-one cabinet ministers—democrats he had appointed on his first day in office. Four more ministers would depart in 1960 as the revolution became more radical.
- Ordered the "trials" and execution of about 600 Batista supporters for alleged "war crimes."

With each of these developments, already strained relations between Cuba and the United States grew more tense. When a Belgian weapons ship, La Coubre, exploded in Havana harbor in March of 1960, killing eighty-one and injuring dozens—huge news in Cuba—Castro blamed the United States. (It was never determined how the ship exploded, although experts speculated that munitions were inadequately secured.)

How could I simply ignore all this? At the end of the day, I reasoned, none of Castro's actions—viewed by many as immoral, if not illegal—affected me personally. I was too busy to give much thought to politics. I had a church to grow, souls to save and—very soon—a wife and family to provide for. In the spring of 1960, I was eager to get on with my life.

Amid the chaotic events in my country, I was ordained a minister of the Evangelistic Association of Cuba on May 14, 1960. At my new church in Lugareno, I embraced the flock with vigor. I loved my congregation and the members loved me. I threw myself into my duties. I was young and skinny, and I thought my small salary was wonderful. The church, it turns out, had seen recent turmoil of its own—the previous minister was alleged to have had an inappropriate relationship with a female parishioner. Although later proven false, the allegations had split the congregation, and membership had fallen off radically. But after only a few months of calling and visiting prospects, I had membership rolls growing again.

Despite my best efforts to stay focused on my church responsibilities, I could not escape the political and social disorder triggered by the Cuban revolution. As Castro's political and economic "reforms" grew more radical, each seemed to elicit a negative response from the United States and other nations (1). Cuba became permanent front-page news throughout the world in the spring and summer of 1960, and an atmosphere of fear, suspicion, and growing isolation began to grip the Cuban people. The escalating events soon began to unnerve me and other Castro supporters.

- June 6, 1960: Cuba requests that two U.S. oil refineries, Texaco and Esso, and one British refinery, Shell, process a shipment of crude oil from the Soviet Union. The companies refuse, and on June 28, Cuba nationalizes the refineries.
- July 3, 1960: In response, the U.S. Congress passes the "Sugar Act," eliminating Cuba's 1961 quota of sugar sales to the United States.
- July 5, 1960: Cuba retaliates for the Sugar Act, ordering the nationalization of all U.S. businesses and commercial properties in Cuba.
- July 6, 1960: President Dwight D. Eisenhower cancels the 700,000 tons of sugar remaining in Cuba's quota for 1960.

- July 8, 1960: The Soviet Union announces that it will purchase the 700,000 tons of sugar cut by the United States. Fifteen days later, Communist China agrees to purchase 500,000 tons of Cuban sugar each year for five years, marking the first commercial treaty between the countries.
- August 6, 1960: Cuba nationalizes all U.S.-owned industrial and agrarian enterprises. The following day, the Cuban Catholic Church condemns the rise of Communism in Cuba. In response, Castro bans religious TV and radio broadcasts. "Those who condemn [the Cuban revolution] condemn Christ, and they would be capable of crucifying Christ because He did what we are doing," Castro says.
- September 17, 1960: Cuba nationalizes all U.S. banks.

In an address to the United Nations on September 18, Castro accuses the U.S. government of causing all the summer's turmoil by undermining Cuban independence. "…Having expelled the dictator Batista, the Cuban people have freed themselves from foreign exploitation, and have taken their fate into their own hands, firmly declaring to the U.S. monopolists: 'No more plundering of our country.' The United Nations must do all it can to remove from Cuba the . . . threat of [outside] interference," he told U.N. delegates.

By the end of the summer of 1960, my mind was in recoil. Castro's actions, and the world's overwhelming condemnation of them, had left me greatly disillusioned about the leader whom I believed held so much promise. I desperately wanted to see Castro deliver on his pledge of free elections. Instead, he seemed to tighten the noose around the remaining freedoms in Cuba during the fall and early winter of 1960 and 1961. With each new restriction, the United States retaliated, and I became more frightened and sick to my stomach.

- September 28, 1960: Castro announces creation of the Committees for the Defense of the Revolution (CDRs), essentially neighborhood watch groups whose function was to spy and report on fellow neighbors' suspicious behavior (2).
- October 14, 1960: The Urban Reform Law takes effect, nationalizing all commercially owned real estate in Cuba and ending landlord ownership of housing for profit.
- October 19, 1960: In response, the United States imposes a partial economic embargo on Cuba that excludes food and medicine.
- October 24, 1960: Cuba, in response, nationalizes additional properties owned by American interests.
- December 26, 1960: A group of Cuban parents, unable to leave the island for numerous reasons, but fearful of Castro's brainwashing techniques, have their children flown from the Havana airport to Miami. The flight signals the start of Operation Pedro Pan, the largest migration of unaccompanied refugee children in the history of the Western Hemisphere (3).

On January 3, 1961, President Eisenhower severed diplomatic relations with Cuba, saying, "There is a limit to what the United States in self-respect can endure. That limit has now been reached."

As 1961 unfolded, I was miserable. My disillusionment with my one-time hero had, by now, transformed into deep distrust, suspicion, and fury. Castro had become a dictator in total control of Cuban society.

That fact was driven home at a neighborhood coffee shop where I, still single, took my daily meals. I had begun sharing mealtimes with two men in Castro's government. They were members of the Communist party who held high positions in the agricultural reform movement, which had seized American-owned sugar cane mills and the private property of the rich. Well-trained in Marxist-Leninist philosophy, they started talking to me more and more about Communism, which, as a child, I had been taught to reject because it was atheistic.

Despite my deep misgivings about the men, I welcomed the opportunity to dine with them in hopes of learning their perspectives on the revolution. When they asked me who I was and I told them, their reaction was instant disdain.

"You are a pastor? You are a minister? You are a Christian?"

They debated me about religion. At first, the conversations were non-threatening, but they gradually turned more hostile as the two socialists warned that the clergy would have no role in the new Cuba. Ministers, the men said, were not "productive." Echoing Karl Marx, they called religion "the opiate of the people" and "a product of the *Yanquis*."

The conversations left me feeling defenseless and downcast. From my heart, I spoke to the men. I tried to present the Gospel to them, but they would not take it seriously. They would only consider things that were objective—objects that they could see and touch. After meeting these men, I was discouraged about Cuba's future. If Castro wanted men who were Communists to manage Cuba, I wanted nothing more to do with the revolution. Behind the hoopla and talk of the revolution—the uprising that was to serve the poor and common folks of Cuba—was a cruel and monstrous political system.

The revolution was like a watermelon—green on the outside and red on the inside. All of us in Cuba had been fooled. If the United States saw fit to overthrow Castro, a charge that the dictator made daily in the Cuban press, so be it.

As the winter of 1961 turned to spring, and I tried to turn my full attention to my upcoming marriage to Jacqui Rosales, I couldn't shake the sinking feeling that now overshadowed all my thoughts about my future in Cuba. My stomach was tied in knots—tension made worse by a growing chorus of family doubts about Jacqui's and my compatibility as husband and wife.

Some family members, among them my mother, had urged me to delay the marriage until Jacqui and I got to know each other better. Knowing my lack of experience in relationships, other family members pointed out some aspects of Jacqui's personality that I might not handle well. My mother knew me well—both positive and negative aspects—and she saw potential flash points of conflict between Jacqui and me. She told me to be careful—to be patient and think more about things. I was aware of some of Jacqui's issues, but I was still immature in the area of love and immature enough to believe that I could resolve anything that stood in the way of my happiness. I would change her once we were married. That was enough. Love would conquer all.

Despite the misgivings of my family, I insisted that the wedding go on as scheduled. On Saturday, March 31, 1961, B.G. Lavastida married Jacqui and me in the church I pastored in Lugareno. After a short honeymoon at a hotel in Camaguey City, we moved into an apartment above my small church.

Almost immediately, our marriage was troubled. During the second week, Jacqui grew furious about how I was conducting things in the church. In a fit of anger, she told me, "I will pick up all my belongings, and I will go back to my home."

I was scared and begged her to stay. A pastor in Cuba, left by his wife after two weeks of marriage . . . that would have destroyed me. Looking back now, I think she saw her behavior as a way to control me. But at the time, I truly thought that our difficulties just needed a period of adjustment.

The continued political turmoil in Cuba exacerbated the stress. Tension hung in the air. The island became ground zero for an international episode of historic proportion two weeks after our wedding. With the world's attention focused on twenty-seven-year-old Russian astronaut Yuri Gagarin's orbit around the Earth—

the first human space traveler, anti-Castro rebels from the United States bombed three Cuban air bases. The attacks on April 15 destroyed five of Castro's planes on the ground, killing seven men and wounding fifty-two.

On April 16, at a funeral oration for one of the bombing victims, Castro compared the air raid to the Japanese attack on Pearl Harbor, proclaiming that "the attack of yesterday was the prelude to the aggression of the mercenaries." His voice rising, Castro declared: "Because what the imperialists cannot forgive us . . . is that we made a Socialist revolution under the noses of the United States . . . and that we shall defend with these rifles this Socialist revolution!" This was the first time Castro publicly described his revolution as a "Socialist revolution."

The next day, Brigade 2506, a U.S. government-trained invasion force of 1,350 Cuban exiles, attempted a secret landing on the swampy beaches of Cuba's southern Las Villas Province—at the Bay of Pigs. Waiting for them were armed forces and citizen militia, led by Castro himself, who defeated the invaders within forty-eight hours, capturing 1,189 prisoners (4). The brief battle took the lives of 106 Brigade members and 161 Cuban soldiers and left another 55 Brigade members and 250 Cuban soldiers wounded.

The Bay of Pigs invasion had been telegraphed for weeks in press reports both in the United States and Cuba. Castro had time to mobilize a regular army of 25,000 troops and a citizen militia of 200,000. As further insurance, he ordered the detention of about 35,000 people he deemed potential collaborators, ensuring there would be no leadership to overthrow his government. When thousands of Cubans wanted to turn and fight against the Communist system, it was too late. Control of the country was in the hands of the Communists, who had planned ahead. In the days after the Bay of Pigs fiasco, Castro's army executed at least thirty-one people "convicted" of aiding in the invasion.

The Bay of Pigs left Castro's opponents bitter toward the United States. I, for one, was critical of the U.S. government. I would write about my feelings two decades later: "This was a defeat for the United States, whose fate was closely related to that of the brave and heroic brigade that could not complete the military mission . . . because the American government abandoned it on those shores without the military protection it had committed to give. It is a tragic chapter."

Meantime, Castro crowed about his victory over U.S. "imperialism." On May 1, 1961, at a 3½-hour televised outdoor rally, Castro officially declared that Socialist Cuba would no longer hold elections, saying, "The revolution does not contemplate giving the oppressive classes any chance to return to power. Do you need elections?" Castro asked the crowd. "No! No!" his audience shouted (5).

In the same speech, Castro signaled his intention to further limit religious freedom, promising early enactment of laws barring foreign priests from the island and nationalizing private schools, many of which were operated by the Catholic Church. Like many of my fellow Cubans, I was outraged, but felt I was powerless to thwart the dictator.

Within weeks, religious freedom in Cuba took a brutal beating. On June 7, Castro made good on his promise to nationalize the educational system, seizing all property and equipment from about 1,000 private schools. All religious colleges were closed and their buildings confiscated by the government—among them Los Pinos Nuevos. Castro claimed religious schools spread dangerous beliefs among the people.

At the same time, the government established a secret police force (the Ministry of the Interior), patterned after the Soviet Union's central security agency, to root out anti-Castro elements. Castro told a group of writers, artists, and intellectuals that there was full creative freedom in Cuba "within the Revolution" but none outside it. The resulting oppressive censorship, which included the jailing of prominent artists, turned Cuba into a cultural wasteland.

On September 10, 1961, Castro's muzzling of religious expression ignited a riot when a Catholic festival in Havana turned into a huge demonstration against the regime. About 4,000 worshipers had assembled for the festival's religious procession that afternoon, only to learn that that the government had canceled the procession. When the furious crowd marched on the Presidential Palace, soldiers and militiamen attempted to disperse the demonstrators by firing rifles and machine guns over their heads. One youth was killed and seven injured.

The peace that had been felt in the churches, among the people and throughout the country was destroyed by Castro's oppression of Christians. Everything was turning against religion. People were killed just because they believed! After the September 10 march, the Ministry of Interior accused the Roman Catholic Church in Cuba of plotting to overthrow the Castro regime. One hundred thirty-six Catholic priests, including the bishop of Havana, were arrested in their churches and deported to Spain (6). Pentecostals and Jehovah's Witnesses also became targets of Castro's hate squads.

Unable to sleep at night, I stewed about the prospect of being jailed and tortured for my beliefs. I was even afraid to talk to other family members out of fear they might inadvertently talk. I feared my phone was being tapped. By late 1961, the clergy in Cuba were in full-blown panic, fearing we would be imprisoned at any moment. Never before had we seen religious persecution in Cuba. It was horrible.

The stress continued to take a toll on my marriage. Jacqui's erratic mood swings would sometimes disrupt church services. A gifted musician with a beautiful voice, Jacqui openly criticized me in front of worshippers one Sunday after I failed to follow her exacting music instructions. The resulting shame from the public dressing down overwhelmed me. I earnestly prayed for my marriage—and for my country. Cuba under Castro slid deeper into isolation—a place I found myself in my marriage.

On December 2, 1961, Castro announced to the world, "I am a Marxist-Leninist and I shall be a Marxist-Leninist to the end of my life." He said that in Cuba "today we shall see to it that to be a Communist is a merit." This was the final straw for us. While Jacqui and I argued about many things, we agreed that we had no future in Cuba under a Communist dictator. Together, we made a heart-wrenching decision to leave our beloved homeland for a new life in a new country.

We thought it would be relatively easy to leave Cuba. We were in for a rude awakening.

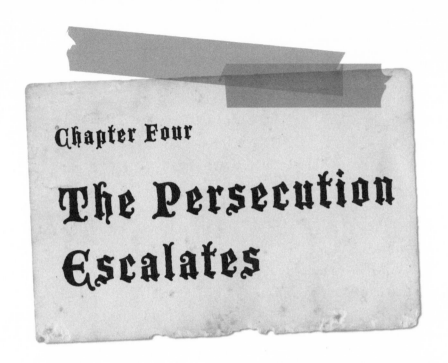

Chapter Four

The Persecution Escalates

Jacqui and I were hardly alone in deciding to leave Cuba. More than 250,000 Cubans fled the island in the first three years following Castro's rise to power. Among those who departed were tens of thousands of middle-class engineers, managers, professors, and physicians who settled in the United States. Although the exodus of hard-working Cubans drained the island of needed skilled labor—Cuba only had about six million residents—Castro seemed not to care. He was glad to get rid of the "management class," which he said was composed of "parasites" and counterrevolutionaries.

Jacqui and I decided we would go to Spain. If that option failed, then we would try to settle in the United States, where relatives had successfully begun new lives. My marriage difficulties with Jacqui, I believed, were due in part to Cuba's turmoil. The cure for us, I hoped with all my heart, was to relocate to a place where we could be ourselves without fear of intimidation, threats, or arrest.

"I came to feel critical of my country," Jacqui said. "I did not want to leave Cuba. But I couldn't stand it anymore under Communism. Life was terrible. There was no medicine. They had rationing, so they would sell us little food. When clothes would come into stores, we could buy one thing, maybe two. You could talk about nothing. If you talked against Castro, they took you to jail."

Once our decision was made to depart, we wasted little time. Under Castro, it was illegal for citizens to leave Cuba without government permission.

I left my small town in late 1961 and traveled to Havana, where I easily persuaded officials at Spain's embassy to issue Jacqui and me a travel visa since my ancestors were from Spain. Armed with the travel visa, I sought an exit visa from the Cuban government. My request was refused with no explanation. By early 1962, despite his public statements to the contrary, Castro had begun to worry about the torrent of people leaving the island and, I would learn later, had secretly enacted a policy ending exit visas. By this time, the newly elected young president of the United States, John F. Kennedy had also grown weary of Castro (1).

I was crestfallen. With legal avenues of departure closed, Jacqui and I decided to make the best of the circumstances. I would embrace my calling as a minister until I could find a way for us to leave Cuba safely. However, by 1962, being a Christian in Cuba wasn't easy. I figured that my request for an exit visa had probably resulted in my being targeted by the secret police as part of the anti-Castro "elements."

My first encounter with official government harassment came in early 1962 when I received a visit from a Communist party official. Increasingly, privately owned homes in Cuba were being converted into houses of worship because Castro had banned construction of new churches. The official wanted to turn a church house used by my congregation for neighborhood worship services into a private home for a woman known to be a prostitute. I told him that he could not have the house. The party official was belligerent. He told me it would eventually be confiscated, and if I resisted, I would be imprisoned. He said, "Ministers are parasites. You live from others who give you money for the church. You aren't producing anything in the Communist system, and you have to produce in order to eat." I tried to explain my duties. I told him that I attend to the spiritual needs of those who came to church, but he refused to understand. I tried to compare what I did to the work of psychologists and psychiatrists, but he said, "You're not one of them. And, we don't like them, either. You have to produce!"

The confrontation left me rattled. Because I refused to sign over the house, I feared I would be watched closely from then on, my every move tracked and recorded. Warranted or not, such fear soon penetrated the very fiber of Cuban life, especially among Christians who could be whisked away to prison at any moment for their religious beliefs.

The harassment continued. A Communist-affiliated union for sugar cane workers opened a meeting hall across the street from our small church. To antagonize churchgoers, union leaders placed large speakers outside the meeting hall's entrance and blasted the Communist party anthem during Sunday services. Their attempts to disrupt our worship failed. Even though it was hot, we closed the doors and windows to shut out the noise. But the union leaders seemed to stop at nothing. They even went so far as to entice church members' children to the hall with hard-to-get candy. Once inside the hall, the children were subjected to lectures on being good Communists. They tried to destroy the faith of these children.

Local Communist leaders also attempted more subtle forms of intimidation. They resorted to sending "visitors" to my church, hoping to entrap me. Following services, the newcomers would attempt to engage me in provocative conversations about politics, Castro, and the Communist party. They posed as false Christians.

I told them I had no problems with the system. I could never tell them, "I know you are a spy, and you're trying to catch me up in something." I would have been thrown in jail. During our conversations, I could feel the tension coming from them. Still, I just preached the Gospel to them.

If it weren't for the prayer and support that my neighbors and I provided each other during this period, the anxiety would have eaten away at all of us. I was known as a caring pastor, available day or night when a need arose. And there were many needs. By the fall of 1962, Cuba's economy was in collapse due to the U.S. embargo of goods to the island.

In a vain attempt to manage the crisis, Castro imposed strict food rationing. Rationing booklets called libretas—still a mainstay of Cuban life today—severely restricted food choices. Everyday staples like eggs, meat, and milk became luxury items. Also imposed were wage scales, which set maximum and minimum salaries. The country's monetary policy was ruinous for many families. When the government changed currency overnight, those who did not have their savings in state-run banks could not exchange old pesos for new ones. Savings kept in private banks were worthless. This devastated many families.

Castro's friendship with the Soviet Union further isolated Cuba. In an effort to stabilize the economic chaos and to fend off further attempts by the United States to invade, Castro sent his brother, Raul, the armed forces minister, to Moscow in July 1962 to secure additional Soviet military backing. Eager to establish a strategic base in Cuba—to counterbalance the U.S. bases ringing the U.S.S.R—the Soviet Union agreed to install forty-two medium-range ballistic missiles on the island.

The plan, of course, erupted into a world crisis when President John F. Kennedy made it clear that Soviet missiles would not be planted ninety miles from U.S. shores. I caught a firsthand glimpse of the secret scheme when, one morning, I and other early risers in my town saw the missiles on transport trains. Black nylon covers hid all but the missiles' tips. I remember seeing them and being scared.

When U.S. intelligence satellites confirmed the presence of the weapons, President Kennedy demanded the withdrawal of "Soviet offensive missiles" from Cuba, and on October 22, 1962, he imposed a naval blockade of the island to prevent further shipments. Kennedy also demanded the withdrawal of Soviet L-28 bombers, and he wanted a commitment from the Soviets not to station strategic weapons in Cuba in the future. For the next twelve days, "the world held its breath," as historian Leslie Bethell wrote. "Not since the dropping of nuclear bombs on Hiroshima and Nagasaki had nuclear warfare seemed so imminent. Poised on the edge of war, the two superpowers jockeyed over their military relationship."

While the Cuban missile crisis received wall-to-wall news coverage in the United States, my neighbors and I were starved for information about the standoff. Castro had muzzled Cuba's last independent newspapers and TV stations. To get news reports about the crisis, we huddled over a short-wave radio, hoping to pick up U.S. broadcasts. We would keep the volume low, not wanting to be turned in to the neighborhood spy watch (2).

As suddenly as it began, the crisis ended. The Soviet Union, without consulting Cuba beforehand, backed down and pulled its missiles and forces from the island in exchange for a pledge from the United States not to invade Cuba. (While there is nothing in public government records to confirm that Kennedy made an explicit commitment not to invade, that has become the de facto policy of the U.S. government.) The Cuban missile crisis left the Soviet Union publicly humiliated. Castro, who had no role in negotiations between the two superpowers, was furious at Soviet leader Nikita Khrushchev—who, politically damaged by the crisis, was replaced two years later by Leonid Brezhnev. But Cuba needed the Soviets, and Castro eventually calmed down and reconciled with his Communist comrades. (To mend fences, the Soviets hosted Castro on a forty-day diplomatic visit during the spring of 1963.)

Resolving the missile crisis did nothing, however, to help Cuba's ailing economy. By the late summer of 1963, my congregation could no longer sustain my small salary, and it was reduced to just a token payment. That bad news was followed by another alarming development: It was disclosed that Castro's secret police had begun randomly arresting Protestant clergy, rounding them up in the wee hours of the night. It was a horrible shock, and all of us were nervous.

With my church salary reduced, I looked for a second job to support Jacqui. I got one from the only employer hiring in Cuba—the government. I sought work not as a bureaucrat, but as a junior high school teacher. There was a great need for teachers, and I needed the money. So in September 1963, I began teaching industrial arts—wood shop, carpentry, electrical repair, and sugar cane production techniques—to seventh-, eighth-, and ninth-graders. I chose to teach industrial arts rather than science or social studies, for which I was more passionate, because the Castro government required all science and social studies instructors to strictly teach the theory of evolution and Marxism and Leninism and to affirmatively disavow religious faith in writing. I refused to do so and settled on a teaching position that didn't require a statement of ideology.

Anything that would force me to renounce my faith was not negotiable. I prayed always to the Lord for help, to give me the strength never to betray Him. You have to abide by the principles of your faith. The Bible asks, "Are you on the side of faith or not?" I never considered rejecting mine.

My students and I were a good fit. I loved teaching them, and they responded well to my instruction. To prepare for my new career, I voluntarily enrolled in education classes that were held on Saturdays in a city about an hour away by train or bus. Upon completing the two-year training program, I received a certificate in secondary education. I also took a typing class during the evenings at a local business college and was certified as typing one hundred words a minute.

To help ward off further harassment from the Communist party, I also volunteered more than three hundred hours in one six-month period on "revolutionary" duties—tasks such as tending government-owned gardens at schools, citrus orchards, and sugar cane fields. I racked up so many volunteer hours that I soon received distinction as a member of Castro's *vanguardia*, vanguard, which entitled me to purchase a refrigerator for my family. Only the favored few could even own a refrigerator.

I came to love teaching. Students thrived in my classes and, as a result, I received a high rating from my school principal.

I kept meticulous records on students' performances so that I could help them and their parents track their progress. However, most teachers were required to record more than just grades. They were also asked to secretly maintain files on a student's "revolutionary integration"—whether the student was a good Communist or not. These records were not shared with anyone but Communist party officials. As an industrial arts teacher, I was not required to keep such records. However, my knowledge of the secret records program would later haunt me.

Despite my success in the classroom, my teaching certification efforts, my exemplary performance ratings, and my work as a volunteer, I could not escape the attention of local Communist party leaders. They tried to have me ousted from my teaching post. The reason: I continued to preach the Gospel and minister at my small church. The Communist party secretary thought I was a dangerous teacher because I was a Christian. I did not talk about Christianity to my students. I did not talk against the revolution. I fulfilled all of my teaching requirements. I even worked extra hard because I knew the Communists were watching me.

Nonetheless, fending off the Communists proved impossible. The situation came to a head when the local party secretary met with my boss, the school principal, in an attempt to have me fired.

"Why is he allowed to work as a teacher?" the party secretary asked the principal, who later recounted the visit for me. "He is a minister!"

But the principal stood up to the party official and backed me, saying I was one of his best teachers.

Even so, the Communists would not give up their efforts to have me fired. They assigned spies to watch me. This fact came to light in early 1964, when I chaperoned students on a trip to a nearby town where they performed a dramatic play. During the performance, one of my students read a poem she had written, using words and themes from one of Cuba's oldest patriotic songs.

Castro considered the song to be against his revolution, and any reference to it was banned. Those watching me reported the poetry recital to the Interior Ministry police, who accused me of staging the girl's performance (3). I was immediately placed under formal investigation. The police wanted to know if I forced the young lady to recite the poem. Of course, I did not. But one had to express devotion to Castro in order not to create suspicions. After this incident, I was nervous as a teacher because I knew so many eyes were watching me.

In fact, the situation was graver than I imagined. Local party leaders wanted me "to disappear." I learned of this from a party official whom I befriended during the 1959 revolution. My friend, Chi Cho, was a self-professed atheist and active in local Communist party meetings. Nonetheless, when Chi Cho was wounded during a battle against Batista's army and sent home to recuperate, I paid him a visit. Although he was an atheist, he was still my friend. I visited him at home, and that touched him deeply. He said to me, "People I fought with won't even come see me. Here you are a minister, and you are visiting me."

Chi Cho told me that the local Communist party secretary would not stand for having a pastor working in his district as a teacher—apparently a one-of-a-kind situation in Cuba. One way or another, Chi Cho said, the Communists would find a way to accuse me of an abhorrent crime and eliminate me. He told me that he was in a meeting where party leaders hatched plots to have me killed or imprisoned for life. The Communist party secretary told Chi Cho that my many volunteer hours were just a front and that I was an informant working for the CIA.

It was a dangerous situation for me—a predicament that took a dramatic turn around midnight one evening when I was awakened by a persistent knock at my front door.

"Who is it?" I asked, not wanting to open the door.

"It is me, Chi Cho."

I let in my friend. I reached for a light switch.

"Don't put on the light," Chi Cho said. "Let me talk to you in the dark. What I have to tell you, I need to tell you man to man. Don't talk about what I am going to tell you or I will be killed."

Chi Cho paused, then continued. "Feliberto, it is very necessary that you try to escape Cuba now. Leave now. You must!"

I shook my head. I wanted to leave Cuba desperately, but not this way. Besides, Jacqui was now eight months pregnant with our first child. I told him, "Chi Cho, you know very well that I am not doing anything against the system. I was a vanguard of the revolution. I am classified a top teacher by my school. I am doing nothing wrong."

Chi Cho replied, "I know. That is why I am here. Take my advice. Try to get out of Cuba."

"I am doing okay," I said. "I am fine with the system. I don't have a problem with anybody but the party secretary."

"But you are a religious person!" said Chi Cho, who then immediately left the house, clearly frustrated by my response.

Two weeks later, Chi Cho came to my house once more around midnight and in the same manner.

"I was in a meeting of the [Communist] elite," Chi Cho said. "You have to be out of Cuba one way or another. You will not have any chance to be accused. You will be killed. You are a very honest person, a hard worker. You have done nothing for which we can accuse you even though there have been many attempts."

Chi Cho got nose to nose with me.

"It is shameful for a Communist party secretary to have a religious person in his region who is also a teacher. And the people love you, and that is very bad. You are seen by the party as a divisionist. You need to go to the airport, take a pistol, and hijack an airplane out of Cuba. Or, go to some fishermen, steal their boat and leave for Miami!"

I was deeply moved by my friend's concern for my welfare. But, I told Chi Cho, "I cannot do that. I have done nothing wrong from which to run. I will leave on my own choice."

Several weeks passed with no further contact from Chi Cho. And for once, anxiety was replaced by joy in the Pereira household. Our first child, a boy named Joel, arrived on May 1, 1964.

The happy occasion was followed by more good news. The local Communist party secretary whom Chi Cho warned me about was himself banished from the region. Apparently, he had a checkered past, which came to light when an old newspaper article was sent anonymously to the Interior Ministry. In it, the party secretary had pledged his support to Batista. He was quoted as likening Castro's revolutionary efforts to "bandits taking cows."

I never found out who sent the article to Castro's secret police. In any case, with my Communist nemesis in exile, Jacqui and I settled into a relatively peaceful routine for the next sixteen months. While both of us still clung to the hope of leaving Cuba some day, we were busy with a baby, the church, and my teaching duties.

Then, in September 1965, another curve ball was thrown our way.

The superintendent of schools in the district where I taught approached me, asking if I would become principal of the junior high. I was more than qualified for the position; I had filled in many times as acting principal. The new job would carry a nice raise and offer me prestige in the community.

Even so, I declined the offer. The position would exact a requirement I would not accept. In order to be approved as principal, I would have to sign a document stating that I was an atheist. As a minister of the Gospel, I could not. I would not.

The school superintendent, who genuinely liked me, appealed to me, asking that I reconsider. I was reminded that as head of the school, I would enjoy extra privileges not available to most Cubans. I was given two more weeks to consider the offer.

I had already made up my mind, so waiting two weeks to tell the superintendent "no" again didn't bother me. But the whole episode took a weird twist a few days later when I received a visit from an agent of the Interior Ministry. The agent was brusque, telling me flat out to sign the forms and take the principal's job. When I politely declined, the agent tried another tactic—intimidation.

Opening a file that he had brought with him, the agent started reading from notes inside. He recited my history. He had a well-documented file. He told me who my friends were and when they visited my home. Although the ploy failed, it made me nervous. I politely declined the job offer once more. But the agent wouldn't back down. As if to sweeten the proposition, he offered me a moonlighting job that would carry additional benefits. The agent wanted me to spy for the Interior Ministry!

"We know that you know persons who are not in favor of the system," he said. "You can work with us. We will assign you a number. You will have good rewards. You will continue preaching, but we want you to inform on other ministers, too." Needless to say, I rejected that offer, as well.

The security agent then told me: "Well, you had the opportunity. And now you will be suffering the consequences." The cruel words lingered in my mind.

By the end of September 1965, I was in prayer daily about what God wanted next for my life. The birth of our son seemed to have stabilized our rocky marriage. Although I turned down the principal's job, I retained my teaching position, which paid the bills. And, I was still pastor of the small church, although I was not content with my part-time status there. My calling was to be a full-time pastor, a position that seemed impossible to achieve in Cuba.

In the deepest recesses of my heart, what I truly desired was a safe exit from Cuba. I wanted a fresh start in a place where my family could live in security, be free to express our thoughts, and, above all, worship God and share the good news of Jesus' saving grace.

I wanted to come to America.

But the big question remained: How? The answer soon arrived in the morning newspaper.

Chapter Five

Tyranny Takes Root

Ever since the missile crisis three years earlier, Castro had refused exit visas to tens of thousands of Cubans, including me. Leaving Cuba seemed an impossible dream. However, on the morning of September 30, 1965, Cuba's government-run newspapers carried a front-page story about an extraordinary offer. If the report was to be trusted, Castro had a sudden and shocking change of heart. The story quoted the Cuban dictator as offering safe travel for any Cuban who wished to join relatives living in the United States.

The government newspaper said Cubans who wished to depart the island would be permitted to leave in small boats at the port of Matanzas, on Cuba's northern coast. Once in U.S. waters off Florida, the travelers would transfer to U.S.-bound boats for the remainder of the journey.

"We do not force—we have no reason to force—absolutely anyone to like our revolution, to like Socialism, to like our ideas and Communist society," Castro said in a speech he had given the day before at Revolution Plaza in Havana. "We have enough people who fight for it and are ready to give their lives for it . . . It is not we who are opposed to the departure of those who want to go. . . . This is our policy. No one who wants to go need go in secret . . . they can go without danger and without risks of any kind."

I was incredulous. Why would Castro suddenly allow what surely would become a mass exodus of hundreds of thousands of Cubans? The offer was just another example of his cruel manipulation of the Cuban people, I concluded (1).

On October 1, the Cuban newspapers carried more news on the offer, to which Castro had added a new twist. Effective October 10, the dictator said, the Cuban government would allow any Cuban wishing to leave the country to fly from Cuba to Miami. The Havana government would pay for the daily flights. The U.S. government would have to cover only the costs of landings and takeoffs at Miami International Airport.

And Castro made a third extraordinary offer: Cubans already living abroad—exiled Cubans—would be granted entrance visas to pick up relatives who wished to leave the country. Excluded from leaving the island, however, would be persons in critical occupations, men fifteen to twenty-six, since they were subject to military service, women with dependent children of school age, and political prisoners.

Castro's proposals left me confused. There had to be a catch. What was it, I wondered? I distrusted the dictator's explanation that allowing the exodus would put a stop to "Yankee propaganda" about the thousands of Cubans who were fleeing their homeland illegally because of oppression.

A few days later, Cuban newspapers carried even more news on the plan. This time, though, I believed what I read. The U.S. government had agreed to Castro's proposal. President Lyndon Johnson announced that the United States would gladly welcome any emigrating Cuban to its shores. ". . . I declare this afternoon to the people of Cuba that those who seek refuge here in America will find it," he said at an October 3 ceremony on Liberty Island in New York Harbor, where he signed a new U.S. immigration law.

President Johnson said arrangements to accept Cuban refugees would be coordinated through the Swiss embassy in Havana (2). The program, he said, would give first preference to Cubans who had immediate relatives in the United States. Second priority would be given to political prisoners of the Castro government—a provision that Castro never seriously considered.

Upon reading President Johnson's words, my body tingled, and my heart filled with hope. Leaving Cuba had been my impassioned prayer for three years. Jacqui and I had long discussed our desire to leave the island with our respective families, and the decision was one both our families supported. The harassment I endured at the hands of Communist party officials had confirmed that Jacqui, Joel, and I would have no future in Cuba under Castro. Jacqui, in fact, had been in contact with relatives in New York City who had made a longstanding offer to sponsor any relative who wished to emigrate (3).

Dubbed "freedom flights" by the press, the movement of Cubans would become the largest airborne refugee operation in American history. And we would be part of it. The Cuban government soon announced how. Any Cuban desiring to leave the island need only visit the nearest police station, fill out some forms, and wait for official word on the flight to Miami. That very week, I went to the police station and put in my application. There were lines of people there.

In mid-November 1965, our notice arrived in the mail. Our family's application for exit visas and passports had been processed. In addition to the three of us, Jacqui's mother, Maria, had decided to leave Cuba, as well. A widow, her husband died when Jacqui, the couple's only child, was a toddler. Maria had been living with us since shortly after we were married. All of us were now officially on the waiting list. Holding that letter in my hand, I allowed my mind to dream. Freedom could be ours in a matter of days, I thought. Overcome with emotion, I wept in thanksgiving.

And then, the other shoe dropped. In Castro's Cuba, there always seemed to be another shoe dropping. Our journey to freedom would not be so easy—or fast.

In late November, the local Communist party made public the names of government workers who had applied for a freedom flight—including schoolteachers. The intent was to publicly shame us. The government wanted our neighbors, our students, and their parents to humiliate us. And in a few days, reports of such harassment surfaced. In a nearby town, several teachers who had applied to leave were taunted as "traitors" and pelted with eggs. It did not happen in my case. My students loved me a lot, as did their parents and other teachers, too.

But the persecution did not end with insults. Across the island, Castro sought revenge against any Cuban who had applied to leave the country. After branding those of us seeking exit visas *gusanos*—"counterrevolutionary worms"—he ordered the firing of all government employees trying to leave. Then he ordered all men who were terminated from government jobs to work at *granjas*— forced labor camps—until their turn to leave Cuba arrived.

Castro's revenge was mean-spirited. He had never disclosed that the offer to leave Cuba carried such dire consequences for those who accepted it. We all expected to keep our jobs until the government allowed us to leave the island. Instead, all of us were expelled from our positions, our salaries taken away. I never expected that kind of retaliation.

In early December, the principal of my school called me in. With great shame, he told me: "I have to do this. I have to fire you. You know this is a regulation of the Communist system. You cannot teach anymore. You cannot come to the school anymore." I was crushed by the words. Although my calling was to full-time Christian ministry, I had developed a love for teaching. And my students loved me. My last day on campus was filled with terrible sadness—for me, my students, and my teaching colleagues. As I packed my belongings, I thought, "When it arrives, freedom will come at a high price." Although I earned but a token salary for my role as a pastor, I was thankful that I could, at the least, cling to it for meaning and hope.

The Cuban government wasted no time re-assigning us *gusanos* to work at sugar cane fields on the city outskirts. It all happened so quickly. Within the space of a few days, I went from being a teacher to backbreaking field labor. I was required to report at 5 a.m. and work a twelve-hour shift, for which I received a few pesos a day. Hour after hour, I hacked and stacked sugar cane stalks. Unaccustomed to such work, my body became traumatized. But I had no choice. I would be jailed if I refused to work. And, I needed the meager subsidy that came with the job—the equivalent of $5 per month in the United States today. As a teacher, I earned an amount equivalent to $34 a month.

The long hours in the fields soon took their toll. I would arrive home each evening, shower, and collapse to sleep, often without eating. The situation was hard on Jacqui and Joel. I was ashamed of my situation. Not wanting to worry my parents, I did not tell them about losing my teaching position or about my new "job."

The Christmas season was far from joyous. Indeed, the Communists did their best to spoil it for us. One cruel example came after I stood in line for hours at a toy store to purchase a rare commodity in Cuba—a small bicycle with training wheels for Joel. It was to have been a wonderful gift for Christmas, even though the holiday was officially outlawed (4). But the next day, a group of uniformed party leaders appeared at my doorstep and confiscated the bicycle.

"You are not allowed to have a toy for your son," one of the men told me. People leaving Cuba did not deserve such prized possessions. He took Joel's bicycle, and I could do nothing about it. Any last doubts about remaining in Cuba were erased that day.

The new year brought more harassment. In early January, local neighborhood spy watch officials came to the homes of those seeking exit visas to make an inventory of possessions. They came unannounced to our home and examined everything we owned. Even if we broke a glass, we were required to save the pieces and show them to local spy watch leaders. Our privacy was subject to invasion all the time.

And there was more humiliation. Families on the list to leave Cuba were forced to wait at the end of the line at their neighborhood grocery store for their chance to purchase rationed goods, such as meat and eggs. Priority was given to residents who were card-carrying Communists.

I allowed none of these ordeals to shake my faith. I continued to believe with all my heart that God would deliver me and my family from Castro's bondage. I knew many others were in far worse circumstances—faithful Christians, political dissidents, artists, intellectuals, and others whom Castro had deemed a potential danger to society. These poor souls had been sent to maximum security camps called Military Units to Aid Production (UMAPs or "Unidades Militares para la Ayuda de Producción")—Nazi-style concentration camps.

The camps, located largely in the rural Camaguey Province of central Cuba, opened in November 1965. Their official purpose—jump-start Cuba's failing economy by putting "troublemakers" to work (5). Men confined there had been officially labeled "socially deviant" and, as a result, subject to harsh military discipline, isolation, and undernourishment. Among those sent to the camps were thousands of homosexuals in need of "re-education."

Also among the detainees were religious leaders, such as Jaime Ortega, now a Roman Catholic Cardinal. Hundreds of Jehovah's Witnesses, Pentecostals, and Protestants were also banished to the camps.

Among the Protestants was a dear friend of mine, Aurelio Lopez, a pastor who was sent to a camp near my town. I knew Aurelio from Los Pinos Nuevos. His only crime—being a Christian. Aurelio had not been allowed visitors in three months and his family, who lived in an adjacent province, had been worried sick about him. When the camp announced it would finally allow visitors on the last Saturday in January, I went to check on my friend so I could let his family know of his welfare.

Given the hostile environment, some might say it was not smart for me to see Aurelio, since I could be recognized as a minister or a "gusano." But I believe that brothers and sisters in Christ are called on to take risks for fellow believers. Aurelio was my friend. He was a pastor.

On Saturday, January 29, 1966, I rode my eleven-year-old motorcycle to a field near the camp, hid it among stalks of sugar cane, and started toward the camp entrance. As I approached the gate, dread overcame me. The camp would have fit in Hitler's Germany. Rifle-toting guards atop watchtowers oversaw the grounds, which were surrounded by high barbed-wire fences. Prisoners, their faces vacant and filled with despair, walked in circles around the main yard. Many of them were filthy and gaunt.

I had disguised myself to look like a farmer. I wore a nondescript shirt, khaki pants, sandals, and a hat made of palm leaves. I carried a fresh loaf of bread Jacqui had baked for Aurelio. After a light pat down, I was allowed inside the camp. The gate snapped shut behind me. Seeing me from a short distance away, Aurelio beamed and walked quickly to shake my hand.

We embraced. Then, just as I handed Aurelio the loaf of bread, a prison guard grabbed my arm. A man behind me yelled, "I know you!" Flipping around, I instantly recognized the man. He was a leader of the local Communist youth league whose headquarters were across the street from my church.

"You are a pastor of a church!" the man said, as if the words instantly sentenced me as a criminal.

In a flash, a half-dozen rifle-toting soldiers rushed toward me. They removed a small Bible and several papers from my shirt pocket and hustled me away. I glanced at Aurelio, who looked on in stunning disbelief.

I was taken to a cinderblock structure not far from the front gate. The guards stood me against a wall facing away from the main prison yard. In front of me, six soldiers, their rifles resting on their shoulders, stood awaiting orders. For the next ninety minutes, I faced a firing squad.

The camp's commander eventually appeared and began an expletive-filled interrogation. He accused me of smuggling in Bible tracts—"CIA propaganda"—aimed at inciting prisoners to rebel. I had brought the tracts and pocket New Testament for Aurelio. In hindsight, it wasn't a smart thing to do, but at the time, I thought only of my friend's spiritual welfare.

The prison commander's grave accusations shook me to my core. He believed the Bible verses contained codes from the CIA, which he accused me of trying to pass to the prisoners. Then he accused me of being a member of the CIA and started cursing at me. In Cuba, at that time, when the authorities made that kind of accusation against you, you knew you stood a good chance of being killed. The commander told me that he was eager to mete out punishment—death by firing squad—for my "crime." He was merely awaiting the go-ahead from his superior, a military captain known to order groundless executions.

My knees quaked from fright. I began to pray. I was sure I

would die. I asked the Lord to forgive me, to receive me, to help me, to keep my family safe. Then, I quieted my fear enough to listen to the Lord for a few moments. Embraced instantly by God, I felt immediate relief and confidence.

Then, all of a sudden, something happened that I have no explanation for. I felt great warmth from my head to my legs. My fear began to disappear. I felt joy and peace. It was like a miracle. I felt taller than all of the soldiers. I began to speak to them in a very fast voice.

Apparently feeling taunted by me, the soldiers raised their rifles as if preparing to fire. I cannot remember exactly what I said to them, but one phrase was: "If you want to know who I am just call"—and then I spoke the name of the local Communist party secretary who had wanted me banished but who himself was later banned from the party. "He will tell you who I am!"

Upon hearing the name of the disgraced party leader, the soldiers instantly lowered their rifles, as if they had just caught a glimpse of an overwhelming power. I continued speaking, but I don't remember what I said. The Bible says not to worry about what to say in circumstances where wisdom is needed—the words will come. I was not in control of my words. All I know is that a peace and joy overcame me and all my fear disappeared.

A few minutes later, the captain known for his cruelty appeared and spoke to the prison commander in a voice loud enough for me, standing 100 feet away, to hear.

"Give him sixty seconds to disappear, or I'll not guarantee his life."

The commander approached me and repeated the instructions. "You have one minute to disappear, or we will not guarantee your life."

Believe it or not, my first instinct was to stay put. There were stories of Cuban authorities releasing prisoners from firing squads and telling them to run for their lives, only to shoot them in the back. When family members or others inquired about the death, officials would have a ready answer: the prisoner was trying to escape, we ordered him to stop, and when he didn't, he was shot.

I thought they wanted to do that to me. But I was in no position to refuse the captain's offer. I peeled away from the camp. I ran like never before in my life. No shots were fired.

I didn't stop running until I reached the motorcycle that I had ditched in the cane field. I quickly pushed it to the road, kick-started it, and sped away. Shifting quickly into high gear, I fishtailed down the bumpy dirt road like my life depended on it. I arrived home a nervous wreck. As Jacqui made me some "nervous tea"—a mixture of Cuban herbs aimed at easing mental strain—I told her what had happened.

There was no doubt in my mind that I had been condemned to die that day and that the Lord intervened to save me. At that time, when the Communists accused you of working for the CIA, you immediately qualified for execution without a trial.

As if the new year had not begun eventfully enough, March of 1966 brought another new trial. I received a letter from Cuban authorities notifying me that I would not be allowed an exit visa until I could verify my age. Apparently, some government records showed me to have a birth date that would have made me twenty-six and, thus, still eligible for compulsory military service in the Cuban army. Castro's offer for exit visas excluded males of military age. A big part of the problem was my boyish appearance. I simply looked much younger than my twenty-seven years. To prove my birth date was March 9, 1938, and not one year later as these documents apparently showed (although I never saw them), I produced an original birth certificate at several government offices.

I finally won my case, and I was fortunate that I had. Castro's exit visa exceptions, such as age restrictions, created hardships for many Cuban families who wished to leave. For example, if you were the father or mother of a boy who was fifteen, the boy had to remain and serve in the military. As a result of these restrictions, many families who had applied to leave Cuba chose instead to stay. And because they had applied for a freedom flight in the first place, they were sent to the sugar cane fields for hard labor.

By the spring of 1966, my life as I knew it before the freedom flights was over. Stress took permanent root in our day-to-day existence as it had for all who applied to leave Cuba. We were treated as traitors by the Cuban government.

Tension permeated my existence. I always felt like somebody was listening to my conversations through the walls. When I greeted people on the street, I was always careful not to say anything against the system. I never knew who might be a spy. Even a close friend could be an informant. The authorities sometimes tried to trap and blackmail ministers by having women approach them and offer themselves. Party officials regularly tried to engage me in political arguments, hoping to provoke an angry response that would justify my arrest.

I tried to direct all conversations to Christ and avoid all political issues. Even so, I was mocked at every turn. The police would say, "What is Christ? Where is he living? Let me see him." They were playing tricks with the Gospel. I prayed always for the Lord to help me, to give me the strength to never betray Him.

On June 7, 1966, my faith was tested again. A letter from the government arrived, ordering me to report in one week for a new work assignment in Nuevitas, a town about twenty-five miles away. The letter sent my heart racing. One of the worst concentration camps in the province was just outside Nuevitas. I dreaded the thought of being sent there. Stories abounded of men killed, tortured, or driven insane at the Nuevitas camp. I knew that if I were sent there, I probably would not get out.

I decided I must share this latest development with my family. I told my parents the full story of what had happened since I filed the application to leave Cuba. My parents, especially my mother, were crushed at the news of the latest volley from the government—that I might be sent to one of Castro's dreadful camps. All signs pointed toward that end. The letter even instructed me to arrive with my hair cut as close to the scalp as possible.

In the wee hours of June 14, I kissed my wife and son good-bye and, following instructions in the June 6 letter, took a bus to the city hall in Nuevitas, arriving at 6 a.m. There, I joined a crowd of about five hundred other men under the watch of armed and uniformed guards. Under Castro, the city hall had been turned into a makeshift detention center. Instructed by guards to assemble inside the building, we were divided alphabetically, then herded like cattle onto trucks for a trip to an unknown destination.

Because there were only a few trucks, it would be a while before the "Ps" would be loaded. I had to wait.

Again I began to pray. Later, I would learn that I was not the only one praying at that moment for my safety. My friends and family had gathered at my church to also petition the Lord. Among them was my mother, who had awakened early. She had been at the church several hours, fasting and praying.

About 10:15 a.m., I heard two men standing in the doorway of the city hall, shouting at the soldiers posted there. I recognized both men as Protestant pastors, and they were challenging the guards. I knew one of them as a former soldier who fought next to Castro during the revolution, but I didn't know him all that well. I certainly had no inkling that he would use his influence on my behalf.

"Why are you taking Pereira? Who authorized his being taken to the camp? Let me speak to the officer in charge!"

Two pastors defending another pastor seemed like a crazy act. This will be a disaster for me, I thought. However, as soon as one of the pastors flashed what appeared to be an identification badge, the soldiers lowered their rifles and ushered the men down a hallway to see the officer in charge. As the men disappeared down the corridor, a strange feeling overcame me. It was a sense of peace.

Back at the church, at around the same time, my mother knelt on a prayer rail in the pew and asked the Lord to spare me. Disconsolate, she leaned back into the pew, reached for a Bible and opened it, hoping to find comfort. It opened to the Book of Acts, Chapter 12. Joy leapt into her heart. Chapter 12 gives the account of Peter's liberation from prison by two angels. My mother wept, knowing at that instant that the Lord would free me.

Back at the city hall, the two men emerged from the chief officer's headquarters and headed toward the building's exit. The man who flashed the identification badge stopped long enough to speak to me. "Don't worry. Everything will be fixed," he said.

A few minutes later, the officer in charge—a man who had interrogated me several times previously and had treated me hatefully— emerged from his office, made eye contact with me, and smiled. I did not know what to make of his sudden charm. The situation turned even stranger when a soldier appeared with a tray of coffee. The commander instructed the soldier to serve me, along with his nearby officers. My first reaction was to decline the drink, fearing it could be poisoned. But I accepted the coffee gratefully and drank it in a few swallows. At no time did the commander speak to me, and I kept quiet. After finishing the coffee, I rejoined the rest of the "Ps" who would be loaded within the next half hour.

At about 11 a.m., my group's turn came. I stood at the back of the line. The commander approached me, looked me in the eye and smiled. Then, he clapped his hands and rubbed them together, as if he was washing himself from me. He spoke no words, but the meaning was clear: I was free to go. As the others in our group prepared to walk to the truck, I quietly slipped from the crowd and, with the permission of soldiers, out a side entrance. I walked quickly to a nearby bus stop where a bus, just then pulling in, took me home (6).

While spared from the concentration camp—at least for the time being—I was forced to return to the sugar cane fields and the backbreaking work of the *zafra*, the harvest. Nonetheless, I was grateful. At least I could return home to my family at night and preach to my congregation on Sundays. I felt terrible for the men who were taken away that day. I prayed and soon found peace. Deep down, I believed that God must have had a greater purpose for me than to have me die in a concentration camp.

As the weeks turned into months and the months into a new year—1967—I still received no word about my freedom flight. I became deeply discouraged. My mind gave birth to fantasy. If only a helicopter would land near the field, scoop me up and fly me to freedom, I thought.

One day, working alone in a sugar cane field, I dropped to my knees in desperation. I looked to the blue sky and pleaded to the Almighty for a signal, some sign of hope that I would soon enjoy freedom. Wiping away tears, I prayed: "Lord, I need to know if I will be here forever or I will be out of here sometime."

Fishing out the New Testament I carried in my pocket, I opened it. My fingers rested on the Gospel of John, Chapter 14. Verse 27 jumped out at me: *Peace I leave with you; my peace I give you; I do not give to you as the world gives. Do not let your hearts be troubled and do not let it be afraid.*

Like ice water on a parched throat, the scripture provided instant relief. "Don't worry about the future." I could feel my body absorb the words. I was overcome by joy, and I began singing the words over and over to a tune that suddenly popped into my head. "Peace, I leave with you; my peace I give to you . . ." I returned to work hacking stalk after stalk of sugar cane, singing at the top of my lungs: "Let not your heart be troubled, neither let it be afraid."

I am not a singer. But I don't know how many hundreds of times I sang that verse that day.

From that point on, I trusted the Lord that some day a miracle would occur, and we would leave Cuba. John 14:27 became my life jacket. I clung to ruthless trust in God through the remainder of 1967 and the early months of 1968, which came and went uneventfully.

On April 16, 1968, joy once again visited our family when Jacqui gave birth to a baby girl, Ruthie. Instantly, she became her daddy's angel. But there was little time to celebrate. A few days after Ruthie's birth, I received a letter from the Cuban government informing me that I was to report on April 23 for a new work assignment. The letter was businesslike, sounding almost as if the government were granting me a job promotion. But I knew better. Intuitively, I knew that it was official notice that I was being assigned to a forced labor camp.

I spent the few days before my departure cradling Ruthie, for I knew that I may never again have the opportunity to hold her as an infant. I figured that, in all likelihood, I would neither see my family nor my church members for many months. And, at my core, I knew this time there would be no rescue party.

Chapter Six

The Prison Camps

On Wednesday, April 23, 1968, I awoke early and, as was my routine, read a Bible devotion and prayed. But this time, I also wept. When time came for me to leave my family for the prison camp, I crammed a small rope hammock and one change of clothing into a pillowcase—the sum of belongings that I was allowed to bring with me. With tears in my eyes, I bid farewell to my wife, my four-year-old son and the infant daughter whom I had known only a week.

At 5:30 a.m., I arrived at the local police station to find a crowd of men from my region who, like me, had applied to leave Cuba. Soon, all of us boarded flatbed trucks and stood for the duration of the ride. We were stuck together like sardines in a tin can. We did not know where we were going. We had no way to communicate with our families. Many of us were praying.

We were driven to a camp near San Miguel, about fifteen miles from Lugareno. The place was eerily similar to the camp from which I escaped the firing squad. Rifle-toting soldiers stood watch from towers—one at each corner of the compound and one in the middle—guarding the grounds, which were surrounded by barbed wire. Dormitories were crude—four wooden walls, covered by a frond-laden roof. There were poles in the floor from which we hung our hammocks for sleeping. Bathroom facilities consisted of a series of pit toilets separated by small wooden walls open to the front. Each man was given a bucket to use for bathing. The five hundred of us would call the place home.

The camp population was made up of political dissidents, clergy, homosexuals, those who had applied to leave the country, and criminals serving sentences for intoxication, theft, and drug use and trafficking. In Castro's world, Christians and criminals were considered the same (1). Inmates were warned: anyone who tried to escape would be tortured or executed.

At San Miguel, my "new" work assignment was the same as at the granja in Lagureno—tending sugar cane fields. Within days at the new camp, the routine had become old. Arising before dawn, we rode in trucks to nearby fields. Once there, we endured a ten-hour day of hacking, hoeing, and stacking. Returning to the camp at sunset, I bathed, using my bucket of water to erase the day's toil from my skin. I was rarely successful. Dinner was a tin plate with small portions of rice or pasta.

There was never enough food to fully satisfy our hunger. Often, only a few pounds of beans or peas were cooked for hundreds of men. There was no bread. What food we were served was often old and spoiled. The meals were terrible, and we passed many nights in hunger. Desperate for nourishment during their shifts in the field, some men hacked themselves pieces of sugar cane and gnawed on them. Many became fatigued from lack of food and would faint on the job.

After supper, we were forced to sit through a thirty-minute lecture on the virtues of Marxism. Most men dozed during the presentations. Around 10 p.m., dormitory lights were turned off. Even following a hard day of work in the fields, however, sleep didn't come easily for many of the men, stretched out in their hammocks row after row. The crowded conditions, the body odor, and loud snoring made for many sleepless nights for me and other camp inmates.

The dreadful conditions were made more tolerable when I met some fellow Christians at the camp. We bonded instantly. At night, after the mandatory lecture on Communist philosophy but before lights out, we would gather in small groups for Bible study, using my pocket New Testament. Among us were Protestants, Catholics, Masons, priests, doctors, lawyers, farmers. There were no cultural, social, or religious barriers. In our prayers, we became one through the power of God.

After a month at San Miguel, I was given a weekend pass home to see my family. The reunion was bittersweet. I was delighted to see my wife, son, and infant daughter. But when time came for me to depart following the short visit, all of us were heartbroken. Jacqui was alone with an infant and a four-year-old. It was terribly painful to have only a few hours to hold Ruthie. My little girl was only a week old when I was taken to the camps. She never knew me as her father until she was eighteen months old. My absence from her seemed like a hundred years.

As difficult as it was to leave my infant daughter, leaving Joel, my son, was the most painful part of the visit home. When the time came for me to leave on Sunday, he grabbed my leg and cried, "Don't go, Poppi. Don't go, Poppi. Don't go!" It was very sad. He did not understand why I had to go, and I couldn't explain it to him. I was so angry when I had to leave (2).

After three months at San Miguel, I and the other men from the Lugareno region were moved to a camp named El Jiqui, about forty miles to the west in a jungle. There were no fences surrounding this facility, and the camp's commander was less strict. At El Jiqui, two faithful Catholic women, a mother and a daughter, befriended me and other Christians at the camp even though townspeople and camp inmates had been warned not to fraternize. The women, who lived adjacent to the camp, hosted us for dinner at their home, which we, under cover of darkness, visited in violation of camp rules. It was a risky outing. The women prepared us meals of *guayaba* (guava) pasta, rice and beans, and special treats of bread and cookies. The meals were in stark contrast to the mushy peas and spoiled rice and meat served in camp. The women were angels risking their lives for us.

After three months at El Jiqui, I was moved to another camp— the third in about six months. I cannot recall the name of the camp, about an hour away from El Jiqui, but I remember that it was near a large sugar mill and that conditions there were horrible. Lacking adequate shelter from the rain, we would see our dormitories turned into mud bogs following daily tropical showers. I vividly remember awakening one morning from my hammock and placing my feet into three inches of mud. At the camp, the food was so awful that I survived on boiled eggs that Jacqui had snuck in on visitor's day and on fresh, edible grass that grew in the sugar cane fields.

After a month at this camp, we were trucked to another facility about an hour to the southwest, a camp called Loma La Rubia. Conditions there were no better. A hard-hearted lieutenant oversaw camp operations, and he required us to awaken at 4 a.m. to start our shifts in the sugar cane fields. While working, we were regularly doused by insecticide sprayed from large trucks. And after putting in a full day in the fields, there was often more work. We had to carry bag after bag of fertilizer—thousands of pounds—from trucks into the fields and spread it. We got no rest breaks. Many men collapsed from exhaustion.

The conditions took their toll. Men in their early thirties looked old and wrinkled; some contracted water-borne diseases and a few, tuberculosis. Lacking food and clean water and poisoned by bug spray, some of the men were driven nearly insane. In the barracks at night, they would sob uncontrollably.

Even if you were sick you had to work, and the guards would keep a constant eye on you. If you didn't work fast enough, they would threaten to kick you or jab you with their rifles. One prisoner, a soldier in Batista's army, became ill. Frightened that he was dying, he pleaded with the camp commander to let him see a doctor, but his requests were ignored. It was not until the rest of us complained loudly that the commander relented and sought medical attention for the man.

The vile conditions bred resentment among the captives, and we became increasingly belligerent toward the guards. We had been warned by the commander that if something happened to one of his officers, all of us would be killed, no matter who was actually responsible. One night that warning was nearly tested. One of the men in my dormitory, deranged with fury, pulled out a machete that he had snuck in and began sharpening it. He promised he would cut off the camp commander's head that night. We had heard that a prisoner did exactly that in a nearby camp. All of us were after this man to stop, and we finally got him to give up the machete.

The memories from those days at the camp still haunt me. A person can never imagine how terrible life is in one of these prisons unless you've been there. Hunger, misery, torture, insults, unsanitary conditions, the hate, the terror.

Through it all, my Christian brothers and I kept our faith alive through clandestine worship and study. When we had a few moments alone, we came together in a group and, one by one, repeated a verse of Scripture. If any of the soldiers approached, we would change the subject to boxing or baseball.

Sometimes, we even wanted to sing hymns. We would do so in hushed voices. Ignoring the stench and the stress of our surroundings, we sang or hummed softly the words to *Leaning on the Everlasting Arms, Sweet Hour of Prayer, Onward Christian Soldiers, In the Cross, What a Friend We Have in Jesus*, and others. Even the men who were not Christians would join in. Many accepted Christ as their Savior with true repentance and tears (3). We let nothing come between us and our faith. When we wanted to celebrate Communion, we used any bread we could find around the compound, no matter how hard or old; for wine, vinegar served the purpose. We received such blessings during these times that tears flowed.

Praise and worship even flourished among the sugar canes. During work breaks in the field, when we could escape the guards' watchful eyes, my Christian brothers and I would form a circle, hold hands, and pray. The Bible was our chief source of strength. We did not know when we would be freed, if we would be freed, or if we would be killed. We had to trust the Lord for our deliverance.

The fall of 1968 marked nearly three years since my family and I had been assured that we could leave Cuba. And, yet, as days turned into weeks and weeks into months, freedom seemed more elusive than ever. One day, amid swaying stalks of sugar cane, at a prison camp where I had no idea how long I would be confined, I prayed the words of God's promise over and over—a pledge found in Matthew 28:20: "*And surely I am with you always, to the very end of the age.*"

Meanwhile, a steady diet of labor camp rations—boiled corn, beans, and pasta, all chased by contaminated water—left me chronically sick to my stomach. The unsanitary latrines and lack of privacy chewed at my self-esteem. After a year of forced labor at Fidel Castro's concentration camps, I, once fit and trim, was skinny and weak. Suffering ruled my days.

Even getting to and from the sugar fields was hazardous. We rode on flatbed trucks with no rails. The drivers often sped, and people were always falling out. One morning, while riding in a farm wagon pulled by a speeding tractor, I was bounced out. Upon hitting the ground, a sharp pain tore through my right leg. In agony, I grasped it above the knee and felt through my pant leg for the place it hurt most. I came upon a tender spot where two bones had separated, but had not broken through the skin. "Aaayeee!" I cried out in pain.

With the help of fellow workers, I was loaded back onto the wagon and driven to the barracks. Once there, camp officials refused me medical treatment, and I was allowed only bed rest. However, the pain was too intense to sleep. The following day, as if to add insult to injury, I was trucked to yet another camp, Quince y Medio, about an hour's drive to the west.

Immediately upon our arrival, my right leg still throbbing, I was forced by the new commander to hoe the fields. I cried in pain all day. By the first night, I asked the Lord to take my life or to save me from the pain by providing relief from the work—one or the other. The Lord's answer arrived early the next morning. One of the lieutenants assigned to oversee our group awakened me and sixteen other men at 4 a.m. and told us to follow him. Apparently, the officer took pity on me. He told us that he was taking a brigade of sixteen model workers, the hardest workers, to another nearby camp. There, the sixteen would not have to work, but only present themselves as a good model to the other concentration camp workers. It would be a mini-vacation of sorts for all of us—a reward for our hard work and cooperation that would serve as an example to other inmates. I was not aware that I was one of the best workers. I thought that I was one of the worst.

After the men climbed aboard a truck for the trip, I counted the passengers; there were seventeen making the trip—not sixteen, as the lieutenant had said. I wasn't going to complain. I bowed my head and prayed in thanksgiving. Only hours before, I was praying for the Lord to take me, period.

At the new camp, near the town of Esmerelda, about fifty miles to the northwest, conditions were no better than at the previous five facilities. But at least I could finally rest. After a week of recuperation, the pain in my right leg dissipated. On the twelfth day at the camp, I was able to walk with only a slight limp. Showing more mercy, the lieutenant allowed me to visit an orthopedic surgeon, a man I knew in Nuevitas, a ninety-minute trip by train. I went to him, but something unbelievable had happened. The doctor said to me, "Pereira, you don't have anything wrong with your leg. I can find nothing." I was in disbelief. I told him, "I felt where part of my bone was separated from the other bone. You could feel it!"

All these years later, the only thing I can say is that the Lord performed a miracle. My colleagues in the camp knew I was unable to work. They saw me in pain. But in the space of two weeks, my leg had healed.

Following the doctor's appointment, I snuck in a quick weekend trip home to see Jacqui and the kids. But when I returned Sunday night by train to Esmerelda, I found the deplorable conditions had worsened. I returned to sweltering summer temperatures, overwhelming stench from open sewage pits—locations of previous camp latrines—and an outbreak of water poisoning, sickness caused by decomposed animal parts in the "fresh" water supply. The ground-level water tank, open at the top, trapped frogs, rats, and other small animals. With my hands, I would try to separate the body parts to get a clear spot for a drink.

"Drink the water or die," I remember one camp commander telling me after I complained of the dirty water. So, in that hot, sweltering summer, we drank the water. So many people got sick. I was filling my stomach and intestines with amoebae. The wretched water even made bathing and washing clothes an ordeal.

When it rained, our campgrounds turned into smelly mud pits. Picture five hundred men crowded into a small space, wet, muddy, and reeking of stale sweat. You cannot imagine how miserable we were.

The horrid conditions created a pressure-cooker environment at the camp. Nerves frayed easily and tempers became short. One day, I watched as a young prisoner carried a machete into the barracks—an infraction of camp rules that could have gotten him severely punished. I followed him inside. "I cannot take this anymore," the young man said, holding the machete to his own throat.

In a gentle voice, I calmed the suicidal man. I shared with him the good news that Christ is hope for him. I told him that there would be a different time in our lives and that suicide was against the law of the Lord. As I talked, the young man put down the machete and prayed for forgiveness. For many weeks following the episode, I nurtured the young man and invited him to our clandestine worship services.

To take my mind off the wretched conditions, I pursued a new passion—learning English. Among my belongings, I had secretly stowed a book of English-language Bible devotions (4). Reading it not only kept my free time occupied, but also kept alive my hopes of going to America.

As the sizzling summer gave way to fall, I was given a new, dangerous work assignment—harvesting timber in the high mountains, lumber to be used for telephone poles. I was one of ten men chosen for the arduous work. We would rise at 4 a.m. for a two-hour drive up narrow, winding, and bumpy roads into the Sierra Cubita mountains. The logging truck would literally drive up the mountainside until it could go no further.

The mountains were steep and made of jagged rocks from which the trees would emerge. After felling the trees with axes, we stripped them of branches, drug them to a clearing and loaded them onto the truck. It was grueling work. As always, food was in short supply. Our meal during the day was salt-cured fish and old bread. The assignment, however, came with two fringe benefits: lots of fresh rainwater, which our crew collected and drank, and many fruit trees from which to snack—mangos, bananas, guava, and mammees.

After work, sore and exhausted, we would climb aboard the logging truck, strapping ourselves to the logs with chains so we wouldn't fall off during the harrowing, two-hour descent back to camp. Most of the men slept. I did not. Always, I was praying—upon waking, before going to work, driving back to the camp. I was praying for deliverance.

We spent thirty days cutting trees in the mountains. From the group of ten, only two of us came back in more or less good health. One man broke both his legs after falling from a tree. Another broke his sternum. Six had severe scars from rock or tree cuts. I only had some scars on my knees.

The good Lord had saved me—literally.

For upon returning to the barracks on the last day of harvesting timber atop the Sierra Cubitas, I was handed a telegram by a camp official. The cable was dated Wednesday, November 5, 1969, nearly four years to the day that I had first applied for a flight to leave Cuba. The message inside would change my life forever.

Chapter Seven

Flight to Freedom

For a few moments, I simply held the telegram in my fingers and stared at it, as if to absorb the shock. The return address said the cable was from the U.S. government and had come via the Swiss Embassy. Near the front door of the dormitory, my Christian brothers circled around me in silence as I slowly opened the envelope and began reading. A tear spilled down my cheek.

In a crisp tone, the telegram stated that I, my wife, two children, and Jacqui's mother were authorized to leave Cuba aboard a freedom flight. The five of us were to report at 10 a.m. on November 10—in four days—at the Varadero Airport, the departure point a few hours away, for our flight to Miami. We would be allowed little baggage, the telegram said. If we wanted to, we could spend the night before our departure in a shelter on the airport grounds.

Chills rushed through my body.

I was unable to speak.

For nearly ten years, I'd been praying for safe passage from

Cuba, and today—this very day—my deliverance arrived. I stood quietly, wiped away tears, smiled, and received hugs and congratulations from the men who surrounded me. Silently, I offered a prayer of thanks. "Praise be to you, Lord."

And then—before I could even leave the front entry of the dormitory—a camp officer, a lieutenant known for his cruelty, confronted me. "You will not be allowed to leave," he told me.

I thought he was making a stab at gallows humor. But the officer's serious expression instantly deflated the joy that had been present only moments before. It was clear that he had seen the telegram hours before.

"Why?" I demanded. The officer stepped close to me so only I could hear his answer. "Because you know too much. You know about the secret records kept on schoolchildren," the lieutenant said (1). He told me that the camp commander made the decision after reading my government file.

Castro had decided that any former government employee who knew of secret practices would be prohibited from leaving. "Pereira will forever be working in the sugar cane fields," the lieutenant quoted the commander as saying.

This couldn't be happening, I thought. Overwhelmed by this latest betrayal from Castro's henchmen, I walked quickly to my hammock and lay down. I began to pray and cry softly. The other men left me to grieve. I skipped the evening meal and fell asleep exhausted from the day's hard work and emotional turmoil.

Around midnight, the same lieutenant awakened me and motioned me to join him outside. What in the world does this man want, I wondered? What worse could happen now? Once outside, the lieutenant spoke.

"I know you are a man who will not talk," he said, as if trying to gain my confidence. "I will get you out of here if you will get a message of mine to the United States." Sensing a trap, I immediately told the lieutenant that I would not meet with him, and I returned inside to my hammock.

He returned around 4 a.m., awakened me again and motioned me to go outside. I didn't know what to make of the situation. My mind raced. What is going on here? I decided to hear him out. Once outside, the lieutenant spoke in an urgent tone. "You need my help to leave this camp. I will tell the captain that we should take this opportunity to get rid of you because you are one of the worst workers we have, good for nothing, and that it is better to let you go. I will secure your release if you take a message to the United States for me."

I did not trust the officer. But if I declined to do as he asked and missed my flight to freedom, I would be stuck in Cuba. If I agreed to his demand, I might have a chance to leave.

Sensing my deep misgivings, the lieutenant explained his request. He told me that he was the brother of an acquaintance of mine, a schoolteacher who had successfully emigrated and now lived in New Jersey (2). In fact, I knew the teacher and remembered her fondly.

The message the lieutenant wanted to get to his sister was simple and heartfelt—get him out of Cuba. He poured out his heart to me. "You see me with this uniform and pistol, but I am not a Communist," he said. "I am an anti-Communist. I belong to an organization that is anti-Communist, and the government is discovering all the members of our group. It is only a matter of time that they will discover me. I must get out of Cuba."

Seeing the man's genuine desperation, I agreed to deliver his message. And he kept his end of the bargain. Around 7 a.m., the camp commander called me into his office and began berating me with insults. "You are good for nothing, and we don't want you here," he said, as if following a script the lieutenant had written. Lifting his right leg as if he was going to kick me, the commander said with hate in his voice, "You are dismissed!"

Showing no emotion—I did not want to display my elation—I hurried back to the dorm where I began stuffing my few belongings into a pillowcase. If I hurried, I could catch a morning train in the nearby town that would stop at Lugareno, my hometown, about ninety minutes away.

Saying good-bye to the men with whom I had been imprisoned was difficult. Over the months, we had shared many tough times. We all cried and hugged. The goal for everyone in the camp was to get out, to leave Cuba, so they were pleased I was leaving. But it was also sad because we all knew it was good-bye. We probably would never see each other again.

Rushing from the camp, I ran the half-mile to the train station, arriving just in time to catch a departing coach home. Once on board, I settled into a seat. Adrenaline coursed through my body. There was so much to be done over the next three days, so many more farewells to say, so many loose ends to tie up. Would I be ready to go? Would I miss my flight? In prayer, I turned my anxieties over to the Lord. God would not have brought me through so much only to have me miss my flight to freedom. "Stop worrying!" I told myself.

When I got to Lugareno, I rushed home to discover a house full of family and friends. Jacqui had received the same telegram at our home on the same day my notice arrived at the camp. She was so happy to see me. After a quick shower, I changed into clean clothing and began greeting my friends and relatives who had crowded into the house. Any time somebody received the freedom telegram, everyone who knew that person would come to give their best wishes.

My friends gave me hugs and kisses—and gifts of money. Before I knew it, my shirt pocket was stuffed full of pesos. Every time I cleared the pocket of cash, placing it in my wallet, the pocket quickly filled again as new well-wishers arrived. These were poor people. But they gave whatever they could.

The gifts totaled nearly 3,000 pesos. I thanked God for the blessings. I would need most of the cash in the next few days. Without reliable public transportation, and with only a short time before our departure, we would need to take taxis to say good-bye to relatives. Taxis—in reality, rented private cars driven by their owners—were expensive.

Jacqui and I decided that our family would leave Lugareno the next day and travel to Zaza del Medio, where most of my family lived. Once there, we would say our goodbyes to my relatives and travel by car to Varadero, the departure point for the freedom flights. My father and brother, Eldo, would accompany us to the airport.

In what seemed like the blink of an eye, the morning of Friday, November 7, arrived and with the sunrise, time to pack for the trip. The five of us would be limited to a total of forty pounds of luggage. We were not interested in taking much with us. We wanted to leave behind what we could for our family in Cuba. We took more clothing for Ruthie and Joel. I took only one change of clothing. We also prepared some sandwiches to take along. No food would be provided at the airport shelter.

As for our house, furniture, and other assets in Lugareno — including about $300 in a savings account—the government would get it. Under Cuban law, ownership of all property and funds of a "traitor" transferred to the Cuban government.

At noon on Friday, the whole neighborhood turned out to say good-bye to me, Jacqui, the two children, and Jacqui's mother, Maria. Among those present were the faithful members of my small church. Throughout my confinement in labor camps, the church continued to pay my family a token salary, even though an interim pastor had been called to serve during my absence. The people of our church knew that what was happening to us was an injustice. They brought Jacqui and the kids food and clothing while I was imprisoned. Thanks to their generosity, my family did not suffer as much as so many others. The congregation considered me their pastor until the day I departed Cuba.

From Lugareno, we took a taxi to Zaza del Medio, about a six-hour trip to the west. We spent the next thirty-six hours saying good-bye to relatives there and in the city of Iguara, a short distance away. Each farewell was sorrowful. I did not know when or if I would see my relatives again. But there was little time to dwell on sadness.

Finally, around 8 a.m., on Sunday, November 9, it was time to leave for the airport (3). Parting from my mother was nearly unbearable. There was loud sobbing between us. My mother said, "Maybe this is the last time I will see you." It was terrible for both us.

When it was time to leave, we five travelers, accompanied by my father and brother, squeezed into a taxi, a large 1950s-era sedan, for the trip to the airport, east of Havana.

The eighty-five–mile trip seemed long, but it was quiet and unrushed. We took our time, stopping for breaks. The past five days had been a whirlwind. I enjoyed the relative calm of the ride. The taxi finally pulled into Varadero around 4 p.m. and made its way to the airport shelter, a shell of dirty brown brick fenced by tall barbed wire, like another Castro prison.

At the entrance to the shelter, we all got out of the car. For my father and Eldo, this would be the end of their escort. A sign said only passengers could enter.

The moment had arrived for me to part ways with my father and brother. Emotion flooded my body once more. What words could I possibly speak to my father, the man who brought me to Christ and whose example sustained me through years of imprisonment and suffering?

He spoke first.

"God bless you, my son," he said. "We will be praying for you. Someday, we will be reunited."

Sadness choked my voice, and I was unable to speak. I could only hug my father tightly and weep for nearly five minutes. Then, it was time to bid farewell to Eldo. I bear-hugged my younger brother. Deep down, I knew I would see Eldo again, our bond unbroken no matter the distance that would temporarily separate us.

At last, we headed down the sidewalk toward the shelter gate.

At the entrance, I handed the guard the telegram authorizing our arrival for the freedom flight. Quickly scanning the document to confirm the date, the guard waved us through. We waved a final time to Eldo and my father before entering the drab and drafty shelter.

Inside, we met another uniformed guard, the check-in agent, sitting at a table. I presented the telegram and five Cuban passports, which the guard opened and examined. Then, picking up a large stamp resting on a black inkpad, he quickly slammed an imprint onto each of the passports. *"Expatriado"*—"Traitor"—it said. The word stabbed at my heart. In reality, it was Fidel Castro who was the traitor, not the hundreds of thousands of Cubans like me who were forced to flee his despotic regime. Castro was the turncoat. Those of us in the shelter were only pursuing the dream he had promised—*la libertad*, freedom.

A quick glance around the shelter confirmed my first impression that my family and I would have to stomach Castro's indignities one more night. There were no beds or cots or even pallets to sleep on—just a chilled and dirty concrete floor.

We found an empty room and settled into a corner around 5 p.m. There was nothing to do but wait for the flight the next morning. The children, Joel, five, and Ruthie, nineteen months, were restless. As the sun began to set, we got out our sandwiches. Jacqui and I were too nervous to eat. Still suffering the effects of contaminated water, my stomach was the battleground for bouts of nausea.

Before darkness, Jacqui and I removed some of the clothing from our suitcases and prepared makeshift beds for Joel and Ruthie. On what I prayed would be my last night in Cuba, I lay on the bare concrete floor dressed in a T-shirt and suit pants. Sleep was impossible. There were many children crying and the floor was uncomfortable. None of us, of course, wanted to draw attention to ourselves, so we kept as quiet as we could.

Around 7 a.m., families began to stir. I got up, changed into a fresh shirt, put on a tie and suit coat. Jacqui wore a dress. We wanted to greet the free world in our Sunday finest. The Cuban government also wanted us nicely dressed because it reflected well on Castro. It was another form of propaganda.

Shortly after 8 a.m., the DC-7 that would carry us to freedom arrived from Miami. Not wishing to attract the attention of guards, I urged my family to show little emotion, even though all of us were bursting with excitement. None of us had ever been on an airplane!

At 9 a.m., two buses pulled up to the shelter. The passengers—there were eighty-five of us—climbed aboard and found seats. We all remained quiet, as if in shock. The moment we had been waiting for for years had arrived! (4)

The bus pulled up next to the plane. The driver instructed us to disembark, line up outside, and stay together. There would be one last check of every family's paperwork. The guards carefully compared travel documents against the official government list of authorized travelers.

My family sat near the back of the bus, which meant we would be among the last to board the plane. As I stood at the rear of the line, I gave our paperwork a close once-over to make sure everything was in order. Then, I saw the mistake!

Suddenly, my heart began to race. I couldn't believe I had not seen the error sooner, while there was still time to correct it! The government had misspelled Jacqui's name on her passport, omitting the "c."

Fear poured into me. I had heard stories in the camps about how families had been separated at the moment of a freedom flight's departure, on the pretext of some minor administrative mix-up, such as a misspelling. The government looked for flimsy excuses to keep people from leaving Cuba. I immediately told Jacqui and Maria about the misspelling, and we all became very scared. The guards may say, "This is not you!"

In fact, such a nightmare played out before our eyes. In line ahead of us was a couple with three children. When they handed the guard their paperwork, he noticed some sort of problem and informed the woman that she would not be allowed to leave until the paperwork was corrected. The couple looked at one another in shock. Through tears, they hugged. The woman told her husband, "Do not stay with me. Go and save them (the children) to freedom." She was then escorted away.

Seeing this event unfold, panic nearly overwhelmed me. As the line inched forward, I hatched a plan.

I said, "Jacqui, you let Maria go first. You get behind her with Ruthie in your arms and holding both your passports. I will be behind you with Joel and our passports. In the moment that we approach the soldier checking the papers, you turn your passport with your picture down. I will accidentally fall into you, and then you move onto the stairway. When you do, I will immediately present him with my passport. He will not have time to check your passport carefully if we do this."

If the plan failed, Jacqui and I agreed that all of us would remain in Cuba.

As we neared the front of the line, I began to pray silently. And within seconds, it was all over! The plan worked flawlessly. The guard did not see Jacqui's passport. As we bounded up the airplane ladder and stepped into the plane's cabin, I locked eyes momentarily with the two American pilots. They smiled, but I could tell they were as nervous as I. They wanted to get out of there.

We found seats toward the rear of the plane. My heart pounded furiously. After the last passenger boarded, the soldier who had checked our passports walked up the stairway and stood inside the airplane door. He peered down the aisle of the plane, as if to double-check a nagging detail that he might have overlooked. But after a moment or two, he turned and headed down the stairway. The pilots closed the door. (There were no flight attendants aboard to welcome the passengers. No welcome was needed.)

The plane's two propellers slowly began to revolve, and in a few moments the cabin filled with a roaring noise (5). What a sweet sound to my ears!

As the plane's engines warmed up, I heard the first of two muffled sounds. The first sound I recognized immediately—crying. The second noise, a whisper, I also recognized. "Holy Mary, mother of God . . ." Then, as the taxiing plane approached the runway, there was a shout from the front of the plane. I couldn't understand what the person said at first, but, then other passengers picked up the chorus. "*Libertad! Libertad!*" the voices shouted—"Freedom! Freedom!"

At 10:17 a.m. on Monday, November 10, 1969, the plane carrying me and my family to freedom lifted from the runway of Varadero airport. The moment we were airborne, the plane became an emotional fireball. Soft crying turned into loud sobs. Whispered prayers became screams of praise. Shouted words were joined by fervent applause. I cried, I thanked the Lord, and I clapped and shouted. The poor pilots! The applause and cheering continued through the entire trip.

Some on board could not forget their fury. Among the shouts of "Freedom!" were a few that said, "Death for Castro! Death for Castro!" God would be the judge of Fidel Castro, I thought. As the plane left sight of the Cuban island and pointed toward Florida, I reflected on what lay ahead. It was difficult not to think the worst—that I may never see my beloved Cuba or the rest of my family again.

Peering out the window at the Gulf of Mexico, I wept softly. I recalled the dreams that I had in seminary—to serve a congregation whom I loved and who loved me; to preach on Sunday mornings and Wednesday nights; to conduct Bible studies, marry young couples, and bury departed elders. I would raise my children and watch my parents age gracefully, and I would grow in faith and maturity with Jacqui. Simple as they were, these were my dreams.

But this day, while on my flight to freedom, I added another ministry to my calling. I had escaped a Castro firing squad; I had been spared a life sentence in the prison camps. And now God had allowed me to escape with my life and dearest loved ones. At this very moment, God was delivering me to freedom—a captive soon to be set free in a land full of promise. At the time, I didn't know the name for what I was—a refugee.

What I knew is that I had been spared. I felt immensely fortunate. God, through Jesus Christ and the Holy Spirit, had sustained me through much suffering in the past ten years. And from this day forward, I decided in my heart that I would respond to such loving grace with gratitude, serving God in whatever way the Lord would reveal.

I would devote my life to help others obtain their freedom from captivity in whatever ways God would show me.

"Here I am, Lord," I prayed.

I glanced out the window again. The view was spectacular! I could see the rounding bend of a huge peninsula, a chain of islands strung like a broken strand of pearls dripping to one side. I was not the only passenger to spot landfall. Just when it seemed as if the freedom-bound passengers could possibly cheer no louder, the sight of Florida triggered a new torrent of emotion. My heart racing, I joined in with the other passengers as we shouted at the top of our lungs: "*Libertad! Libertad! Libertad!*"

Chapter Eight

Freedom's Ring

An extraordinary thing happens when you ask the question "Who am I? " and leave it to God to answer. The result will be a calling, an identity that is revealed in service to others.

"Who am I in freedom?" This was the question I mulled as our DC-7 prepared to land at Miami International Airport, one hour and seven minutes after leaving Cuba. I had no idea what the future held for me, Jacqui, and our family, but I knew that God would carry us along our journey one gentle step at a time.

Greeted by a brilliant sun and a cool breeze, our plane touched American soil and taxied to a terminal and stopped. In moments, three buses pulled alongside the plane.

When the plane door opened and the breeze of freedom touched our faces, the shouting began anew: "We are free! We are free!" *Somos libré! Somos libré!* Eager to embrace America's promise, we quickly gathered our belongings. The plane emptied in ten minutes.

Jacqui's mother led our group, followed by Joel whose hand

Maria gripped tightly. Next went Jacqui, who held nineteen-month-old Ruthie in her arms. Then, it was my turn. As I stepped onto the oil-stained tarmac, ignoring my Sunday suit and with tears streaming from my eyes, I kneeled and kissed the concrete. *Gracias, Señor. Gracias, Señor.* "Thank you, Lord. Thank you, Lord." Jacqui felt the same overwhelming gratitude. "I am in heaven!" she said.

As we walked into the terminal—I would later find out it was named "Freedom Gate" (1)—a uniformed receptionist smiled and said, "Welcome to the United States." *Bienvenidos a Estados Unidos.* Upon hearing the words, I burst into tears once again.

I didn't know what to expect upon our arrival. Would we be placed in detention? Jail? Only ninety minutes earlier, we were captives of Communism. Now, we were free, welcomed by the world's greatest democracy. It soon became clear to me: There would be no punishment by the government here, no detention, threats, or intimidation. My family and I were secure. Only God could have delivered such a miracle.

We were directed to a sitting area to await processing by U.S. immigration officials. I was glad to sit for a few minutes and collect my thoughts. Soon an attendant came by and, speaking in Spanish, pointed to a nearby table of sandwiches and soft drinks. The generosity nearly overwhelmed me. Because of my stomach sickness, I had little appetite, until I saw a piece of fruit that I had not eaten in years because of the embargo—an apple.

Once our name was called, a polite agent who spoke Spanish saw to it that we were photographed, fingerprinted, and issued identification. The process took about an hour. Our official immigration status as political asylees took effect immediately—a gift, I would learn later, that the U.S. government gave to hundreds of thousands of Cubans fleeing Castro's regime (2). We would not be returned to Cuba involuntarily.

Following our processing, we were escorted to meet a representative of the Church World Service, the ecumenical agency formed
after World War II when U.S. churches came together to respond
to the needs of war refugees in Europe and Asia. It was through
this wonderful agency—the doorkeeper of freedom for hundreds
of thousands of refugees—that my family and I were permitted to
come to the United States.

The young woman from Church World Service—an angel of
the Lord, in reality—had many surprises for us. The first was a
reunion. She took us to a large waiting area separated by a glass
partition. On the other side of the glass, we instantly spotted some
dear family members—Juan Luis Dominguez and his wife, Iris,
cousins of Jacqui who lived in the Miami area. They had come to
greet us at the airport. Juan Luis was the nephew of our official
U.S. sponsors in New York, Jacqui's uncle Miguel Dominguez and
his wife, Lolita. We had never met Juan Luis or his wife before and
only knew them from photographs. But that didn't matter. It was as
if we had known them all of our lives.

Later, I would find out that Juan Luis heard our names announced
over a local radio station (3) and drove to the airport, where they
waited hours to see us.

After a few minutes, our Church World Service angel announced
that she had another errand for us. Juan Luis, needing to return to
his job, said he would come back at 6 p.m. to pick us up for supper.
He knew where to find us, he said. Iris remained with us as we
climbed aboard a passenger van. Five minutes later, the van pulled
up in front of a large warehouse on airport property. Inside was a
sight to behold—row after row of tables stacked high with clothing
that appeared mostly new and categorized by gender and size.

Because of the baggage restrictions, Jacqui, Maria, and I had
brought only one change of clothing. The Church World Service
representative told us to take whatever we wanted, as much as we

could carry. After being forced to wear just one set of clothing every day for eighteen months, I was overwhelmed by the generosity, thanking God and praising his name. I took six pair of pants, four shirts, and multiple pairs of socks and underwear. Then, as we prepared to leave the warehouse, the Church World Service representative handed us an envelope with $600 inside—$200 for each adult. This was seed money to begin our new lives. It was more than double the amount of cash we were forced to leave in our Cuban bank account.

Our arms loaded with clothing, our wallet containing more money than we'd ever had in our lives, we were taken to an apartment building near the airport operated by Church World Service and other agencies. It was called "Freedom House" *La Casa de Libertad* (4). We were greeted warmly by staff members, who took us to a small but clean furnished two-bedroom apartment, which would be our home for the next four days. A spirit of joy and freedom filled the air at the complex, and through the generosity of Americans living in Miami, there was plenty of food for us.

At 6 p.m., Juan Luis arrived in a large sedan to pick us up for a short ride to the suburb of Hialeah, where he and his wife owned a home. Like many Cuban exiles in Miami (5), Juan Luis and Iris had found the American dream, and this night they would share with us a wonderful home-cooked meal.

Staring at the sights of Miami from the front seat of the car, I was overwhelmed by how new and clean everything appeared. In what seemed like only a few minutes, we sat down to a wonderful supper in a cozy dining room—a stark contrast to the cold concrete floor of the Varadero airport.

My battle with nausea kept me from eating much of the meal. After 1,431 days—three years and eleven months—in Castro's prison camps with little food and drinking contaminated water, I weighed forty-five pounds less than my normal 150.

Jacqui said, "He was so skinny. Praise God he didn't get sicker drinking that nasty water."

We returned to our apartment after 11 p.m. After we tucked the kids into bed and made out the couch for Maria, Jacqui and I retired. The moment my head hit the pillow, I fell asleep. The next morning, Tuesday, November 11, the first order of business was to visit a tailor to take in my clothing, which fell off my skinny frame. The following days were uneventful. Mostly, we rested and visited with some extended family from the Miami area. Mostly, I slept. I was physically, emotionally, and mentally exhausted.

On Friday, November 14, our stay in sunny Miami, where the high temperature reached 83 degrees, ended all too soon. On Friday night, the time came for us to leave for our permanent place of residence, New York City. We would fly there with tickets provided by Church World Service. This was another act of generosity by one of God's greatest service organizations.

At the Miami airport, while waiting for our flight to New York's JFK Airport, one of my distant cousins came to bid us farewell. Before I knew it, he had taken off his heavy overcoat and placed it over my skinny frame. I disappeared into the coat. The cousin said it would be very cold in New York and that I would freeze without a heavy jacket. "You're going to need this," he said. As our plane was called, we said good-bye and hugged. My Miami relatives could barely find me in that oversized coat. I was grateful to have it when we arrived in New York, because the temperature was near freezing.

We landed at JFK around midnight. Miguel and Lolita, Jacqui's aunt and uncle, were there to greet us with hugs and kisses. They had legally immigrated from Cuba in the late 1940s and had subsequently helped more than a dozen family members settle in America. Miguel was a dishwasher at a New York City hotel. Lolita was a seamstress. Humble and faithful believers, they were active in their church, Mount Sinai Christian Church of Brooklyn (Iglesia Cristiana Sinai), a congregation of the denomination called the Christian Church (Disciples of Christ) (6). This congregation would formally serve as the sponsoring church for me and my family. Miguel was treasurer of Iglesia Cristiana Sinai, which, to this day, I consider my home church in the United States.

Because of the late hour, we hurried to get our luggage and make our way to the family's apartment in Brooklyn, a half hour away (7). From the front seat of the large sedan that Miguel had borrowed to pick us up, I stared in awe at the Manhattan skyline—and, though warm in the heated car, shivered from the thought of the outside temperature. Never in my life had I been in such cold.

The Dominguezes lived in a small but comfortable one-bedroom, one-bath apartment on the third floor of a building on Jefferson Street. It was after 1 a.m. when we finally collapsed into borrowed twin beds that Miguel had arranged. I spent the next few days as I had in Miami—resting and adjusting to the whirlwind changes of the past week. The cold of New York was one of the most difficult adjustments. I found the falling snow, which I had only read about but had never seen, delightful to watch. However, after a few days of snowfall, no sunshine, and seeing the gray sky turn dark at 4 p.m., I knew living in New York would be a difficult change for me. Nonetheless, I was so grateful to Miguel and Lolita, our guardian angels.

In no time, we met many new friends from the church and neighborhood. Many of them wanted to know of my experience in Cuba, and I found myself—without merit—suspicious of some of their questions. The intimidation I felt in Cuba I carried to the United States. I couldn't yet speak of all I had seen and experienced. I remember one man telling me, "You are in America. You can speak the truth." I tried to be trusting, but so much fear and pain from Cuba lingered in my heart. Even to this day, I must confess that I feel suspicious of strangers who want to engage me about Cuba.

After only a week in New York, I felt compelled to get a job—even though I was chronically sick to my stomach. "I have two arms," I told Miguel, "and I want to work." Miguel said what I needed was rest. One man told me that the U.S. government would pay me welfare until I got back on my feet. I said, "I don't need welfare. Save it for a mother with a baby."

Miguel was right about needing the rest—and time to adjust to my new life. I soon found myself awaking every night from nightmares. I was sick with nausea and throwing up. I found myself ridden with fear, pervasive fear. Every time a stranger spoke to me, I was suspicious. If people were friendly to me, I was anxious. I thought they might be spies out to hurt me and my family. I was fragile, and I didn't know why. I felt trapped and panicky. Doctors today, I believe, would diagnose my condition as post-traumatic stress disorder, which can afflict people who have witnessed or experienced traumatic events (8).

I had a classic case. For me, the condition manifested itself in both predictable and unpredictable ways. One Saturday, only a few weeks after our arrival in New York, the congregation at Mount Sinai hosted a "welcoming shower" for our family. More than one hundred church members attended, offering us food, new housewares, and other gifts to help us start our lives in the United States. We received dishes, blankets, utensils, and many other gifts.

Long tables of food—turkey, dressing, vegetables—stretched the length of the church basement. However, when I got up to get a plate, I couldn't proceed through the line. I started to sob. I thought of my family in Cuba, the sacrifices they were enduring. I thought of the men in the camps. I said to myself, "Here I have so much food, surrounded by people I love, and there are the others left behind in Cuba; they are ones who don't have anything." One of the men from the church took me into another room and stayed with me while I broke down—part of the healing process, I would later discover.

The nightmares continued. There were recurring images— armed soldiers coming for me, wherever I was. They would take me into interrogation rooms and tell me that I would never leave the concentration camps. My digestive system was a wreck. I prayed for the Lord's mercy. Slowly, after many months, recovery began to take hold. I began to open up to some of the dear church members who reached out to me. My irrational fears began to abate. My stomach began to heal. I started gaining weight from a steady and healthy diet.

To my last breath, I will always be grateful to my brothers and sisters at Mount Sinai Christian Church in Brooklyn. This congregation opened its doors and received me and my family with love. They made me feel that I was no longer a stranger in a strange land. They made me one of their own. They helped me spiritually, praying and reading the Bible with me, counseling me and sharing love, kindness, and tenderness when I needed it most.

By the end of the second month living with Miguel and Lolita in their one-bedroom Brooklyn apartment, Jacqui and I were ready to find a place of our own. Maria, Jacqui's mother, remained with Miguel and Lolita.

January 1970 brought a new year full of promise, but it was in a place that I didn't like at all. I loved New Yorkers—the people. But the place itself was strange for me, so compacted, so expensive, and with so little sun. I yearned for warm weather, brilliant sun, and open spaces. Complicating matters was the fact that I knew very little English. Although I read English in the camps, my vocabulary was extremely limited. I could say, "Good morning," "Good afternoon," "How are you?" "Yes," and "No." But my pronunciations were awful.

With the help of church members, who provided our first month's rent and security deposit, along with furniture, we found a two-bedroom apartment in an old building a few blocks from the Dominguezes. The apartment was shabby, crowded, cold and, much to Jacqui's terror, infested with cockroaches and rats. The heat didn't work, and we suffered through weeks of cold nights. But at $195 a month, the place was affordable.

Equipped with a work permit, a Social Security card, and a few leads from church members, I went in search of a job (9). I was hired as the pastor of a small Hispanic congregation, affiliated with the Southern Baptists, in Corona, Queens (10). I received a generous salary of $200 a month. The congregation met in the basement of an Anglo church for Wednesday night services, Bible study, and Sunday morning services. On Saturdays, I would call on church members at their homes. I loved being in ministry again, although it was not full-time.

I took a second job in a factory in Queens that made kitchen stoves. I welded stove parts for the minimum wage—$1.45 an hour in 1970. My shift was from 6 a.m. to 2 p.m. I arose at 5, walked to a subway station three blocks away, and rode the train twenty-five minutes to the factory. In the winter, I wore three shirts and two pairs of pants, but I still froze. And, as I would learn later, the factory—which hired recovering drug addicts in rehabilitation—was unsafe.

The job I truly desired, the calling of my life, was to return to full-time ministry as a pastor. I prayed to God, expressing my heart's desire. In late January, I was approached by the general offices of the Christian Church (Disciples of Christ) in Indianapolis, the mother church of Mount Sinai. The denomination was seeking Hispanic pastors (11). In my interview with a church executive, I learned that my evangelical background would be welcomed. I admired the inclusiveness that the Disciples of Christ showed toward me and other minority group members. Very quickly, I became convinced that the denomination was one where I could worship and pastor while being myself.

I was certain a full-time return to ministry was the direction God wanted me to pursue. However, Jacqui seemed as certain in her opposition to that plan. "The people will always have you, always be calling you, and keeping you occupied," she said. "What about me?" There were better-paying opportunities, she said. And, while Jacqui cared no more for the cold weather than I, she liked New York—the excitement, variety, and pace of the big city. I disliked it intensely. I continued to pray for reconciliation with Jacqui.

In early March, I received word from the Disciples of Christ of what was, to me, an unbelievable opportunity—to revive a small church in the South Texas town of San Benito, near the border with Mexico. The church had twenty-eight members and a parsonage— a home—on the church grounds. The congregation could afford no salary, but the Indianapolis office would pay to move us there and provide $350 a month for expenses. However, what I remember most from the conversation was this: "There is hot weather and the people speak Spanish."

I said, "Send me there, please!"

Jacqui would have none of it. She saw the pay I was earning in New York from the factory and from the Baptists and compared it to what we were earning in Cuba. She said, "This is good money." She was right. But the future for me wasn't about money. It was about serving God.

I had so hoped that our newfound freedom would mean a new beginning for Jacqui and me. But once again, I found myself in despair, this time in New York, on my knees seeking God's guidance. I asked Him to show me his will for my life. Was Texas the location he was calling me to serve? I prayed for my marriage.

Meanwhile, I had a family to support, and I went to my factory job every morning. Several of the men there, supposedly in rehab, came to work doped up on drugs. One day in April, the situation nearly turned tragic for me.

On my way to a coffee break, in a room just off the main factory floor, a young woman tried to stop me. I went around her, and, just as I did, a man who was high on drugs came from behind and tried to rob me of my wallet. He held a switchblade to my throat. Reacting on instinct, I elbowed him in the stomach and turned around quickly to face my attacker, only to see him lunging at my stomach with the knife. I jumped back, screaming at the top of my lungs. I ran into a room next door and locked the latch. I was crying and screaming.

In an instant, the fragile scab that had begun forming over my experience in Cuba was ripped away. Supervisors from the factory found me and tried to comfort me. The two culprits would be captured and prosecuted for assault and attempted robbery, they promised. They urged me to go home and come back the next day. But I knew what I was to do. I took this episode as the sign I had asked God to give me.

I went home, told Jacqui what had happened, and informed her that I was quitting the factory job and moving to San Benito. I phoned Indianapolis and accepted the offer. Jacqui was very angry, but after some conversations with her mother, the pastor of Mount Sinai, and her uncle Miguel, she relented. She would go to Texas, too.

We prepared again for a move to a strange place. However, one family member would remain in New York: Jacqui's mother Maria. After many years alone, she had found love in New York. Her first husband died when Jacqui was a toddler, leaving Maria a widow at sixteen. In New York, she had fallen in love with Lolita's brother. Although we would miss Maria terribly, Jacqui and I were delighted that she had found a life for herself.

As we packed for the move to Texas, I felt assured that this was the call of the Lord. I had a few moments of doubt, however, when some people in New York told me: "You are going to a place that has no culture. You are going to a region where the Mexicans fight for everything. They use pistols and knives, and they will kill."

At the time, the only Mexican I had ever met was one of the leaders of the Communist party in Cuba. People lived in fear of him and his family. But then I met a woman who had attended a Bible institute in Edinburgh, Texas—about forty-five miles from San Benito. She told me, "If you treat people there with love, you will have them in your pocket." She added, "There are lots of Mexican festivals. It's not so bad."

The day of our departure was May 14, 1970. The kids and I were excited, and even Jacqui seemed okay with the relocation. The moving company had come the day before to pack our few belongings and ship them to Texas.

We would fly from New York to Houston and then on to Harlingen, about six miles from San Benito. At JFK airport, where just six months earlier we had arrived as refugees, Miguel and Lolita held us in their arms once more. This time, their hugs would bid us farewell on our journey's next leg. We were refugees no more.

As I hugged Miguel and Lolita, feelings of gratitude coursed through my body. If not for these humble servants—he a dishwasher, she a seamstress—I would not be alive today. God, in His mercy and grace, had saved my life, and now I was off to a place I had never seen to assume my call as a Cuban minister of a Mexican congregation.

I could hardly wait to get to the place I would call home.

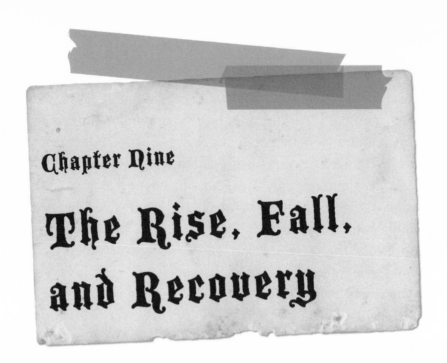

Chapter Nine

The Rise, Fall, and Recovery

From the window of our jet, for as far as I could see, green carpets of croplands bordered by swaying palm trees stretched across the landscape in all directions. For a moment, I thought we were returning to Cuba. When we left New York early that morning for Texas, I didn't know what to expect upon my arrival in the Rio Grande Valley (1). Although the church executive who offered me the position had tried to describe the place, I had focused only on his depiction of the climate and language of the Valley, not its geography. From my window seat, I thought the flat and lush green landscape was beautiful.

As the plane pulled into our gate at Valley International Airport and the flight attendants opened the cabin door, a rush of sticky, humid air baked by the brilliant afternoon sun hit my face. Startled by the warmth and texture of the breeze, tears filled my eyes. I found myself filled with unanticipated joy. As we walked toward the terminal in 80-degree weather, Jacqui smiled at me, and her look described what I felt: "We have found our new home."

Immediately, upon seeing her face, my senses united in delight. I had not felt so much happiness in years. I was concerned that Jacqui's initial refusal to come to Texas might resurrect itself after she saw the place, but my worry was for nothing. When I observed her reaction, I knew instantly that this was the place that the Lord was asking me to be, the land that he chose for me to live out my days. In my mind, I recalled the Lord's words from Genesis, Chapter 12, concerning the call of Abram:

The Lord had said to Abram, *Leave your country, your people and your father's household and go to the land I will show you.*

I didn't know what lay in store for me in the Valley, but I knew deep in my soul that some special purpose was planned.

I knew little about the church in San Benito, the Second Christian Church (*Segunda Iglesia Cristiana*). It had been closed for several years, but was recently restarted by Eliseo Rodriguez, pastor of a Christian Church in nearby Brownsville. The church itself, the sanctuary, and the parsonage next door, were in need of work, I was told. Still, I was excited that the official rolls of the Second Christian Church listed the names of twenty-eight members.

Inside the airport terminal, Eliseo and his wife Elizabeth greeted us with hugs. Anxious to see the church and our new home, we asked Eliseo to take us straight to San Benito, then a town of 15,000. As we drove, I noticed that almost all the people we passed had brown skin like us. Eliseo, a Cuban, said that almost everyone in the Valley spoke Spanish. I found his words reassuring, because my progress in learning English had been painfully slow.

In the time it took us to drive the six miles from the airport to San Benito and park in front of the church, at 335 Corral Street in San Benito, our family had worked itself into a collective frenzy. I got out of the car and gave the surroundings a quick once-over. I noticed right away that the aging buildings were in need of improvements, but my overall impressions were positive. The grass and weeds would need cutting; the fading and chipped wooden buildings needed repainting; and the barren grounds cried for some trees and flowers. Hard work was nothing new for me.

We carried our luggage into the parsonage, our new, two-bedroom, one-bath home. It was in sorry condition, but it had potential. My mind went to work. I would start by repairing the roof and ceiling, where cracked plaster and water stains greeted us from one corner of the living room. Next, I noticed something I had overlooked at first—almost all the windows in the house were broken. I would need to replace the panes. As I continued walking through the house, I cringed. The entire place needed a thorough scrubbing and paint job. The home was bare; it had not one stick of furniture. For the short-term, I would see about getting mattresses for us to sleep on.

Concluding our tour of the parsonage, we walked the few steps over to the sanctuary and opened the doors. I was shocked by what I saw. There were no pews—a few chairs, but no pews. I saw a small closet in the corner and opened the door. I was surprised to find a hole in the floor, until a pungent odor told me that the closet had once been a bathroom.

Retreating hastily from the stench, I turned back to the sanctuary just in time to watch a marble my son Joel had accidentally dropped race on its own momentum to the front of the church. I immediately saw why—the floor was sloped.

Soon, however, we were warmly greeted at the parsonage by two ladies and six children who had brought food. They were members of the church who dropped by to welcome us. Sitting on the floor of our new home, Jacqui and I ate a simple but wonderful supper of Mexican rice, pinto beans, and tortillas. After we cleaned up, we made our way back to the sanctuary for a special worship service, during which the members of the church were supposed to formally greet us.

When we arrived, the two ladies and six children who had brought us our dinner were waiting inside—but there was no one else there. I greeted them again. I looked at my watch. It was past time to start the service. I was a little surprised that the other twenty members of the church had not been able to attend, but I didn't think much more of it. Those of us there had a wonderful service.

For our first night in Texas, Jacqui and I made up pallets for the kids and ourselves. On the floor of the old, beaten-up parsonage, we had our most peaceful night of sleep since our arrival in the United States six months earlier.

Over the course of the next few weeks, I gained a clearer and deeper understanding of the circumstances at Second Christian Church. To his credit, Eliseo had tried to revive the church, but the needs were too demanding for one person, much less someone who already had a thriving ministry in Brownsville, twenty miles away (2).

The facts were these:
- The two ladies and six children who had greeted us so warmly were, in fact, the entire church membership. There may have been twenty-eight names on the official rolls, but only these eight remained active members.
- The church, built in 1935, had closed in 1966—literally shuttered. There was no budget and no functioning church board to raise or develop one. The pews were gone because they had been given to a growing church in Reynosa, Mexico, about forty-five miles away.
- Before my arrival, the church had nearly been sold to the Jehovah's Witnesses. They had plans to develop a thriving congregation at the site. However, their purchase contract with the regional office of the Christian Church allowed us to re-take the facility with thirty-days' notice—which had been done. The local leader of the Jehovah's Witnesses told me, "There is no chance to build a successful

Hispanic church in this area. It's been an impossible job for many other ministers, and it will be for you. Go to another place!" I replied, "I will do my best here with the help of the Lord."

I must confess that upon learning the truth of the San Benito situation, I was frustrated. When I accepted the call to come to the Valley, I was led to believe that there was a church already established. The labor needed to repair the parsonage and church was not the issue; it was that I had no real congregation to serve. And, yet, a voice inside told me, "Pereira, you will have a church. You will have a congregation." From that point on, I prayed and worked with great enthusiasm. I was certain that the Lord would provide.

On my first Sunday in San Benito, we held services, and three former church members joined my family and the two ladies and six children for worship. The Sunday after that, five more adults visited. Once a total of ten church members joined the congregation, we named one of them church treasurer. I think it is best to not have the pastor involved in managing church finances.

Encouraged by this early growth, I decided to embark on a strategy that would bear wonderful fruit. I would personally visit every home within one mile of the church. I had no car or other transportation, but that didn't stop me. I walked the streets of San Benito. When I called on folks, I identified myself, told them of the new Christian Church I was starting and gave them my card. I issued them a warm invitation to visit our Sunday service. Every week, several of those I had called upon came. I gave God the glory for making this occur. One day, I called on a wonderful Pentecostal lady. Upon learning that I was making my visitation calls on foot because I had no transportation, she gave me a bicycle that she no longer used. I was grateful for the gift, and it contributed greatly to our evangelism efforts.

However, not everyone in San Benito welcomed my initiative.

My door-to-door visitations infuriated the Jehovah's Witnesses, who accused me of stealing members from them. They threatened to sue my church superiors to force a sale of Second Christian Church. Surprising even myself—I realized I was healing from my experiences in Cuba—I didn't run from the conflict, but rather stood up to them. Attempting to intimidate me, they began following me, calling on the same people I had just finished visiting. They told people that I was crazy and that our church would not make it—they should join the more stable Jehovah's Witnesses.

I confronted one of the men and engaged him in a theological discussion. Finally, I said, "I notice you are going to the very same people that I am coming to. Why do you do that?" I added, "If you want to compete for visitations, I will do the same with your prospects. I will visit all of them!"

Finally, the district leader of the Jehovah's Witnesses, a Cuban man, came to see me. I said to him, "You know that I am a Cuban, too. You know how Cubans can be. If you want to play this game, I will play it, too." It wasn't long before the Jehovah's Witnesses dropped their efforts to purchase Second Christian Church and evangelize the neighborhood. They took their efforts across town.

The first few months in San Benito were difficult. However, from the beginning, the Lord provided for our needs. In a matter of weeks, I secured the donation of seating for our sanctuary—rows of chairs from a closed movie theater. With help from our small but dedicated congregation, we painted the sanctuary and parsonage inside and out. Rotting boards, broken windows, and ripped screens were replaced. Plumbing was repaired.

One of our visitors, a young man from Mexico, painted a colorful scene in the baptistry. Outside, I cut down the tall weeds and planted trees and flowers. I erected a fence around the parsonage, built a garage and attached a carport to the house. As hard as I worked on the church facilities, Jacqui labored equally on the parsonage. She cleaned and sewed beautiful curtains and bedspreads and clothing for the children, as well as costumes for a Christmas pageant. Our start was made easier by many generous Anglos, Christians of many Protestant denominations. They brought to our church material for Bible classes, as well as furnishings for the sanctuary and our house.

While our $350 monthly salary was considered subsistent for that time, I thought it generous. We were able to pay our tithe and cover our expenses. When we needed a few extra dollars, I would mow lawns in the neighborhood. Economically, Jacqui and I fit perfectly into the neighborhood. Our salary was probably more than that of many parishioners in our neighborhood (3).

At 3 p.m. on Sunday, July 12, 1970, I was formally installed as pastor of Second Christian Church. I told the congregation: "Brothers and sisters, before you and with you, I affirm my desire to be your pastor. I promise with the help of our savior Jesus Christ that I will live an exemplary life for you and I will be diligent and faithful to fulfill my ministry as a good servant of Jesus Christ for the congregation and to the glory of his name for the edification of the church."

Important to Jacqui and me was getting Ruthie and Joel settled in the elementary school, located across the street from the church. Neither of the kids spoke a word of English, but God sent us an angel by the name of Anna Cora Rush, an Anglo teacher who took our children under her wing with great love and taught them English and so much more beginning in the late summer of 1970. She and her husband John were very kind to me and my family, and I will always consider them a gift from God.

By the end of 1970, our church had grown to include about fifty members. As a congregation, we made the decision to grow aggressively. We set a goal to baptize ten new members every three months. We drew our inspiration from the words of William Carey, the English Protestant missionary and Baptist minister known as "the father of modern missions." He said, "Expect great things from God. Attempt great things for God (4)."

I became involved with the San Benito Ministerial Alliance, an ecumenical group of Anglo ministers from across the Valley, even though I was unable to stitch together a complete sentence in English. (I used a lot of smiles and hand gestures.) By the reaction I received from my listeners, I seemed to communicate just fine.

Some of my Hispanic colleagues in ministry told me that they wouldn't try to speak English, since they couldn't do so without an accent. Others, however, said that if I wanted to achieve success, I should try to speak English no matter how poorly I did so at first. I chose this route. To this day, I always apologize for my poor English before speaking to a group. As for my Cuban accent, I don't even try to cover it up. When I first arrived in the Valley, even some of my church members couldn't understand my Cuban-accented Spanish.

In South Texas in 1971, I found myself bridging two like-hearted groups of ministers, Anglos and Hispanics, whose cultural and language differences kept them apart. In Cuba, I had known neither Anglos nor Mexicans. My cultural background was different from either group's heritage. What I knew then—and certainly know now—is that Jesus' love unites us all. I emphasized this to both the Hispanics and the Anglos when I came to San Benito by always trying to be polite to any person I met. But I also believed that we needed to proactively address this split between our backgrounds, starting with our youth. I proposed a joint Anglo-Hispanic camp for youth, a concept that was greeted with enthusiasm by all.

As I approached my first anniversary in San Benito, I knew that the United States would be my permanent home. In early March of 1971, with the Vietnam War in full swing, I went to the post office in San Benito and attempted to register with the Selective

Service. I was ready to pledge my loyalty in the event that my service was required. My application was rejected. In fact, I think the postmaster thought I was *loco* for even trying to register. At thirty-two, I was too old to serve, and my immigration status made me ineligible. To this day, however, I carry my Selective Service card in my wallet, No. 4116381519, and I am ready to defend my country if ever needed.

I loved my new country and all the opportunities it provided. In my first five years in San Benito, I became enthusiastically involved in many civic and church-related activities. I was an officer or director on five different church boards. In 1972, I was elected president of the Spanish convention of Texas churches of my denomination. I was also president of the San Benito Ministerial Alliance.

Through the alliance, I helped develop an ecumenical chaplaincy at the Dolly Vinsant Memorial Hospital in San Benito. I viewed this as part of my calling to minister to the sick and the poor in spirit. I also told every funeral home in San Benito to inform families who did not have money for a funeral service to call me. I would gladly perform a service at no cost, no matter the family's religious background. I applied the same policy to weddings. And if I was offered a fee for my services, I told the bride's father to contribute it to the church. I figured that if people at weddings have money for drinking, they can just as well give to the Lord.

To everyone I called upon, I extended an invitation to visit our church. Motivated by the Spirit of God, I made 260 separate calls on people in November 1972 alone. I believe that evangelism must be conducted in the streets, in homes, in hospitals, and in jails. We cannot evangelize from behind our desks, cranking out e-mails. Following the example of the Lord, it must be done with a personal touch.

At Second Christian Church, we who began as a mission church were being transformed into a missionary congregation. Despite the poverty of many of our members—some still had only out- houses in those days—we worked to provide ministry wherever it was needed.

In March 1971, with the gift of a passenger van from our denom- ination, we started a bus ministry, transporting twenty-five to forty passengers to and from church every Sunday. During the rest of the week, we used the van to drive those who needed transportation to the hospital or pharmacy. We also delivered clothes, food, and furni- ture to the needy. In less than two years, we wore out a set of tires.

We also opened "home missions" in our members' residences to reach friends and relatives who did not attend church services. For our new converts, we put into practice a "big brother" system, in which established church members agreed to shepherd new members. Every first Sunday of the month was "friendship day." Every member was to invite a friend to our services. Twice a year we held revivals. We also formed a jail ministry to reach out to those behind bars.

In September 1971, we launched a radio ministry, *The Christian Hour* (*La Hora Cristiana*). I had no experience in radio—beyond my childhood fantasies—but I knew from my days in Cuba as a listener how powerfully radio can carry messages of hope, victory, and faith. With the help of supporters, *The Christian Hour*—in reality, a fifteen-minute broadcast—became one of the most suc- cessful Spanish-language religious programs in South Texas (5). The program aired at 9 p.m. Sundays on KGBT (1530 AM) in Har- lingen, a 50,000-watt station that blanketed much of South Texas and Northern Mexico.

The program addressed thousands of listeners craving spiritual food. With God's help and support from generous contributors, we expanded the reach of the broadcast. Eventually, *La Hora* reached 15 million people in two-dozen countries—from the southern tip of

Argentina to as far north as Canada—on more than fifty stations.

At the end of every broadcast, I invited the audience to write to us for a free Bible correspondence lesson, written in Spanish. Eventually, we developed eighteen different Bible lesson booklets, which became popular throughout Latin America and the Caribbean. By 1985, we had 50,000 listeners studying the Bible by correspondence, even though it was a great challenge to raise our needed monthly operating budget.

I have no accurate record of how many programs of *The Christian Hour* we completed over the years, but it was well more than five hundred. I prepared the messages so they could be heard any time of any day of any year. I was careful not to mention the hour of the day, the month, or the year. I wanted these to be timeless messages that could be replayed in the years to come. Although the hundreds of programs were hard work to prepare, distribute, and publicize on a regular basis—at the peak we produced a new program every week—the experience was a glorious one.

By early 1973, our church—dead just three years before—was open most nights of the week. On Mondays, we held church board and committee meetings. On Wednesdays, we had Bible study; on Thursdays, we trained teachers in preparing lessons for evangelizing; on Saturdays, we gathered for prayer in preparation for the Lord's Day. On Sundays, our worship services went well past noon; then, in the evening, we gathered again for more worship.

I believe when we serve Christ faithfully, He manifests Himself. In our congregation, we prayed and we fasted and we preached what the Scripture says. I believe that's why people sought us out.

To our great surprise and delight, the monthly magazine of our church's denomination, *World Call*, published an article entitled "Rebirth in San Benito" in June 1973. The article began: "Together, Segunda Iglesia Cristiana in San Benito, Texas, and its Cuban pastor, F. Feliberto Pereira, have been reborn. The vibrancy of the congregation belies its deadness three years ago, when its building stood gutted and decaying." To have my photo on the cover of the magazine was an unbelievable honor. The national attention prompted a speaking invitation in October 1973 before the International Assembly of the Christian Churches in Cincinnati, Ohio. I spoke at a workshop called "Renewal of the Church."

By the end of 1973, attendance at our Sunday services averaged about one hundred. We had a thriving youth group of about thirty, and several young people participated as teachers of children's classes and song leaders. I worked diligently with our youth, teaching them to be proud of being Christian—and Hispanic.

When I first arrived in San Benito, I noticed that many of the teenage Mexican boys, especially in the presence of authority figures, stood with slumped shoulders and heads bowed, never daring to make eye contact. They seemed resentful and without pride. One day, when I came across this in a young man, I jammed my hand under his chin, forced his head up, and made him square his shoulders. I told him, "You may be poor and brown, but you are a man of worth and loved by God!"

I started doing the same thing with other young men. Fellow church members, following my lead, began doing it as well. It worked beautifully.

Young people who discover themselves as persons of value and who are proud to be who they are in Christ are the finest and most promising anywhere. Oh, a few are full of mischief and they bring trouble to our hearts when they make poor judgments, but they are also the joy of our lives. I have seen young people care for the elderly, take food and clothing to the poor, clean and work around the church, and give many hours of hard work on behalf of others. They stand proud of their heritage in Christ and are a blessing to the entire community. Now when I make eye contact with them, I see in their eyes dancing lights of joy and anticipation.

In January 1974, the church board and I challenged the congregation to set a record attendance of 150 before the end of the year. By October, we were busting the seams of our forty-year-old facility, enjoying an average Sunday attendance of 210. The month before, in September, the congregation stepped out in faith, voting to build a new sanctuary and to give our church a new name: Emmanuel Christian Church (*Iglesia Cristiana Emmanuel*). Emmanuel means "God with us." To be candid, I never liked the name Second Christian Church. Within a year of my arrival in San Benito, I wanted to change it, I told the church board, "We are not second at being Christian." I was happy the congregation embraced Emmanuel as the name of the church.

Although our church members were largely poor, most of them tithed faithfully. But even more important than our financial growth was the number of conversions to Christ. For without bringing people to Christ, our offerings of money would have little meaning. From July 1974 to June 1975, forty people were baptized in submission to the Savior.

We launched a building campaign fund and every member gave sacrificially. One single mother, who received an income of $189 a month, gave $19 of it to the church without fail. One elderly member received $143 a month in income. She faithfully gave 10 percent to the church. For the building campaign, she went into a partnership of sorts with God. She made and sold tamales and other food. From her efforts, she contributed $200 a month—every month. Any remainder from her sales above $200 was hers.

We praised the Lord because we only had to borrow $48,000 of the $125,000 actual cost for a new sanctuary and an educational building.

In June 1976, with permission from the national church office, we relocated the parsonage to a five-acre plot that I purchased about three miles from the church. Then we constructed the education building on the site of the former parsonage. Once the education building was completed, we demolished the old sanctuary, moving our worship services to the education building while the new sanctuary was constructed.

On Sunday, June 19, 1977, at 3 p.m. with national, state, and local dignitaries present, we dedicated our new sanctuary and education building. In his remarks, my friend and brother, Lucas Torres, then director of Hispanic programs for the Christian Church (Disciples of Christ), summed up my feelings about our growing church and those I was called to serve there:

"This building will be a visible reminder to every Mexican, Mexican-American, and Hispanic-American in this community, regarding the potentials hidden in each one of them, and all that can be achieved when a people are united in one spirit," he said. "These stones will offer every day a challenge more eloquent than all the words."

Overcome by emotion, I spoke only a few words at the dedication. The new facilities were a dream come true, the result of prayer, sacrifice, and the united efforts of the congregation of Emmanuel Christian Church. God was truly with us. We were given fifteen years to repay the $48,000 loan; we repaid it in four. On November 8, 1981, during a Thanksgiving service, I was privileged to lead the congregation in a ceremonial burning of the mortgage.

We would eventually grow to have 425 baptized members, the largest Hispanic church in the Disciples denomination. But as wonderful and exciting and fulfilling as were these years at Emmanuel Christian Church, I would have gladly traded every moment to save my marriage to Jacqui.

I had hoped with all my heart that we would find a fresh start in the United States, but it was not to be. A healthy marriage takes two people willing to mutually submit to one another, to support each other through good times and bad, and to be united in spirit and flesh. It is a mutual commitment blessed by God that both husband and wife honor until death.

In 1978, Jacqui made a decision to leave our marriage, and in 1979 she filed for divorce. It was granted in March 1980, without my participation in the proceedings (6). It was the most painful experience of my life—worse than anything I endured in the prison camps. I was taught that divorce was unacceptable.

Today, I recognize that every coin has two faces. I accept responsibility for my role in the failure of our marriage. I was very involved in being a minister. I must confess that I enjoyed our church's heady years of triumph. But, as great as the experiences were for me, they came at a tremendous cost—time away from my wife and two children. In retrospect, I recognize that during those first years in the United States, I neglected my family. I made a mistake, so clear in hindsight, by abandoning my family emotionally during these years. I wanted to do so much for the Lord, but in the process I wasn't doing enough for my family. It was not intentional. Nonetheless, I am sorry for the hurt I caused. If I have learned nothing else, I know that if a person is to heal from painful experiences, he must be honest with himself, no matter how difficult the truth.

In the early 1990s, Jacqui and I were able to resume our friendship. In an interview in June 2001 with my co-author, Jacqui took responsibility for the collapse of our marriage. "My plan was to finish my life with him," she said. "But I ended the marriage. He didn't give me the attention I wanted and needed because he was giving his all to the Lord and to the people. All the time he was busy with the people. I needed more attention, but I didn't wait for it. I became very tired, and I didn't wait on the Lord's answers to my prayers. What I did made me guilty. And I will feel guilty all my life for that. I know the Lord forgives me. I forgive Feli, and

I know Feli forgives me, too. Feliberto is a good man who has devoted his life in service to the Lord."

In 1990, Jacqui was diagnosed with multiple sclerosis. As the disease progressed, she was confined to a wheelchair and eventually to an assisted living center in Harlingen, where Maria, her mother, visited her daily. I, Joel, Ruthie, and other relatives visited her on a regular basis.

Through the collapse of my marriage, the congregation of Emmanuel Christian Church rallied behind me. Some churches, especially in a small, conservative town in South Texas, might want to sever ties with a preacher going through a divorce. But the leaders of my church, in the manner and ways of Jesus, embraced and comforted me.

As I grieved the end of my marriage, I also cried for the church that I had worked so hard to build. The church board, believing that I might leave San Benito because of my personal situation, raised my salary and provided me with a car. The church did not want me to leave. I will forever be grateful for the support of my congregation during the toughest period of my life. I love them with all my heart.

One of God's many promises is that He will open a new door whenever we find one suddenly bolted shut. And so it came to pass that as the 1980s unfolded and a fog of grief infiltrated all aspects of my personal life, God revealed a new mission for me.

As a young minister, I told God, "Here I am, Lord."

Now, as a divorced minister in my early forties, I knew that God was doing the talking.

"Feliberto, are you there?"

Chapter Ten

The Good Samaritan

In 1980, Central America stood in chaos—a region wracked by war, civil strife, and widespread human rights abuses. Violence had driven hundreds of thousands of men, women, and children through Mexico and across the border to the Rio Grande Valley—a migration of mass proportion that the United States had never seen at its border with Mexico before (1). What began as a trickle of refugees, arriving in 1979 from El Salvador, turned into a torrent a year later. The tidal wave of fearful, hungry, thirsty, and emotionally wounded refugees overwhelmed our local public agencies, charities, and churches. They were simply not prepared to cope with the scope and scale.

Even as my heart ached over the breakup of my marriage, my spirit hurt for these poor souls. I saw these brothers and sisters in bus stations, in airport parking lots, in our parks and orchards. Driving home, I found needy men, women, and children crowded near our church doors and, eventually, at my front door. In all candor, I was initially at a loss as to what I could do for these strangers seeking protection from the violence in their homelands. I must confess that I saw them as foreigners. We should be visiting them as missionaries, I thought, not hosting in our country without an invitation.

Overwhelmed, I pondered, "What is my responsibility to these strangers among us?"

A turning point for me came when I visited the sheriff of Cameron County, a border county, at his invitation. He wanted to show me photographs of dozens of bodies of men, women, and children who had drowned attempting to cross the Rio Grande.

My heart ached as I viewed the images of these dead refugees from El Salvador and Nicaragua, who had wanted the gift of freedom, the asylum I had been given by America. The scale of the challenges hit me like a bolt of lightening. We were the closest region of America to their home countries. *Of course, they would come to us* (2)*!*

As I looked at the photographs, I paused to pray for each of the victims and their families. I battled both tears and anger. Tears for the suffering they had obviously endured, anger over the popular terms of the day used to describe these brothers and sisters— "illegal aliens" and "wetbacks." Upon seeing these photographs, I viewed the refugees not as "illegal"—God does not consider any human being "illegal"—but as gifts brought to us at a most opportune time. It occurred to me that whereas God may have called us at one time to minister to those in foreign lands, the foreigner was now visiting us, challenging all churches near the border with Mexico (3).

I found myself overwhelmed by the evidence I encountered— the tragedy of the refugees who died in search of freedom and the considerable needs of those who safely made it across the border. They needed food, clothing, shelter, and spiritual care—needs reflected by the pile of messages on my desk at the church office.

None of us in the Valley were prepared to house, feed, or clothe tens of thousands of brothers and sisters for long periods. In reality, their needs were not going to be met quickly, not with hundreds more refugees arriving each week.

One day, I prayed in frustration, "God, who will do this work? Who?"

God answered: "You!"

"Me? You want me, God? Well, okay. Here I am. Let's go."

Some may think me crazy for accepting this appointment based on a conversation with the Lord. But that day, at that hour, the Lord placed on my heart a burden for refugees. However, God did not send me an instruction manual to go with it. I knew just three things: I was to continue caring for refugees, enlisting others to help me; I was to release my worry and anxiety over managing the intense needs of refugees, turning the burden over to the Lord; and I was to trust God to provide the path and open doors for the new ministry to which He now so forcefully summoned me.

As a result of this expanded mission, my attitude and approach to refugees completely changed. I rid my vocabulary of the label "illegal alien;" I made a choice to love the refugees for who they were in their current circumstance—not as I wished they were or would become. I would treat each person as an individual, taking each seriously, and I would, to the best of my ability, prepare each to pursue citizenship in our nation if they so desired.

I believe with all my heart that when our love frees the refugee of his or her strangeness to us and we overcome our strangeness to him or her, then we both begin to grow in the Lord. I've never wavered from these principles.

I began educating myself on the complexities of mass migrations of people, on U.S. immigration law, and of the special needs of refugees. My enthusiasm soon became known among churches of all backgrounds in the Valley, and I began receiving many calls for assistance. Then, as now, most refugees are referred to me by other churches, social service agencies, and from the U.S. government.

In general, when I come into contact with a refugee whom I know to be a victim of persecution, I first meet any emergency needs such as a meal, clothing, medical attention or prayer. Then, I seek legal assistance for the refugee from one of our partner agencies in the Valley to begin the process of applying for political asylum. Asylum granted by our government offers immunity from extradition. Those seeking asylum aren't officially categorized as refugees until that status is granted by the government.

In the early 1980s, local immigration detention facilities were at capacity due to the influx of Central American refugees. As a result, many refugees were "paroled" to my custody while their cases snaked through the soon-backlogged pipeline of asylum applications. I found myself on the phone day and night trying to find "room in the inn" for these brothers and sisters. At any one time, our church in San Benito hosted as many as twenty refugees. I took another six home to live with me until other arrangements could be made. Eventually, I found emergency housing for all the refugees with whom I had contact.

At night, I was blessed to listen to their stories—to the experiences and fear that drove them to seek protection in America. I cringed at the details of the physical attacks and of the armed conflicts where rape, torture, and ethnic cleansing were part of military strategy. I learned of their escapes from bullets, human traffickers, and bandits; I held their hands as they recounted how they risked their lives crossing stormy seas on leaky rafts. My tears ran heavy alongside theirs. I identified completely with their stories of torture, oppression, and humiliation—experiences I had known firsthand in Cuba.

Fulfilling my promise to God aboard my flight to freedom, I threw myself into trying to meet the needs of these brothers and sisters. I saw my involvement in this new ministry as the grace of the Lord at work in my life. While struggling with the grief of my divorce from Jacqui, God called me to a new beginning. Driven a final time to my knees in despair over my failed marriage, a church in turmoil, and hurt and confused children, I felt God's call to trust in Him to guide me through the tough days, just as He shepherded me through the harsh times in the prison camps.

As God called upon me to help refugees rebuild their lives from the ground up, I asked God to help me rebuild mine.

After Jacqui left our marriage (though she continued to live in the parsonage), I moved into my office at Emmanuel Christian Church, sleeping on a couch. Ashamed, I tried to keep this a secret. However, when Eliseo and Elizabeth Rodriguez, the couple that had greeted us upon our arrival, learned of my situation, they graciously invited me to live with them. Two months later, I received what I consider a miracle. That's when a brother from Costa Rica—a legal immigrant to our country—asked me if I would help him by taking over the monthly payments on six acres just outside town—and the mobile home that sat on it. I gladly did so, and the small ranch became an ideal home for me.

Soon after that, I met a man at a regional meeting of our church denomination in Harlingen who was a strong Christian. In his hotel room, during a long break in our meeting, I poured out my grief and shame over the breakup of my marriage. His compassion, understanding, and guidance served as another turning point in my healing.

He explained what the Bible teaches on divorce. Naïve as it sounds, divorce was such a foreign concept to me because I had never thought it would affect me personally. The man told me: "I believe that what God has joined together, no man can put asunder. Since God's blessing is no longer on your union, the most loving thing to do is to acknowledge that fact and to allow two children of God to go on their separate ways." This new knowledge sealed by prayer through a river of tears, blessed me tremendously, helping me finally accept my divorce, distasteful though it was and remains. Equipped with this new understanding, I could move forward with healing.

Deep down, I understood my new call to refugee ministry would require me to sacrifice what was familiar and comfortable. Consequently, I decided to leave my position at Emmanuel Christian Church. In November 1983, I announced that I was leaving, effective in January. My decision shocked many people. A few of my friends and colleagues told me I was crazy. With 425 active members, Emmanuel was thriving. It had its largest budget ever.

"How will you ever again have a church like the one you have now?" a friend in the ministry asked.

Despite the warnings, I knew I was following the Lord's will. I had spent hours in prayer before making my decision to leave Emmanuel. When God calls, one must listen and act on what one hears. The time was right to make the move. Not only was I ready for what would become the biggest professional challenge in my life, I also was ready for a fresh start.

Emmanuel Christian Church was not built by one person. It was the result of an enterprising and innovative fellowship of concerned people walking with the Holy Spirit. Today, I can tell you with all my heart that I don't regret leaving the pulpit at San Benito. In fact, I remain a regular visitor at Emmanuel Christian, participating in special services or when I am called upon by church leaders there for special assistance.

On January 15, 1984, I delivered my final sermon at Emmanuel. You can imagine the tears shed that day in the standing-room only sanctuary. During the service, the congregation presented me with a plaque that said:

In thankfulness for your work in service of the Lord,
which has been a blessing and inspiration to the people of
God. God Bless you always in the preaching of the Gospel.
If God is with us, who will be against us?

We love you in Christ,
—Iglesia Cristiana Emmanuel
San Benito, Texas

Upon my resignation from Emmanuel, I assumed new responsibilities as director of Hispanic ministries for the Southwest region of the Christian Church (Disciples of Christ). The salary was significantly less than what I earned at Emmanuel, but it provided enough to meet my needs. In my new role, I would be responsible for both "planting" new Hispanic churches and nurturing existing ones in Texas, New Mexico, Louisiana, and a small part of Kansas. I would continue my radio ministry, *La Hora Cristiana*. And I would work with churches to coordinate services for refugees.

Two other tremendous events would occur in 1984: I would remarry, and I would become a U.S. citizen.

In early 1983, nearly three years after my divorce from Jacqui, I sought God's counsel in rebuilding my personal life. During this time, I had not dated anyone. Instead, I prayed for guidance, all the while yearning for the companionship of a wife. "Lord, if it is your will, please provide me a woman who wants to be my wife, who will be supportive of my ministry as my wife first and foremost," I prayed.

Following this time of intense prayer, I immediately began envisioning one particular woman as my wife. Prior to that time, I had never considered her in a romantic way. When I shared my feelings for this person with my closest friends, some questioned my sanity. Some even became angry.

I would surprise many in the church—and in my circle of friends and family—by marrying Micaela Salazar, a member of Emmanuel Christian Church. Born a U.S. citizen on a ranch near San Benito on July 10, 1953, Mica was raised in Matamoros, Mexico, by her mother. Her father had abandoned the family when Mica was an infant. Desiring a better education for her daughter, Mica's mother arranged for Mica to live at the home of her sister (Mica's aunt) in San Benito to attend school. Her mother remained in Mexico, working as a housekeeper.

During the summers, Mica worked as a migrant farm laborer, traveling with her extended family to Ohio to pick cucumbers and tomatoes and, later, to Florida picking oranges. Rising before the sun, she often worked twelve-hour days in poor weather conditions, leaving her exhausted.

By her early twenties she was on her own, with a full-time job, a car, and her own place (a small travel trailer). "I know what it means to work and to obtain something," she told a friend once. Mica and her aunt were early members of Emmanuel. I baptized Mica as a young woman of seventeen. She was a very faithful person. She became a driver of our church bus, bringing and taking home church members on Sunday. In 1974, she began as secretary of *La Hora Cristiana*, reporting to the director of the program, where she worked faithfully for nearly twenty years before taking a better-paying position in 1992 with the Harlingen public school system.

I understand how strange our union might appear to an outsider. I am the first to say that our decision to enter marriage seemed unlikely and, to be sure, appeared unusual—suspicious, even, to some. Mica was quiet and retiring; I had an outgoing personality. She was fifteen years younger. I was a divorced minister with two teenage children. As you might imagine, not everyone approved of our marriage.

The turning point for me to seek Mica's hand in marriage came when I shared my feelings with older, wiser people whose opinion I respected tremendously. One was an older woman, a church member, who told me that, in prayer, she had a vision of Mica as my future wife. The other person was my father, who came to visit in February 1983 on a visa from Cuba. At the time, he was losing his eyesight due to cataracts, so I also arranged for him to undergo eye surgery in the United States, which was successful. During the recuperation time with me on the ranch, I told him of my feelings for Mica, whom he had met. He was pleased and gave me his blessing to move forward in marriage.

I proceeded to ask Mica to marry me. Before my proposal, she knew nothing of my feelings for her. As you might imagine, she was surprised to hear me tell her of my love for her. You could say that my marriage proposal shocked her. In fact, her first reaction was anger.

"When he told me his feelings for me, I told him immediately, 'No, you don't like me!'" Mica said. Shaken by my declaration, she left the Valley the following weekend for the seaside city of Tampico, Mexico, to visit relatives—and, she said, to forget about me.

"He was there when I got back—he and that smile of his," Mica said. "The next Sunday, I allowed myself to feel for him. I remember saying, 'Boy, he is handsome.'"

We finally talked at length about our futures—by telephone. We never met in public. "Why me, Feliberto?" she asked me. "There are ladies who sing, who are more dedicated than I am. I don't have a degree. I don't even go out much." She told me that she had only seen me as a minister of the church.

As it was for me, the visit with my father was the turning point for Mica. "In February 1983, I met with Feliberto's father who was visiting him from Cuba. He told me, 'Stop worrying about what others think.' He said it is God's will for you to be together. 'You have my blessing.'"

After several months of prayer and low-key courtship, Mica agreed to be my wife. At first, I was hurt by gossip that Mica and I had been having an inappropriate relationship before our marriage. Many of my friends, some of whom were ministers, told me I could not overcome the appearance of impropriety—marrying a church member fifteen years my junior—and still remain in ministry in the Valley. If I married Mica, they said, I should move and start fresh in Miami, Los Angeles, or New York.

I prayed for God's guidance, and I received the direction I needed. I had nothing to run or hide from. I had done nothing wrong for which I should be ashamed, falling in love with Mica after prayerful consideration. The people who were critical of me were not going to be the ones who make me happy, I decided. What makes me happy is Christ in my life and being married to a woman I love, who loves me, and who is as committed to loving God as I. Furthermore, my children needed me. I wasn't going to move away and abandon them in order to placate lies. I could not do that to them, to Mica, or to myself.

On Tuesday, February 14, 1984, Mica and I were married at the First Christian Church of Harlingen (4). Officiating at the ceremony were seven of my dearest friends. One of them, my brother David Vargas, who is co-executive director of Global Ministries of our denomination, joked: "If this marriage is good, all of us will take credit; if it doesn't work out, all of us will be blaming each other"(5).

After our marriage, a few people turned their backs to Mica and me. However, after some time, as they saw the Lord's blessings at work in our ministry, they came to me and sought forgiveness. And now, as Mica and I prepare to mark nearly twenty-five years of marriage, some of our former critics treat Mica and me as extended members of their family.

The other great event of 1984 occurred on Independence Day—the day I became a U.S. citizen. Although I had been in the United States a total of fourteen years, I had delayed applying for citizenship. I did so because I was conflicted. I thought, as many Cubans did, that Castro's revolution would eventually fail and, if we chose, we could return to our homeland. For many years, this dream remained in my heart. However, after twenty-five years of Castro's rule, I knew what I had to do—what, in reality, I had wanted to do for many years: Give my allegiance to the country that provided me its greatest gift.

To become a citizen, one must meet several requirements and take the oath of allegiance. In taking the oath, an applicant swears to:

- Support the Constitution and obey the laws of the United States.
- Renounce any foreign allegiance and/or foreign title.
- Bear arms for the armed forces or perform other services for the government when required.

Dressed in a suit, and with tears tumbling down my face, I gladly—and gratefully—raised my right hand and took the Oath of Allegiance on July 4 with about four hundred of my fellow U.S. citizens at the Fort Brown Memorial Center in Brownsville.

I was accompanied to the ceremony by Rush Barnett, a retired minister from the Anglo First Christian Church in San Benito, a dear brother of mine and my official witness of citizenship. Becoming a U.S. citizen was a great moment for me. After suffering so much in the Communist system for my religious beliefs, I was welcomed and embraced by the United States of America with opened arms. My new country made me feel like somebody. Upon becoming a citizen, I was able to vote in federal elections, serve on a jury and help decide how my tax dollars are spent. I could express my ideas and worship the God of my choosing, which I could not do in Cuba. Freedom is a glorious feeling for me, and I wish it for everyone in the world.

By mid-1984, I was feeling the call to return to the pulpit on Sunday mornings. I had been a guest preacher at many churches, sitting in the pews as a visitor until I was called to deliver the sermon. These opportunities were precious to me, and they confirmed my desire to have a regular pulpit once again.

I felt a particular calling to serve in Los Fresnos, Texas, then a city of 2,200 about twelve miles from San Benito and about twelve miles from the Port Isabel Processing Center, from which asylum seekers were released to our custody. Los Fresnos is just seventeen miles north of the Mexican border.

I discerned that Los Fresnos is where God wanted me planted, and soon He showed me why. In mid-July of 1984, I was invited by an independent Christian Church in Los Fresnos, an Anglo congregation with no denominational ties to a national church, to establish a Hispanic mission, using their aging facilities at 205 First Street.

Our first Spanish-language service was held on August 5. I, Mica, and two families, about seven of us all together, attended. The mission was greeted warmly by Los Fresnos residents, and by the end of December, we attracted about forty regular worshipers, mostly people of Mexican heritage and modest means. We outnumbered the Anglo congregation's twenty members.

In January, the Anglo minister told me that his church was no longer able to survive. The sanctuary was old and crumbling and needed to be restored or torn down and replaced, he said. Exacerbating the situation was high unemployment in the Valley. Church members were moving away for new opportunities. The congregation, the Anglo minister said, had expressed its desire to disband. They would turn the property over to us, if we agreed to assume the debt of the church. Without knowing the amount of the debt, I immediately said yes. Only later did the ramifications of my impulsive decision hit me. I said to myself, "Feliberto, my goodness, you don't know how much the debt is. How will you pay for it?"

Sometimes, God wants us to say yes, trusting Him to provide the means to accomplish the yes. I believed with my whole heart that this was one of those times. I told our church members, after the fact, what I had agreed to, even though I didn't know the cost. They were even more enthusiastic than I.

We learned the amount of the debt when we went to the bank to close the deal: $1,900.

As small as the total was, for us it was something. Immediately, we formed a fund-raising committee to retire the balance as fast as possible. We staged one fundraising event: selling homemade barbecue and tamales. News of our delicious food spread by word of mouth, and within six months, we paid off the debt.

Immediately following this milestone, we formed a new committee, this one to raise funds for a new sanctuary. We decided to build the facility ourselves. The Bank of Los Fresnos loaned us $16,000 to demolish the old sanctuary and buy materials for a new one. The general office of our denomination arranged for twenty-eight volunteers—carpenters, masons, engineers, and electricians—to help us.

Many of the refugees in my custody also volunteered to help. It was a wonderful experience to see English-speaking volunteers working side-by-side with Spanish-speaking refugees, using only hand gestures and facial expressions to achieve the common goal of building a church.

We began construction in the spring of 1986, and we dedicated our church, a new congregation of the Christian Church (Disciples of Christ), in May 1987. We named the church Iglesia Cristiana Ebenzer (Ebenezer Christian Church). In the Old Testament, Samuel gave the name Ebenezer to a stone set up in recognition of

God's assistance in defeating the Philistines. In 1991, we paid off the debt on the new church and an educational building.

Even before we started construction of Ebenezer Christian Church, it became clear that we needed to establish a more formal approach to our myriad efforts to help resettle the growing population of political refugees streaming across the border.

In January 1985, with the assistance of Jennifer Riggs, director of refugee and immigration ministries of our denomination, and David Vargas, who later became president of the division of overseas ministries, we established a formal ministry, building on a proud tradition established by the Disciples of Christ following World War II (6). At Vargas' suggestion, we called it the Good Samaritan Project. I was named its executive director.

At first our volunteer efforts were limited to helping refugees with immediate and basic needs—food, clothing, legal assistance, and spiritual guidance and counseling. But the refugees also needed a place to stay—besides my living room couch and floor—while their cases for political asylum were processed. I did not want them to endure immigrant detention centers. Refugees are not prisoners.

Our mission has remained the same over the years—to provide assistance to the thousands of needy refugees in the Rio Grande Valley, especially Central American political refugees and others who legitimately fear persecution in their homelands.

Immediately, God blessed our ministry. It was embraced by a few faithful men and women who helped me establish sustainable programs to feed the refugees with rice and beans and provide them with emergency clothing and toiletry supplies. We also organized an annual Christmas toy and clothing drive for refugee children and other poor living in the Valley.

In 1990 and 1991, the United States faced a new refugee challenge when tens of thousands of Nicaraguans began pouring into the Rio Grande Valley because of political violence in that country.

Our small church did what it could to feed, clothe, and shelter these brothers and sisters. The larger church universal did not want to take on this responsibility directly during this period. It had plenty of committees study the issue—committee after committee after committee. I remember attending many meetings only to observe nothing was actually accomplished for refugees.

I learned much during these years, when I saw intense concern expressed for refugees but little in the way of action to meet their needs. Sharing with "foreigners" is not always easy, but the members of Ebenezer Christian Church remained faithful to God's call to welcome the stranger. I would rather have a hundred active members, like we have at Ebenezer, than a thousand asleep in the pews.

With the help of work groups of all ages from churches throughout the United States, we began in 1991 to build small dormitories on the grounds of Ebenezer to house refugees paroled to our custody. In addition to Latin American countries—El Salvador, Nicaragua, Guatemala, Honduras, Peru, Cuba, and Haiti—we also assisted refugees from as far away as the former Yugoslavia, Russia, Libya, Nigeria, Ethiopia, Uganda, Iran, and the Palestinian territories. Because 99 percent of refugees arrive with absolutely nothing but the clothes they are wearing, they earnestly need our assistance. Hungry, frightened, and bearing marks on their bodies that testify to the torture and mistreatment they endured in their countries or on their long journeys, refugees most often arrive traumatized.

Jesus teaches us what our response should be to these brothers and sisters in Matthew 25:44–45:

. . . *Lord, when did we ever see you hungry or thirsty or a stranger or needing clothes or sick or in prison, and did not help you?" He will reply, "I tell you the truth, whatever you did not do for one of the least of these, you did not do for me."*

We are also to follow the example of the Good Samaritan, whose story is told in Luke, Chapter 10:

A man was going down from Jerusalem to Jericho, when he fell into the hands of robbers. They stripped him of his clothes, beat him and went away, leaving him half dead. A priest happened to be going down the same road, and when he saw the man, he passed by on the other side. So, too, a Levite, when he came to the place and saw him, passed by on the other side.

But a Samaritan, as he traveled, came where the man was; and when he saw him, he took pity on him. He went to him and bandaged his wounds, pouring on oil and wine. Then, he put the man on his own donkey, took him to an inn and took care of him. The next day he took out two silver coins and gave them to the innkeeper. 'Look after him,' he said, 'and when I return, I will reimburse you for any extra expense you may have.'

A friend in ministry once told me: "Jesus reminds us that it is in offering water from our well to another that we find springs of living water. When we open ourselves to the needs of our sisters and brothers, we find those springs filling the parched hollows of our own soul." This is true for me and the hundreds of other workers and volunteers from faith-based and secular organizations that assist us with refugees in our care.

Refugees stayed with us anywhere from a few days to a few months while awaiting progress on their applications for asylum. A travel permit is usually one of the first freedoms granted a refugee, allowing him or her to reunite with relatives and friends already in the United States. I have had the great joy on several occasions of seeing displaced and thought-to-be-dead family members reunited.

Imagine a loved one you thought was dead or you couldn't locate suddenly phone you—a mother, father, sister or brother—seeking an immediate reunion. Imagine the tears of joy! I've been blessed to see this happen time after time.

God will work miracles in spite of our doubts and lack of understanding. For Mica and me, this occurred on February 9, 1991, when we experienced a great blessing with the arrival of a baby daughter, Sarah Elizabeth, whom we adopted. Sarah, who will graduate from high school soon, is a wonderful young lady whom we (and her *padrinos* or godparents) adore and spoil.

In April 1996, on the occasion of the Good Samaritan Project's eleventh anniversary, we established it as a stand-alone nonprofit organization, retaining its faith-based affiliation but governed by a separate board of directors. Our first board chairman was Robin Hoover, who later founded the life-saving group Humane Borders Inc, a ministry dedicated to reducing the number of migrants dying while crossing the border near Tucson, Arizona (7). We also changed the name of our ministry to Southwest Good Samaritan Ministries to better reflect all the sub-ministries we have been instrumental in starting. And we developed a formal mission statement.

The mission of the Southwest Good Samaritan Ministries of the Christian Church (Disciples of Christ) is to teach the love of Jesus Christ by building a renewed wholeness and dignity and by standing with those who are broken, especially among refugees and those who are disenfranchised and displaced. The Good News of salvation is lived out by addressing spiritual and material needs, including emergency food and shelter, clothing, transportation, legal aid, advocacy and job referral through a cooperative effort with other agencies and religious organizations.

In October 1996, our ministry was extraordinarily blessed by the arrival of Raquel Garcia, who, as assistant director, oversees all daily administrative operations (8). Previously, Raquel had been administrative assistant for more than fourteen years with the Latin American/Caribbean office of our denomination in Indianapolis. Raquel said of me one time: "Feliberto doesn't know how to say

'No' in English or in Spanish." I suppose she is right.

Today, we support the Casa Bethel orphanage in Matamoros, Mexico, which is also home to a highly successful training program (Instituto Biblico Ebenezer) for young evangelists (some raised at the orphanage) who are called to grassroots ministry in Mexico. We support an annual Christmas toy drive for poor children on both sides of the border. The program, called "Mike's Kids," has become a national model. We also assist with a Bible Institute (Berea Bible Institute) in Monterrey, Mexico, to train future ministers. (More than 850 students have graduated since its founding in 1977.) And we support medical and educational programs at *colonias* in Mexico and South Texas. The *colonias*, small residential communities that develop outside municipal boundaries, often resemble Depression-era shanty towns, with no running water, no sewer system, no paved roads, and no electricity. With hard work and dedication at all levels of government, and with assistance from private agencies, two-thirds of *colonia* residents in six border counties now have access to water and sewer lines. In 1990, only a handful had water and sewer service.

In recent years, we have been blessed to be invited to assist the residents of a primitive *colonia* in Matamoros called Derechos Humanos ("Human Rights")—a poor neighborhood that began to assemble in 1997 on the site of a former landfill. Efforts there are overseen by a "sister" organization *Juntos Servimos* (Together We Serve), led by a dear brother from the United Methodist Church named Larry Cox. Larry is a remarkable man with a heart of gold who traded a six-figure income as a business executive for work gloves and sweat to serve the poor at the Mexican border (9).

We are the grateful recipients of year-round clothing and food drives sponsored by churches in Texas, Oklahoma, New Mexico, and Kansas. These congregations provide rice and beans, which we distribute to refugees, Mexican orphanages, and others in need on both sides of the border.

None of these additional ministries would have been possible without the generosity of others from many different denominations and religious organizations. God is the provider of our every blessing and to Him goes all the glory (10).

On October 9, 1999, I had the tremendous opportunity to share the message of our ministry and recount a few of the stories of the refugees we have served before the General Assembly of the Christian Church (Disciples of Christ) meeting in Indianapolis. Delivering the speech in Spanish (with an English translator) was a highlight of my life.

This morning I stand before you not as the pastor of Ebenezer Christian Church . . . of Los Fresnos, Texas. Nor do I come to you as the executive director of Good Samaritan Ministries of the Southwest. Rather, I stand before you as the exiled Cuban who came to the shores of this land in 1969 desperate, thirsty, hungry, disoriented, alone, and sick of the mistreatment I received in the Communist detention camps of my country.

But one day I was rescued and I was received into this beloved Christian Church (Disciples of Christ) in the same way that the man who was attacked on the side of the road between Jericho and Jerusalem was embraced and healed by that famous Samaritan when he least expected it.

Although from an early age at home I was taught the Bible, learned the hymns of the Christian tradition and was part of the community of faith known as the church. . . . it really wasn't until 1969 that I understood not only in my spirit but in the whole of my being what church truly means.

To be hungry and thirsty and then to be filled to overflowing.

To be a stranger with a different language and then to be embraced.

To be mistreated and to suffer illness and then to be rescued by an unknown hand and taken to a clean and safe place.

To be naked and cold and then to be covered with a cloak of protection and clothing.

It is precisely that community of faith, the one I believed I knew well before 1969 . . . but that I truly discovered the day I became a political refugee. . . .

If we the church are going to serve as a community belonging to God, a community of love and justice, a great challenge for the church is to respond not only with programs and projects controlled by those of us with power and money but also to learn to walk the road with the poor. . . .

I can say to you this morning, for us it is a blessing to have the opportunity to see Jesus' face every day: in the face of the immigrants, the displaced and the homeless, in the face of those who come to our doors still wet from the waters of the Rio Grande or the Rio Bravo, if we see it from the Mexico side.

Seeing the face of the God of Jesus in the face and the journey of each of these—the least of these brothers and sisters in the work of our creator—makes us feel like we are always in touch with the anguish of the cross but also with the hope of the resurrection.

And hearing from the mouth of one of the least of these a word of gratitude for a pound of beans or a mattress to sleep on or a change of clothes or for a simple toy that brings a smile is like hearing once again from the lips of the master his beautiful words of reconciliation, "You did it to me, to me, to me you did it."

It is possible that I have a love for the United States that many who are native born do not understand. But you must realize this: I know what it means to be captive and to be freed and, now, an American. In the final analysis, I represent the refugee as his or her advocate through what is often a gut-wrenching process. Because I am a former refugee, I see these brothers and sisters as my peers. It is the stories of the refugees that we must hear and to which we must respond. For this is what Jesus teaches us.

Chapter Eleven

Strangers Among Us

For the past twenty-five years, God has blessed me with the opportunity to serve others in whose shoes I once walked—those whom I believe Jesus calls "the least of these, my brothers and sisters." I stand at the door to greet these strangers with God's welcome at a place where the world's longest border separates a rich country from a poor nation.

We invite asylum seekers, paroled to our custody by the U.S. government, to our new five-acre compound, *Casa Compasión*—House of Compassion. The facility is located twenty miles north of the Mexican border and just three miles from one of the largest immigration detention centers in the United States, the Port Isabel Service Processing Center, from which those who qualify are released to us (1).

With the U.S. government as our partner, Southwest Good Samaritan Ministries offers refugees food, clothing, shelter, counseling, and, with partner organizations in the Rio Grande Valley, legal assistance with their applications for asylum (2). While asylum seekers from Latin America and around the world wait for the often long and demanding process of immigration to work, we offer them a safe place away from the violence and persecution in their home countries.

Our efforts in welcoming and assisting these refugees have been so successful that I have worn out six cell phones, three beepers, seven answering machines, and nine large passenger vans!

Our ministry is largely devoted solely to those seeking refugee status. These are brothers and sisters who come to our country with nothing and who expect nothing except the protection of our government. It's a common misperception that everyone who comes to the United States does so for a better job, for money. The people we work with come because they have no other option. They seek not economic benefits, but rather to save their lives and those of loved ones. Because I am a former refugee, I know how to spot the frauds who claim asylum merely to take advantage of our economy and our welfare system.

Asylum is granted to persons who have a well-founded fear of persecution in their homeland due to their race, religion, nationality, membership in a particular social group, or political opinion. An ancient judicial practice, asylum is a long-respected route to freedom in the United States.

However, in post-September 11 America—where the debate over illegal immigration dominates the national conversation—asylum as a legal path to freedom appears to be vanishing for hundreds of thousands of refugees. As the United Nations High Commissioner for Refugees noted in a 2007 report, "More and more asylum seekers are portrayed not as refugees fleeing persecution and entitled to sanctuary, but rather as illegal migrants, potential terrorists and criminals—or at a minimum as 'bogus.'"

I support stringent investigations and background checks on any person making a claim of asylum. I do so because it is a matter of life and death for some refugees. I knew a twenty-three-year-old man from El Salvador who made a claim of asylum but after an inadequate investigation was immediately deported from our country. He was murdered within a week of his return by the guerillas from whom he sought protection.

Illegal immigration is a problem that no country can ignore, but we Americans must distinguish between illegal migrants seeking a better way of life economically and individuals in need of protection. Each of us struggles with our moral and political beliefs about illegal immigration. As a legal topic, immigration is as complicated as the U.S. tax code. My hope is that through understanding legal immigration—specifically, the stories of refugees seeking asylum—we will better understand the larger issues of immigration (3).

I personally screen every one who comes to us. I generally know when refugees truly need what we have to offer. Every refugee has an important personal story. But we are all bound together by a central shared experience: To save our own life or the life of a loved one, we left everything familiar for a life of complete uncertainty. It is a decision of epic proportion for any human being.

I think it is difficult for Americans to imagine the plight of a refugee. People who decide to leave everything they have ever known, fleeing with what they can carry to begin an unknown future in a new country, usually making the decision only when there seems to be no other option for survival or when the kind of survival they can expect at home is brutal and stark. Common to all is that they are desperate and willing to endure just about any hardship to obtain a sense of security.

Today, nearly ten million refugees—a population larger than that of New York City—roam our world in dozens of countries (4). More than 70 percent live in developing countries and nearly all of those refugees—more than six million people—are "warehoused" in camps and holding areas. There they face extreme and protracted conditions of poverty, dependency, and idleness—a massive waste of human talent by anyone's measure. Half the world's refugees are women and children in urgent need of assistance and protection. Adolescents are particularly vulnerable to violence, neglect, sexual exploitation, and other abuses.

Tragically, only a relative few of these refugees will gain means and choice in their lives. But I won't give up on these brothers and sisters, just as I didn't give up on myself. America is the world's beacon for hope, and I am a living proof of freedom's gift. We are a nation of immigrants, many of them refugees. Our generosity in taking those who flee persecution is evident in every community across our nation. Since World War II, more refugees have found homes in the United States than in any other country. More than two million refugees have arrived since 1980 alone. Of the top ten countries accepting resettled refugees in 2006, the United States took in more than twice as many as the next nine countries combined.

Some refugees have become household names: Albert Einstein, Sigmund Freud, and Gloria Estefan. Other well-known refugees include Jackie Chan, Henry Kissinger, Madeleine Albright, and U.S. Senator Mel Martinez and U.S. Representative Ileana Ros-Lehtinen, both of Florida.

God's son—my Savior—was a refugee. Mary and Joseph, with their infant, were forced to flee to Egypt to escape the wrath of Herod. What if they had not been offered safe haven? Just as Jesus and His family went back to their country when the danger had passed, most current refugees want to return to their own countries when it is safe for them to do so.

Generally speaking, a refugee applies for protection from the U.S. government while outside the United States. Refugees typically apply in refugee camps or at designated processing sites outside their home countries. In some instances, refugees may apply for protection within their home countries, such as in the former

Soviet Union, Vietnam, and Cuba, which is the procedure I followed. If accepted as a refugee, the person is sent to the United States and is eligible to receive assistance through a refugee resettlement program. (For its 2008 budget year, the U.S. government has authorized the resettlement of 80,000 refugees).

A person seeking political asylum—such as those we serve at *Casa Compasión*—first comes to the United States and, once here, applies for protection. At any given time, about 170,000 people are seeking asylum in the United States (new and pending cases), according to the United Nations. Asylum is generally granted on a case-by-case basis following a lengthy interview and background check, although some groups are granted asylum by the U.S. government in special circumstances. In the post-September 11 era, waits of up to a year or longer are customary. Only about one in three people applying for asylum receives it.

I was lucky to be one of those.

Exhausted, penniless, and emaciated, I arrived in Miami on that November day in 1969 with only a change of clothing and a promise in my heart: to help bring others the gift I had been given—freedom from persecution, a place to heal wounds, and, with God's help, the chance to discover joy once more in my life. I arrived bruised and battered, physically and emotionally. But others saw me not as a stranger, but as a brother. I was the man on the side of the road whom the Samaritan happened upon. I was the man who had been beaten and robbed. And, like the Samaritan had done for the man on the side of the Jericho road, the Americans who embraced me ignored my national origin and showed me compassion.

Emma Lazarus' poem, engraved on a tablet within the pedestal on which stands the Statute of Liberty, spoke to my condition:

Give me your tired, your poor,
Your huddled masses yearning to breathe free,
The wretched refuse of your teeming shore. Send these,
the homeless, tempest-tossed to me,
I lift my lamp beside the golden door!

This is not just an image that speaks to our interconnectedness as the family of God. The verse reflects my experience as a refugee embraced by love! I am breathing evidence that when we allow it, the flow of life and grace from Christ empowers, emboldens, and equips us to do the work that must be done. This work, the last teaching of Jesus before His Resurrection, becomes a reality in the midst of a hurting and hurtful world when we see glory on each face—*whatever you do for the least of these my brothers and sisters, you do to me.*

Today, my phone rings day and night. Many of the calls concern the routine matters of a pastor's life in a small town: the need of an elderly church member, a youth group activity, a wish for special prayer. But, regularly, the calls are from a stranger, the lost and forsaken refugee calling from the immigration prison or from a pay phone near the border.

"*Hermano Pereira* (Brother Pereira)?" the caller will ask.

"*Si, bueno* (Yes, speaking)," I reply.

The caller will identify himself, explain how he got my name, and, summoning all the courage possible, explain his situation and ask for help. Asking for help is difficult for any human being; it is more so for the stranger.

I am blessed that so many refugees phone me. I used to wonder how it is that my name got to those who needed our services before our ministry was listed with U.S. immigration authorities. In 1986, one refugee told me that my name was selling on the streets of Managua, Nicaragua, for $50. "I was told that you are a brother who can help us. We would have been killed if we had remained in Nicaragua," the man told me when he phoned me from the immigration prison near *Casa Compasión*. At that time, Nicaragua was embroiled in a civil war fought between the Sandinista government and the counterrevolutionaries (Contras) supported by the U.S. government.

On two separate occasions years apart, I had refugees tell me the same amazing story. They were a man and a woman who had never met. Upon meeting me, each of them nearly fainted. The man was speechless for several minutes. Each of them told me how, in desperate prayers for their safety, they had asked God to provide them a sign. My face appeared to each of them in a dream. As you can imagine, this is something for which I have no explanation—other than that our Lord works in wondrous ways.

I have been blessed to assist thousands of refugees from more than forty countries and of all religious backgrounds. I have assisted Muslims, Jews, Christians, and atheists. As a Christian, I am called to practice the love of Jesus to all. The success of refugees in the United States depends greatly on the welcome they receive when they arrive. From the very beginning, I have considered our ministry a full partner of the U.S. government to help those who are seeking freedom from persecution and oppression. The Immigration and Customs Enforcement branch of the U.S. Department of Homeland Security operates the detention center near our facility and oversees immigration services and enforcement in our country. Immigration officials have referred many political refugees to us, and on several occasions in the past, they have transported refugees to our facilities. Refugees may be released or have needs at any time of the day or night. Therefore, our ministry is on call twenty-four hours a day.

In 1998, six Muslim brothers from Bosnia were released to my custody while their applications for asylum were processed.

Like other refugees, they were scared and suspicious of authority figures. During the first hours with me, I asked one of the men who spoke a little English if I could help the men with any special needs. Sheepishly, he asked me if they could have room at our church in which to meet for daily prayers and readings from the Quran, the religious text of Islam.

"Yes, of course," I replied. "Whatever you need from me, I will help you."

Appearing shocked by my kindness, the man graciously thanked me.

The next day, I checked with the man to see how he and the others were faring.

The man asked: "Why are you taking such an interest in us? Why are you so friendly?"

I replied with words that came to my heart. "Jesus loved me, and I love you."

"We don't know this Christ," the man replied. "At home, the Christians are trying to kill us."

"Here," I told the man, "Jesus loves you."

By the third day, the men called me "Imam," which caused me to blush (5).

God has called me to have concern for the whole human society in which I have been placed. The person in need is my neighbor—the neighbor to whom Christ sends me in response to His love.

In our country, there has been no conflict since the Civil War that has divided the nation, resulting in great disruption, poverty, and loss of life. Because those of us alive today have not lived the experience, we find it almost impossible to really understand the great psychological and emotional toll that refugees know firsthand. Yet, the presence of refugees in the world indicates that something has gone seriously wrong, and we need to understand why people are forced into the desperate decision to flee their homelands. Among the most common causes of refugee and immigration movements

are failed political leadership, war, poverty, human rights violations, and mistreatment of minorities. These causes are most often
found in combination with each other. Ethnic cleansing leads to
war, for example, and human rights violations lead to poverty.

Each year, under the cover of night in a desperate attempt to reach
U.S. soil, hundreds of refugees from Cuba, Haiti, and the Dominican
Republic secretly leave their homelands on rafts lashed together with
pieces of wood, used inner tubes, large pieces of Styrofoam, plastic
bathtubs, and surfboards. Since 1990 alone, about 30,000 Cuban *balseros* (rafters) have been picked up by the U.S. Coast Guard while
attempting the ninety-mile journey across the Florida Straits in hopes
of drifting into the Florida Keys five to seven days later. Hundreds of
balseros have died from shark attacks, drowning, exposure, starvation,
or dehydration. In March 2001, the sole survivor of a ship that failed
to reach America from the Dominican Republic told how people on
board resorted to cannibalism to stay alive.

Roberto traveled from Cuba on a raft made of a tractor chassis
and inner tubes. On the journey from Cuba, westward through the
Gulf of Mexico, he witnessed fellow rafters suffer horrible deaths
from shark attacks. Through the grace of God, Roberto was able to
save the life of an eleven-year-old boy after his parents sacrificed
themselves to sharks in order to prevent further attacks on the raft.
Needless to say, when Roberto arrived in the United States through
Mexico and phoned us from the Port Isabel detention camp, he was
traumatized. We took him in and immediately began caring for him.

Mariela and Alberto, * a young couple, also fled Cuba on a raft.
The raft drifted until it came upon the Cayman Islands, where the
couple lived several months before they were ordered to leave.
Without any funds, they were forced back to the open sea, where
they soon ran out of food and water. Just a day or so from death
by exposure and dehydration, the couple landed on the shores of
Honduras. Hoping to reach San Antonio, where they had relatives,
they walked across Guatemala and into Mexico. It was a difficult

* To protect their privacy, some refugees have been given pseudonyms.

journey because Mariela was pregnant.

On a mountain path, some corrupt Mexican immigration offi-cers robbed them of what little money they had and gang-raped Mariela, who, by this time, was seven months pregnant. The sexual assault prompted the baby's premature delivery on the side of the mountain. When the couple and the baby arrived in a nearby vil-lage, they were imprisoned for being in the country illegally. When some other Cubans living in Mexico learned of the family's plight, they came to their aid. Mariela, Alberto, and their baby were taken to the International Bridge between Matamoros and Brownsville. There, the family presented themselves to the U.S. Border Patrol as asylum seekers from Cuba. They were transported to the Port Isabel detention camp, from which the couple contacted me. The family was paroled to my custody and with assistance from our ministry, Mariela, Alberto, and the baby were able to get to San Antonio to join their relatives.

Miguel, a man from El Salvador, lived at our facilities for sev-eral months. A member of a political party seeking peace amid the civil war in El Salvador in the 1980s, he had witnessed many sad events in his country. He told us that around midnight on December 29, 1988, four armed men entered his home while his family slept. They took him and his brother-in-law to the back patio and began shooting at them with rifles. The two men ran for cover behind large rocks. A bullet hit Miguel in the right hip, but he was able to scamper into the dense jungle behind the family's home. However, his brother-in-law was unable to escape.

The next morning, after the sun rose, Miguel counted seventy bullet wounds in the body of his brother-in-law. Traumatized, Miguel, the bullet still lodged in his hip, ran to a nearby cemetery where he hid for two days. Incredibly, he slowly made his way through Guatemala and Mexico and across the border into the United States. In late January 1989, he came to our church. Once he was stabilized, we took Miguel to the U.S. immigration office, where, with the help of a lawyer we had arranged for, he initiated the process of seeking refugee status. Soon, he was able to write to his mother, wife, and children in El Salvador, who were relieved to learn he was alive. However, in their letter of reply, they told him he could not return to El Salvador or he would face certain death because of his political views.

Mina, a fifty-two-year-old woman from Nicaragua, came to us in 1989. She arrived in a state of great anguish, crying uncontrollably after witnessing unspeakable crimes during the civil wars in her homeland. She saw with her own eyes her brother killed and his body dismembered by political opponents. She saw her father tortured and his body only half-buried so its remains could be eaten by animals. Only God knows how Mina managed to survive this torture.

Terrified, she fled to Mexico with her six children (her husband had already left the family, fearing for his safety). Because the journey was so difficult, she was forced to leave her four youngest children at refugee camps along the route—her two youngest children at a refugee camp in Guatemala, the third-youngest at a camp in El Salvador, and the fourth-youngest at a camp in Honduras. Mina and her two oldest children continued their journey through Mexico, where they were robbed of what little money they had. After suffering great hunger, dehydration, and exposure, they eventually crossed into the United States and arrived at our church with, literally, rags hanging from their skinny frames.

Seeing Mina and her children in that condition reminded me of a scene from a horror movie on late night television. We immediately got them food, clothing, shelter, medicine, counseling, and legal assistance. Best of all, we showed Mina and her children how much God loved them. They stayed with us for several months, during which time we worked with refugee organizations to locate her younger children and assist in arrangements to reunite the family once more.

Ivan, a Guatemalan, and a companion came to us during Christmas 1989 on one of the coldest nights we have ever experienced in the Valley, with temperatures hovering in the 20s. Around 10:30 p.m., I received a telephone call from a lady in our church, informing me that she had seen two young men staggering along a road. She feared for their lives in the freezing weather. I went to find these two young men, discovering them huddled together on the side of the road. I ascertained that the two men had left Guatemala to escape the political violence there. Once in Mexico, however, they had been robbed and tormented. Ivan's companion was thin and frail. On the verge of collapse, he could barely stand. I took the men to the church, offering them warm showers, clothing, shoes, blankets, and a hot meal. The next morning, I took Ivan to the doctor because he was unable to sit without trembling. Our church took these men into our care, and they participated in our worship services while awaiting the asylum process.

One of the most difficult situations I've ever faced in ministry involved a brother and two sisters escaping the political violence in Nicaragua. Having successfully endured the journey through Mexico, the three were attempting to cross the Rio Grande when they were attacked by river bandits and robbed. The two girls, sixteen and eighteen, were raped. Their brother was shot and killed trying to defend his sisters. The younger girl was fatally shot in the stomach and head. The eighteen-year-old, having suffered a chest wound, was left to die next to the bodies of her siblings.

Miraculously, this young lady, wounded and naked, managed to get to a house on the Mexican side of the border, where she received medical attention. Within weeks, she was able to continue her journey to the United States and eventually made her way to our ministry. With God's help, we were able to place her in the home of a Christian family with whom she recuperated. Some women from our church and I spent hours with this young girl, holding her as she sobbed. The pain was so intense, she sometimes threatened to take her life. The healing process will continue the rest of her life.

Danger is ever-present for refugees. We see on those who come to us the anguish in their faces, the scars on their backs. The "least of these" and their needs are everywhere. Our mission as people of God is to respond to those needs whenever, wherever, and however we can.

In my experience, we are quick to label the foreign-born. As long as the stranger who crosses the border is labeled a "refugee," some feel comfortable responding. If the stranger is labeled "illegal," however, people are more apprehensive. Some find excuses not to see, not to hear, not to respond. We need a revival of Christian compassion that sees beyond the prejudice and stereotypes. We must see Christ in the faces of these refugees and respond to God there. Together, we must lift our voices to eliminate the obstacles that prevent these, God's people, from achieving freedom and liberty (6).

An old rabbi once asked his pupils how they could tell when the night had ended and the day had begun. "Could it be," asked one of the students, "when you see an animal in the distance and tell whether it's a sheep or a dog?"

"No," answered the rabbi.

Another asked, "Is it when you can look at a tree in the distance and tell whether it's a fig tree or a peach tree?"

"No," answered the rabbi.

"Then when is it?" the pupils demanded.

The rabbi answered: "It is when you can look on the face of any woman or man and see it is your sister or brother. Because if you cannot see this, it is still night."

I Was a Stranger
A Pictorial History

Brothers Eldo and Feliberto Pereira sit for a portrait.

Feliberto, Eldo, Hermenegilda Navarro,
and Juan Francisco Pereira.

Emerging from seminary class, Feliberto
mugs for a student photographer.

Third in his seminary class, Feliberto speaks at
Los Pinos Nuevos graduation ceremonies.

Feliberto's Cuban Ministry of Education
teacher identification card.

Feliberto's Cuban driver's license.

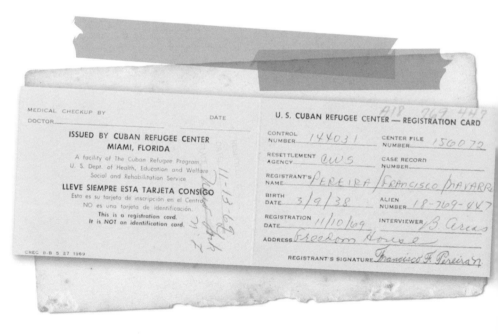

Feliberto's refugee card, which also covered his family.

Feliberto, Jacqui, Joel, and Ruthie
at JFK before departing for Texas.

In March 1971, with the gift of a passenger van from the Christian
Church (Disciples of Christ), Second Christian Church of San Benito
transported 25 to 40 passengers to and from church every Sunday.

June 1973 *World Call* details Feliberto's
turnaround of San Benito, Texas, church.

As minister of Emmanuel Christian Church, Feliberto saw the
congregation grow by 1984 to include 425 members, the
largest Hispanic denomination in the Christian Church (Disciples of Christ).

Feliberto in his new study at
Emmanuel Christian Church.

La Hora Cristiana reached 15 million listeners in
15 Latin American countries at its peak.

Casa Compasión at Bayview, Texas, hosts
refugees and mission trips.

Feliberto preparing for a Sunday sermon.

Raquel Garcia oversees day-to-day administrative operations
for Southwest Good Samaritan Ministries.

Feliberto takes a call while checking on the fish in the resaca (pond) near his home. He has worn out six cell phones, three beepers, seven answering machines, and nine large passenger vans in his role as executive director of Southwest Good Samaritan Ministries, which cares for refugees.

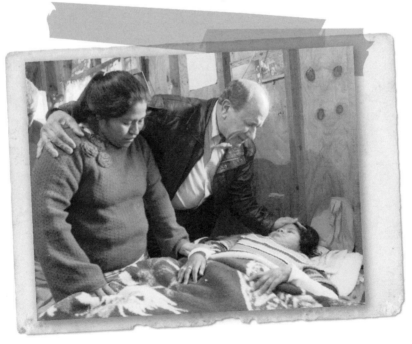

Feliberto prays with Angelita, who has spina bifida, and her mother at their Derechos Humanos (Human Rights) colonia home in Matamoros, Mexico.

Feliberto and a refugee from Honduras stack "Disciples Rice"
and "Disciples Beans" contributed by congregations of the Christian Church
(Disciples of Christ) throughout the southwestern United States.

Mike's Kids annual Christmas-time campaign provides
new toys and clothing for thousands of poor children on both sides
of the U.S.–Mexican border.

A close colleague and friend of Feliberto's,
Sister Margaret Mertens (the Sisters of Divine Providence),
oversees the refugee center La Posada Providencia
in San Benito, Texas.

"With God, all things are possible," reads the marquee of
Ebenezer Christian Church (Disciples of Christ).

Feliberto prays at the church altar every morning
when in Los Fresnos.

The Guerreros—Irene (top left), Felix (top right),
Katherine (bottom left), Rocio (bottom right) and Omar
(not pictured)—escaped Shining Path terrorists in Peru and
received political asylum in the United States
with Feliberto's assistance.

Feliberto, Mica, and Sarah Pereira.

Children from Casa Bethel orphanage in Matamoros,
Mexico surround Feliberto.

Feliberto Pereira and Chris Kelley, January 2008.

Chapter Twelve

America's Gift

Since the September 11 terrorist attack on our country, the number of refugees both seeking and being granted political asylum has fallen by double-digit percentages. Many of us who work with refugees are trying to determine how much of the drop comes from a lower demand for asylum and how much from stringent legislation and changes aimed at keeping people from seeking protection. What we do know is that our government has broadened grounds for placing refugees in detention. That alone has probably kept many in perilous conditions in their homelands, when they might otherwise have sought protection in the United States.

Under current law, all who come to our country seeking asylum are subject to mandatory confinement in immigration detention centers—including entire families. On any given day, roughly 3,000 asylum seekers are detained (the exact number is unknown), often in remote areas with limited access to legal counsel. Many are confined with criminals in county jails. Many have little, if any, access to health care. It is sad that we, the loving people of the United States, are locking up entire families while their applications are processed.

While asylum seekers may request release on what amounts to parole once they pass through a screening procedure, release policies vary widely across the country. In some areas, asylum seekers are rarely released. Furthermore, there is no process for appealing a decision by the Department of Homeland Security to initially detain asylum seekers or to deny parole. And there is no limit to the length of time that asylum seekers can be detained. The average is sixty days, but more than one-third are held for ninety days or longer— in prison-like conditions that are inappropriate for the population. This results in some asylum seekers suffering depression, painful anxiety-related symptoms, and post-traumatic stress disorder. The U.S. Commission on International Religious Freedom, a bipartisan commission, has documented and condemned these practices. The Department of Homeland Security has promised to address these concerns, but had not as of March 2008.

Furthermore, our nation's immigration courts are treating asylum seekers with great disparity, with the outcome of cases influenced by factors such as the location of the court and the gender and professional background of judges. These disparities, reported in a study by three law professors published in November 2006 in the *Stanford Law Review*, were gleaned from data on asylum decisions from January 2000 through August 2004. According to the study, female immigration judges grant asylum at a 44 percent rate higher than their male counterparts. One explanation is that 27 percent of the female judges in the study had previously worked for organizations that defended the rights of the immigrant or the poor, while only 8 percent of the male judges had similar experience. We must correct this kind of injustice, and, working within the system, I know we will.

Tragically, asylum is being lumped together with all forms of immigration. It is often viewed as just another reason for concern in our country that we've lost control of our borders, even though asylum adds but a fraction to the overall number of immigrants. "The necessary public support for the reception of asylum seekers has continued to be hampered by the tendency of certain elements in the media and some politicians to misrepresent the issues of illegal migration and refugees without sufficient concern for accuracy," states a 2006 report from the United Nations.

An undocumented immigrant is one who enters the United States illegally or refuses to leave after his legal permit or visa has expired. Generally speaking, illegal immigration is driven by a strong desire for better economic opportunities and better living conditions. Often, an undocumented immigrant is from a country whose quota for legal entry into the United States has been exceeded. While I have certain views about economic immigrants, let me be clear about one thing: I love my country too much to disregard its laws, and I would never damage my relationship with the U.S. government by not strictly following its immigration rules and regulations.

In our post-9/11 world, we are rightfully concerned about protecting our borders, which many people believe leave America vulnerable. All nineteen of the hijackers on September 11, 2001, had come in on temporary visas, as students, as tourists, or on business, and had illegally overstayed them. Our nation has done much to plug these holes in our immigration system, and we are all safer as a result. However, as a nation, I believe we have not yet adjusted our levels of fear accordingly.

Fear and freedom are at war in our country, and we must not let fear win. We must find smarter, more humane ways to manage the threat of terrorism than by simply shutting out foreigners, especially refugees who need freedom's healing embrace, or locking up mothers and children who have legitimate claims for protection

(1). I've seen up close what chronic fear of persecution does to a person. At certain times in Cuba, I was that man. In my heart, I believe we have inadvertently allowed our collective fear to fuel a backlash—hatred on the part of some—against the undocumented immigrants in our country.

Some "illegal aliens" are sacrificing their lives for our country. The first soldier killed in combat during the 2003 invasion of Iraq had once been an undocumented immigrant. Lance Cpl. Jose Antonio Gutierrez, a proud holder of a U.S. green card, was a Guatemalan orphan who eventually obtained legal residency and joined the Marines.

Much of the anger over immigration, I believe, is a manifestation of great anxiety that many in our country are feeling over the globalization of our economy, which is fueled by expansive new technology. For example, the historic levels of change introduced by the Internet just since 1990 have resulted in lifestyle changes that are so different than what many of us have grown up with, leaving all of us feeling less in control of our lives, our culture, and our country.

During earlier times of great economic change, we have historically treated immigrants as a convenient scapegoat. We, as a nation, have become intolerant. The United States is now experiencing a wave of immigration comparable to the largest in its history. More than one million immigrants enter the country legally every year, compared to about 300,000 in the 1960s (2). An estimated 500,000 undocumented immigrants also enter every year, according to the Pew Charitable Trust. The effect of this influx on pay and future prospects for nonimmigrant workers is a contentious, polarizing issue for Americans who have, historically, built an economy large enough to easily accommodate newcomers.

In this environment, reasonable solutions based on fact have been replaced by fear-mongering and political gamesmanship.

Think of how much energy and money we now spend fighting over illegal immigration. Then imagine what results we would achieve if we spent just a portion of the energy and money finding ways to help the nations from which the migrants are coming. By investing in their home countries, providing needed skills and technology, I believe we could reduce the desperation that drives so many people to emigrate in search of a living wage.

I pray that our nation's Congress and president will arrive at reasonable reforms that humanely address illegal immigration while providing immigrants the opportunity to become Americans.

I agree with the director of U.S. citizenship and immigration services, who said it is the obligation of the government "to ensure that law-abiding immigrants who seek legal channels into our nation are met with the necessary scrutiny so that we do not admit individuals who seek to do our nation harm or are threats to public safety." Once we properly vet these applicants, he added, it is also incumbent on our government "to promote an awareness of U.S. citizenship to every new arrival and help cultivate an understanding of what it means to become an American (3)."

But we mustn't treat refugees like terrorists in the meantime. Instead, what we must do is process asylum claims and background checks faster. And we must address the complexity of the asylum application forms themselves for non-English speakers.

The asylum process starts with the completion of Form I-589, a twelve-page form supplemented with eleven pages of instructions. Comprehending these instructions would be hard for many native U.S. citizens. The form is written for people for whom English may be a second language. But English skills are not commonplace among asylum seekers. I tell all the refugees with whom I work that their first order of business must be to learn English.

Contrary to popular opinion, most asylum seekers are highly educated. That's why they often end up opposing the oppressive governments in their home countries. That's why oppressive regimes target them. But they can't be expected to understand a process conducted in a language that they don't speak.

Language barriers are but one hurdle. Often, refugees must grapple with the difficult discrepancy in their social status here, compared with where they were in their homelands. I have counseled many doctors, engineers, and other educated professionals who, in the United States, are forced to take jobs as meat packers, truck drivers, or fast-food workers.

If they have extended family in the United States, most asylum seekers wish to stay with them. A main part of our refugee ministry today is to arrange transportation for them to join relatives or friends once they are authorized to travel. This also involves getting a change of venue for their court hearings. A few years ago, the local U.S. immigration office asked me to accompany about twenty refugees to the bus depot in Harlingen. Once there, I purchased bus tickets to their various destinations, gave them enough money to eat along the way, and gave them phone cards so they could call relatives or sponsors along their journey. Many hours into the night, I saw each of them off to his or her destination with a wave and a smile. I consider it a privilege to serve others in this way because I believe God walks with me at all times.

I don't want to paint a perfect portrait of refugees. A few are lazy and want others to provide for all their needs. I once told a man seeking refugee status who behaved in this way. "I am not giving birth to you! If you don't want to help yourself, I certainly have no obligation to try to assist you." I have also known a few refugees who are filled with rage and hatred for those who tortured them. One man from El Salvador in my custody who had been assaulted and forced to watch women sexually assaulted said he couldn't wait to obtain permanent residency in the United States so he could return to Mexico, where he believed the perpetrators resided. "I will take my revenge on them one way or another," the man told me. I counseled him and we prayed and prayed together, but to no avail. "These kinds of people don't deserve to live," he told me. "They need to learn their lessons." I know this hatred all too well. Several times in Cuba, I asked God to take away the hate from my heart.

From the moment refugees begin life anew, each day brings struggle, rejection, doubts, fears, and loneliness. These are people in need of God's Shalom—His sweet peace. Jesus understood those to whom he ministered. Even the feeding of the 5,000 was done by breaking down the mass into smaller, identifiable groups. So, too, must we seek to understand and come to know those that we seek to serve.

Children who are refugees need our special attention. Each year, thousands of kids show up in the United States without families and are detained, according to the U. N. High Commissioner for Refugees, which has been working to ensure greater protection for unaccompanied children.

According to U.S. immigration officials, 6,460 unaccompanied and undocumented minors from Central America alone were detained in 2005, a 35 percent increase over the previous year. While stepped-up border enforcement is probably a key reason for the increase, it also may reflect growing desperation on the part of foreigners eager for freedom in America.

In South Texas, unaccompanied children who are undocumented immigrants are placed under the supervision of the U.S. Department of Health and Human Services. International Educational Services Inc. is the nonprofit agency, one of more than thirty under contract to the government, that cares for the children, nearly all of whom are from Central America.

The children are assigned to foster homes until they can be united with a sponsor, usually a friend or relative. It is up to sponsors to see that children attend court hearings related to their immigration status. The foster care program emerged from the 1997 settlement of Flores vs. Reno, a class-action lawsuit against the former Immigration and Naturalization Service. The suit argued that it was wrong for children caught by the Border Patrol to be imprisoned like adults.

Exploitive smugglers have been known to tell parents to separate from their children once they cross the Rio Grande. "Even if they are caught by the Border Patrol, the children are all but guaranteed to be in a safe, comfortable home within a day or so and placed with a relative or friend within a few weeks or months," the Associated Press reported in July 2007. "The parents can meanwhile seek voluntary departure, which means they can leave without a deportation order on their record—which would prohibit them from entering the United States within the next ten years and subject them to jail time if they are caught. They can then try to qualify for a visa or attempt to sneak in again."

If families are caught together, they mostly likely would be detained at one of two new family facilities. One, the T. Don Hutto facility in Taylor, Texas, is a former prison and has been heavily criticized for its conditions.

Before the 512-bed facility opened in May 2006, U.S. immigration officials routinely separated parents from their children upon apprehension. Infants and toddlers were placed in foster homes; adolescents and teenagers were placed in contract facilities. Parents went to adult detention centers. Immigrant advocates have decried the Hutto center as "fundamentally anti-family and anti-American" because of its prison-like style, lack of educational services for children, inadequate health care, and other shortcomings. The Women's Commission for Refugee Women and Children in New York and Lutheran Immigration and Refugee Service in Baltimore have recommended that ICE parole asylum seekers while they await the outcome of their hearings. Immigrant families not eligible for parole should be released to special shelters run by nonprofit groups (like Southwest Good Samaritan Ministries), the groups said (4).

Frequently, I am privileged to respond to the needs of an entire family, such as the Felix Guerrero family of Lima, Peru. Felix, his wife Irene, son Omar, and daughters Katherine and Rocio arrived at our ministry with literally the clothing on their backs.

A Christian minister, Felix brought a message of hope to a poverty-stricken indigenous population living in a small village outside Lima. His ministry, however, was viewed as a threat by terrorist guerillas operating in the region, members of the Shining Path (Sendero Luminoso) (5). Felix was seen as a threat to the terrorists' ability to control the tribe for political and economic purposes. He knew it was dangerous to continue to minister to these poor people, but he loved them and they were responding to his Christian teachings.

In March 2003, two masked gunmen paid a visit to Felix at the home of relatives in the village where he preached. After shooting the family's two dogs, they burst into the home and pointed their weapons at Felix. "If you keep preaching, trying to brainwash these people, we will kill you like the dogs." A month later, Irene received a phone call at home. The caller said, "If your husband doesn't stop preaching to the Indians, we will kill your family. We have targeted your children. We know where they go to school."

The family knew the threat was serious. Two uncles, leaders in their communities, had opposed the Shining Path and were killed by the terrorists in the mid-1990s.

When the authorities said they could do nothing to protect the Guerreros, their only option was to flee Peru and seek asylum in Mexico. Scraping together all the money they had, Irene, Katherine, and Rocio, mother and two daughters, flew to Mexico City to hire an immigration lawyer to help the family obtain asylum. The plan was for Felix and Omar to join them in Mexico after they found housing, which didn't take long. The lawyer warned the family that asylum in Mexico would be difficult to obtain, and after nearly a year of waiting, the family's petition was rejected (6). Fearful for their lives if they returned to Peru, they prayed for guidance from God. "The message all of us received gave us the courage to continue our efforts to find protection," Katherine said. "God said through prayer to all of us: 'Trust me. You are my children.'"

Believing they had no other option, the family paid a "coyote" $1,500—$300 per person—to smuggle them from Mexico into the United States, where they hoped to reunite with distant relatives living in North Carolina (7). (For the record—I despise coyotes.)

The coyote drove the family in a van to the Mexican border and dropped them at the banks of the Rio Bravo (the Mexican name for the Rio Grande) just outside Reynosa.

Katherine told me what happened next.

The river is very large and dangerous. Heavy vegetation grows on both banks of the river. Dead tree branches stick up from the water. Sharp rocks cover the river bottom. At dusk on April 17, 2004, we approached the river and then our coyote told us the truth: There would be no boat to cross the river.

"How are we to cross?" my mother asked him in a panicked voice.

"You will float across on garbage bags, which I will blow up with air," he said. "These will be your flotation devices."

"What?" my father said. None of us could believe it, and my mother, sister, and I began to cry and pray.

The coyote left the Guerreros at the river and went to purchase a box of thirty-nine-gallon garbage bags at a nearby convenience store. Irene and Rocio wept. Katherine prayed: "God, we can't go back home. In Mexico, there is no safety for us. I know how you held Abraham from danger. Please keep us from danger. If you don't approve of this, please tell us now. Only you can understand us, God."

Then, Katherine said, she felt the peace of God surround her and her family. "I listened and I received his assuring words. 'I can understand your plight because my son was a refugee. He was an immigrant, escaping danger. I know you completely.' I felt God give us a promise: He would guard all of us as we crossed the river."

The words of Psalms 126 came to her heart. *"Restore our fortunes, Lord, as streams renew the desert. Those who plant in tears will harvest with shouts of joy. They weep as they go to plant their seed, but they sing as they return with the harvest."*

The coyote returned with the garbage bags and began blowing them up with his breath. Holding one of the bags, he told the family, "We are going to cross like this." He showed them how they are to place as much of their body on top of the bag as they could. He tied the bags together with some rope. He would go first, followed by Felix, Irene, and the children. Each of them carried a change of clothing in a small plastic bag tied to their waists.

It was dark when they approached the river—the six of them, each with a blown-up garbage bag as their transportation across the Rio Bravo. They were quiet. All were aware that only Omar knew how to swim, and he was very frightened.

Katherine said:

I walked into the water. It was cold April water. We got on top of the bags. The water became very deep and I couldn't feel the ground. Suddenly, we could feel the river current pulling us, and we were helpless to stop it. We could see tree branches a short distance away. My mother and sister began to cry. I prayed:

"God, please help us. You are God and only you completely understand us at this moment. You know how much I love you and you are with me completely. I trust you completely."

Instantly, peace came to me. I knew we weren't going to die in the river.

We reached the other side. We were in America, and, apparently, no one saw us enter. In the bushes, along the river bank in the dark, we changed into dry clothes. We climbed to the top of the river bank, and following our coyote, we ran and ran. My brother suffers from asthma, and as I was running behind him, I noticed that he could hardly breathe. I slowed to walk with him.

The family made their way across a field, careful not to damage the crop rows. They met up in a nearby cemetery and hid there for a while. Their coyote, who had friends on the U.S. side, arranged for a van to pick them up and drive them to the home of a family (part of the coyote's network) in Pharr, Texas, about five miles from the border.

In Pharr, the Guerreros hoped to make contact with some distant relatives in the United States who might be able to help them start a new life there, but they could not find them. They knew no one else. But they were grateful they had each other. The woman they stayed with in Pharr had cancer and they prayed for her. Grateful, the woman invited the Guerreros to stay with her.

However, after two weeks with the woman, the coyote transferred them to a home in Mission, Texas, about ten miles from Pharr. But the woman who was to be their host was cruel. Katherine said she told the family: "We don't pray for illegals. How can I pray for you when you are crossing illegally. I should tell immigration you are here." Katherine said she figured the woman "thought we could pay her some money to not tell. We had no money."

After a few days, the woman took them to the house in San Benito, about fifty miles away. The homeowner, a woman, had a small camping trailer, which became the cramped home for the family of five. By this time, Katherine said, "We all felt lost in our journey to a safer life. I prayed for two days. 'God, we are lost. We don't know what to do. Please help us.'"

A few days later, the family met a plumber who had come to fix a problem at the woman's home. He told them about me and our church, which was only eight miles away in Los Fresnos. I knew the man because he had asked me and others in our church to pray for his little boy, who had leukemia.

That day, Felix Guerrero called me and told me the family's harrowing story. I made arrangements to meet them at the church in Los Fresnos. When I met them, each was physically and emotionally exhausted. As they wept, I prayed with them, thanking God for their deliverance. Based on the facts, I knew they had a good case for political asylum. I made arrangements for a lawyer to represent them before U.S. immigration, which I contacted on their behalf.

Katherine said of that day:

We cried and cried. Brother Pereira told us, "The first refugee was Jesus. You have nothing to be ashamed about. I am going to get you a lawyer to work on your case for political asylum." We cried some more, but this time in joy. God used the heart of a plumber to answer our prayers. We felt peace like never before. We knew God would guard us from now on (8).

I believe America is blessed by God because of its founding principles—freedom, justice, and compassion. The wonderful men and women who escaped religious persecution and political oppression and banded together to form our great nation should remain our example. The wish I desire from the depths of my soul is that each of us sees each immigrant as a human being created by the same God that created us.

Chapter Thirteen
Stranger No More

I am blessed to work with refugees who are just like you, just like me—only placed by life in circumstances that none of us would ever freely choose. I follow the Bible command to "welcome the stranger" just as she or he arrives—not as I would like them to be or wishing they had taken another route.

Even more than food, clothing, and shelter—though they need these, too, desperately—what a refugee needs is to be wanted. It is their outcast state that their poverty imposes on them that is the most agonizing. I know this feeling firsthand. I have a place in my heart for all refugees and immigrants and if you allow yourself to see in them Christ's face, you will, also.

When we serve others, we save ourselves and touch the face of God.

Today, our *Casa Compasión* campus is as much a place where we teach compassion as where we receive refugees. Volunteers have built new and larger dormitories to house both refugees paroled to our custody and for work groups. We have a kitchen, dining and bath facilities, a warehouse, an office, a caretaker's cottage, a garage for tools, mowers and food supplies, an educational building, and a chapel. On the grounds, we also added an outdoor chapel and prayer garden and a volleyball court.

Every spring and summer, during school breaks and vacations, we host youth and adult mission groups from all over the United States. Our ministries keep them busy building new facilities, making needed repairs, and conducting classes at our affiliated orphanage, colonias, and Bible institutes in Mexico (1). Everyone who comes participates in daily devotions and prayers. For the teens, we leave time for a trip to nearby South Padre Island at the conclusion of their stay with us. *Casa Compasión* is also used for weekend spiritual retreats for people of all faith backgrounds. When invited, I relate my personal journey of redemption and freedom.

When possible and appropriate, I like for the mission team members to work side by side on projects with the refugees. This forces both to work to overcome challenges of language, culture, and socioeconomic differences. In my experience, when the refugees, who are poor materially but rich in God's love, mingle in a Christian environment with Anglo adults and teens who may not recognize their vast blessings, life-changing results occur for both groups.

In working with the poor, the young people (and their adult sponsors) who visit us meet the God who parted the Red Sea, who cared for the prophets and patriarchs, who gave up His son to die on a wooden cross and resurrected Him so that they might have eternal lives. Author James Finley captures this transformative experience in *Merton's Palace of Nowhere*. "Christ has identified himself with the human family, especially the poor and the forgotten. In loving them we love Him in them. And they, in turn, encounter Him in us in the love we give them. And in this the bonds of charity are formed, building up one Christ unto the eternal glory of the Father," he wrote.

Over the years, I have been privileged to hear or read of these experiences of the men, women, and young people of high school and college age who visit us. They tell how they have learned new lessons in human dignity, in courage, in achievement, and in love (2). None of us is so mature that we cannot use more understanding in these areas.

From business executives with six-figure incomes to church ministers, from freshmen in high school to college professors with PhDs, a common theme has emerged: redemption comes through freedom and security of the Gospel made flesh in service to others. A man from Bloomington, Illinois, summed up his mission trip experience this way: "It is a unique feeling to suddenly realize that you are an answer to prayer."

I especially admire the young people who work with us out of true sacrifice. Many students, instead of partying during spring break, give their time, talent, and money to others. They learn that full joy has nothing to do with materialism, which has for too many in our society become a god. A person doesn't have to live behind bars to be in prison. Many people are in a jail of their own making as they seek to fill voids with material things. Only God can plug these holes within mankind in a lasting way.

I've seen young people become blessed by poverty. Having arrived with every good intention, their minds made up to "help those less fortunate," they are clobbered by the sights, sounds, and smells of the poverty of South Texas and Mexico—and by the smiles, the hugs, the pure unfiltered joy of an orphan who has one change of clothing, or an elderly widow whose bathroom is an outhouse.

In seeing the richness of their lives, we are inspired by the joy that exudes from them because they have Christ as the treasure of their lives (3).

Following a mission trip, one man from Kentucky wrote, "The

people we met at *Casa Compasión* are people who only have the shirt on their back and who are literally wondering where their next meal is coming from. They are wondering how they are going to care for their children; wondering how they are going to get through the next day. They don't live in a war zone (some have come from one), but their living conditions were just about as bad as living in one. These are people not out bumming for a meal—not saying 'poor little me'—not saying 'if you give me a meal today, I'll pay you back tomorrow.' These are people who for economic reasons, for political reasons, geographic reasons, family reasons, health reasons, a multitude of reasons, have fallen into being the poorest of the poor—who have only the dignity they can muster. Yet, these are people who have a faith in God stronger that some of us will ever know."

A man from a church in suburban Fort Worth, Texas, wrote: "For me immigration reform has been a remote, abstract conundrum. But things changed during mission week. The debate raging in Congress and in the media certainly kept the issue on the front burner of my brain; but faces, voices, miracles touched my heart. Orphan girls sing and joke about boys. Reverend Pereira gives money to a woman living in a plywood box. God appears in the tear-filled eyes of a couple getting a donated mobile home. My brothers and sisters from Azle Christian Church sing, 'Gracias, gracias, el Señor' with the congregation at Iglesia Cristiana. Around this troubled world, crafty, resolute idealists like Feliberto Pereira turn problems into opportunities, curses into blessings. Sunflowers thrive in garbage dumps. Miracles occur. Sometimes power hears truth and things get better. We just have to believe."

Over the past twenty-five years, our ministry has been blessed— I have been blessed—by the generosity of so many who give of their time, talents, and money. No ministry like ours is built by one person. On a regular basis, I am, as Christian author C.S. Lewis wrote, "surprised by joy."

In the early months of the influx of refugees from Central America, feeding so many hungry brothers and sisters became a daily challenge. My prayers were answered one day by an angel of justice sent by the Lord—a church leader named Frank C. Mabee, area minister of the Christian Church (Disciples of Christ) in the Houston region, who visited me in 1980, at my invitation (4).

I believe only God could have brought Frank and me together. The truth is that my first encounter with him was not easy. At that time, I was so extremely right-wing conservative and he was very extremely leftist. We butted heads on many political issues. But when I saw how much he loved the people, and he saw what I was doing, how much I loved the refugees, we put our political views aside and worked for the same purpose.

I took him to the Oscar Romero Center, a roadside shelter operated by the Brownsville Catholic Diocese where hundreds of refugees stayed pending asylum hearings.

Determined that no one at the shelter go hungry, Frank decided on the spot to purchase ten fifty-pound bags of rice from the Port of Brownsville and take them to the shelter. Prepared that evening, the rice was blessed by a Catholic nun who prayed, "Let us give thanks for this Disciple's rice." That's how the "Disciples Rice" program got its name. It's a ministry that has fed hundreds of thousands of refugees, orphans, and members of impoverished communities in Texas and Mexico over the past twenty-five years. In 1992, the High Plains Area of the Christian Church (Disciples of Christ), located in the Texas Panhandle, initiated the "Disciples Beans" program, contributing funds to purchase 30,000 pounds of pinto beans—a truckload of needed protein for hungry refugees (5). The program continues to this day.

Very soon, Frank would call me from Houston and say, "Pick me up at the airport in forty-five minutes." I said, "Frank, you know you always have a room here." We became very close, like brothers. Frank told a friend about our political differences: "Both of us have given in. He's come my way, and I have come his way."

One of the greatest surprises—and joys—of my life arrived in early November 1988, when a thirty-six-year-old man filled with God's spirit visited me to learn firsthand how his organization, the Christian Men's Fellowship of the North Texas Area of our denomination, might assist us. Mike Slaight arrived alone in his van. I introduced him in Spanish to the refugees in our care. Mike doesn't speak Spanish. I'll always remember how instantly he greeted the refugees with a big smile and a bear hug. In those few moments, I knew God had sent another angel.

I soon learned that Mike was a giving person from the very early years of his life. One day, when he was in the third grade, he came home without his jacket. When his mother, Virginia, asked him what happened, he said, "There was a new kid at school today who didn't have a jacket. So I took mine off and gave it to him."

On his short visit to the Valley, Mike saw our urgent need for food, clothing, and toys for the growing population of refugees and their children—children who, despite the chaos of a refugee existence, maintained their innocence and love. Seeing how much these children loved God in spite of their conditions, Mike was driven to tears and action. Returning to his suburban Dallas home, he came back to the Valley days later accompanied by his young family in a van full of food, clothing, and toys.

As you might imagine, this was a great surprise for me. Mike asked, "What else do we need for the refugee children?" I thought a moment. "We can always use shoes," I said. Without hesitation, Mike sat down and began removing his size 13s. My jaw dropped, and I burst into laughter. "I think we will need some smaller sizes, too," I said.

"This is what we're going to do," Mike announced to me. "Our men's fellowship is going to provide new clothing and toys for as many kids as we can at Christmas."

The following Christmas, Mike, his son Mark, and his father Hank Slaight rented a U-Haul truck and with the help of men in the North Texas area collected new clothing and toys from several churches. Then they drove the truck, packed to its roof, to Southwest Good Samaritan Ministries. With the truckload of clothing and toys, we provided a joyous Christmas to hundreds of refugee children who would otherwise have gone without gifts.

Today, when I think of "calling," Mike Slaight immediately comes to mind. In superficial terms, Mike was an Anglo, a professional with a good job who lived in the comfort of urban North Texas. Yet Mike yielded his life to the Lord and received a calling that transcended the racial, ethnic, and social categories that so often define and, too often, limit us. Mike saw the need to provide Christmas gifts to poor children in the Rio Grande Valley and followed God's call. In doing so, he enabled the churches of the North Texas to get involved as well. Mike is an example of compassion for all of us.

Six months after making Christmas 1989 a reality for hundreds of poor children, Mike died of an aneurism at the age of thirty-eight. His only brother, Mark, had died of a similar cause in 1986 at thirty-one. Their parents now grieved the loss of both of their boys.

As I stood graveside with Mike's family at his burial on a muggy June day, I cried for the loss of this big man who never knew a stranger. Earlier, during the memorial service, I wept from the pulpit as I spoke about Mike and the impact he had on all of our lives—especially mine. I miss him terribly to this day.

However, in suffering God works miraculous wonders, and so He has in Mike's going home at such a young age. Every year since Mike's first trip to the Valley, a truck bearing gifts of new clothing and toys arrives in South Texas just before Christmas. These gifts for "Mike's Kids" are collected by churches in North Texas. We distribute them to the glory of God (6).

By giving to others, we receive. Even the poorest among us who know God's love understand this. I have had the great honor to experience, with great humility, acts of generosity from the poor themselves.

Juanita was a single mother of seven. Her husband abandoned the family shortly after the birth of their last child, and she was filled with shame as a result. She had few skills, never having attended school. She spoke no English and her Spanish was poor, as well. We welcomed Juanita to our church, where she began attending services. She became a Christian and was baptized.

Juanita worked twelve hours a day Monday through Saturday as a domestic worker to support her children. I've never known a harder worker. One year, as we started our annual campaign to raise our church budget, knowing of her poverty, I took her aside and told her to keep her tithe for her needs. She looked at me in disgust and without hesitation spoke words that still ring in my ears, "No, this 10 percent is not mine. It doesn't belong to me," she said. "I don't want to be a thief of the Lord's money. It belongs to Him!"

As her children grew, I encouraged Juanita to pursue an education. She taught herself to read, write, and speak English. Eventually, she became a nurse's aide and received a decent paycheck and benefits. After her children married, Juanita, who would never remarry, would even travel.

A similar story comes from Clinton Looney, the minister and brother who ran the daily operations of our radio ministry, *La Hora Cristiana*. Over the years, we have received dozens of wonderful personal letters from listeners throughout Latin America, telling us how the weekly broadcasts touched their lives. While traveling through Mexico on his way to Belize, Clinton stopped by a village outside Vera Cruz to meet a couple who had written to *La Hora*.

"I met them outside their small home, a mud hut really, and they invited me in," he relates. "They had almost no furniture. They had two chairs and a board laying across it. They were an old man and his wife. My wife was with me, and we had arrived at meal time. The couple had a cup of something sitting across the board. They begged me to take their meal and eat it. We didn't and wouldn't. We stayed for a short visit, and when it was time to leave, the old woman pressed, at that time, a $5 peso coin in my hand. I begged her to take it back. She swelled up and big tears ran down her face. She said, 'But, Brother. I want to help with the Lord's work.'"

Sometimes, events occur that, at first sight, appear not to be blessings but burdens. Such was the case for me in 1995 when God brought to our ministry a dedicated and committed couple, Ismael and Lorena Sifuentes, who responded to a calling to establish an orphanage for the homeless children of Matamoros, Mexico.

Ismael, with a master's degree in education, and Lorena, who had a degree in nursing, could have enjoyed a six-figure income lifestyle if they had wished. But they had begun feeding orphans regularly on the street corners of Matamoros—a gesture of good intent from a young couple with everything in life to look forward to. The plight of these orphans forced them to their knees. "Giving food was not enough," Ismael said. "God was asking us, 'Where are they going to sleep tonight? Who will give them an education?' I talked about these things with my wife, and we agreed that it should be us."

They hoped to secure a bank loan to buy property, hire architects, and in orderly fashion build an orphanage over a three-year period. But, Ismael said, "God had a faster timetable in mind." A man who heard of their desire to open an orphanage leased them property he had owned for twenty-five years—at no cost. The five acres, fourteen miles south of downtown Matamoros, once housed a juvenile detention facility, but it had been closed for twelve years. The property was overgrown with weeds, the buildings filled with trash.

Surprising Ismael and Lorena, the property owner brought to the couple thirteen orphans whose parents had died in a recent hurricane. Casa Bethel Hogar ("The House of God") opened its doors in August 1996 without water service, electricity, or furniture. A friend of the couple from Monterrey, Mexico, brought thirteen blankets—enough for each child to have one at night. "We made our bed from bags of rice," said Ismael. The couple only had a small savings, which they quickly exhausted.

"The conditions were so bad in the beginning that the Mexican government said we can't live there—and, brother, if the Mexican government calls something bad, you can imagine our situation! We were given ninety days to make improvements or shut our doors."

A woman living across the border in Brownsville learned of conditions at the orphanage. She arranged for power and water. "And then Feliberto came into our lives," Ismael said." A man who worked with us at the orphanage as a volunteer told us that his sister's husband knew of a pastor in Los Fresnos who could help us secure some rice and beans for the children. So, I phoned him and went to visit him at the Ebenezer Christian Church in Los Fresnos."

I asked if I could see the orphanage. "Gladly," Ismael said. It was December 1996.

"We worked very hard to clean for his visit," Ismael said. "But when Feliberto saw the children sleeping on the floor, God touched his heart."

When I visited Ismael and Lorena that first time, I found a young couple with a three-month-old baby of their own, living in a place with no windows and doors, only a partial roof, in terrible conditions, caring for needy children. I knew immediately God called me to this place to support this young and dedicated couple who had given up everything to care for orphans. The children were so skinny. On some of them, I could count the ribs. I know what starvation means. I made the decision on that first visit that I would be involved with the orphanage from that day forward. With winter coming on, I knew time was of the essence.

Ismael said, "Feliberto's army (of workers) arrived from the United States and began helping us. . . . And as our orphan population expanded, even more help started coming from across the border. The door I asked God to open for this place was opened the day Feliberto came. Everything changed. Everything became different. I am so grateful to God for how he has worked through Feliberto and others to make this place possible."

In 1998, the orphanage was re-inspected by the Mexican government, Ismael said. "The inspector said, 'What happened here?' I told him, 'We've been working.' He said, 'When you want your permanent license to run an orphanage, we will give it to you.'"

In 2003, Casa Bethel moved to a new facility on seven donated acres about ten miles closer to Matamoros, nearer its schools. The new campus includes separate dormitories and bathrooms for boys and girls, laundry and kitchen facilities, an office and director's house, and a large cafeteria area that can be converted into a worship space. The orphanage is home to about seventy-five children (the population fluctuates) ages six to eighteen—orphans who have been abandoned, abused, neglected, and are from extremely impoverished households. The new facility was built by volunteers who continue to actively support the orphanage (7).

For the past twenty-five years of our ministry, so many have shown how the love of Christ can make a difference in the life of a refugee, an orphan, or a person living in poverty. These givers have allowed themselves to be used in order to bless others (8).

It is a privilege to serve those who come to us in search of love, understanding, and assistance. I am ever mindful of St. Paul's message, ". . . You are no longer foreigners and aliens, but fellow citizens with God's people and members of God's household, built on the foundation of the apostles and prophets, with Christ Jesus himself as the chief cornerstone." Let us carry this Gospel message to all who will hear. For we, the people, are America. And we, the church, are America's conscience. I pray that you will see refugees as members of God's family and pray for them. In the same manner, I ask for your continued prayers that God will give us the strength and undivided commitment to continue serving "the least of these."

I am so grateful to God for the freedom in which He has allowed me to live. Because of His great mercy to my family and me, I want to continue to serve Him with all that I have: mind, soul, strength, and love. Joshua 1:9 contains a message I try to live by: *"Have I not commanded you? Be strong and courageous. Do not be terrified; do not be discouraged, for the Lord your God will be with you wherever you go."*

Throughout my life, this verse has been a source of hope and help, sustaining me whether the times were rough or smooth. God has taught me that while we walk in His way, we should be valiant regardless of the circumstances that surround us. The promises of God are not vain promises, but are sure to us who trust in Him. What else could we desire when the King of Kings and Lord of Lords has promised: *"And surely I am with you always, to the very end of the age"* (Matthew 28:20).

Some have asked me if I will ever retire from Southwest Good Samaritan Ministries, or leave to take a better-paying position— say, at a church in Miami, Los Angeles, or Houston. I have been blessed to have many offers of higher-paying jobs with lots of benefits. It's not that I have not wanted these opportunities. Rather, I am fulfilling the call God gave me. I will move from the Texas-Mexico border when we no longer have refugees coming here. On that day, I will move to another ministry. Until then, I will be here to welcome the stranger, serving our brother and sister in need, until God calls me home.

I stand with all the refugees around the world—those who, at this moment, are on a trail of tears in search of freedom from persecution and violence; those who are in refugee camps; and those whose immigration status is being processed by governments that honor asylum rights. I greet them with open arms, as an American proud to live in a country that embraces me, a stranger no more.

When I close my eyes and remember the moment when God tapped me on the shoulder beneath a mango tree, I still feel the awe coursing through my body—sixty years later. I remember, too, the words spoken by my mother—the truth that I pray you will take into your heart, no matter your station in life, and claim as your own:

"*Dios te quiere*. God wants you!"

Epilogue

In 2007, Southwest Good Samaritan Ministries welcomed 157 asylum-seekers from ten countries, among them Cuba, Colombia, Bolivia, Ecuador, and Venezuela.

More than 800 volunteers from nine states built a dozen new homes and delivered 50,000 pounds of rice and 30,000 pounds of beans for the poor on both sides of the border.

More than 2,000 of "Mike's Kids" got toys the week before Christmas—for the eighteenth consecutive year.

Thirteen students completed three years of study at Berea Bible Institute in Monterrey, Mexico. Another ten students completed a year of study at the Matamoros institute for the Ebenezer Movement.

Six orphans at Casa Bethel graduated from high school. Twelve more will graduate in 2008. Nearly all of them plan to attend college.

On July 23, 2007, the Guerrero family from Peru received asylum from the U.S. government after the U.S. Board of Immigration Appeals overruled the local immigration judge. Felix, Irene, Omar,

Katherine, and Rocio plan to become U.S. citizens as soon as the law allows them.

Feliberto celebrated his seventieth birthday on March 9, 2008.

Other Updates:

Amado Rodriguez, the minister in Cuba who introduced Feliberto's family to Christianity and helped Feliberto enroll in seminary, died in 2002 at eighty-two.

Aurelio Lopez, the Christian pastor whom Feliberto was visiting in a Cuban prison camp when Feliberto was placed before a firing squad, arrived in the United States with his wife in 2005 as refugees. They are pastors of La Trinidad, a Hispanic congregation in Corpus Christi, Texas. The couple's grown daughter and son and their families arrived in the ensuing years under the U.S. government's family reunification program.

With funding support from the Week of Compassion humanitarian assistance program of the Christian Church (Disciples of Christ), David Welch, an ordained minister, joined Southwest Good Samaritan Ministries in July 2007 to oversee the new "Casita Project" devoted to building emergency housing in northern Mexico.

Miguel Dominguez, Jacqui's uncle, who along with his wife Lolita, were the Pereiras' U.S. sponsors, died in 1986 at eighty-two. Feliberto was at his bedside. Lolita Dominguez, ninety, is living in Hialeah, Florida, with her daughter.

Eliseo and Elizabeth Rodriquez, the couple that welcomed the Pereiras to San Benito, are retired from the ministry and live in Orlando, Florida.

Fidel Castro, who turned eighty-one on August 13, 2007, resigned as president of Cuba on February 19, 2008. The resignation ended nearly a half-century of rule. His younger brother, Raul, became his successor. Castro had transferred his duties to Raul in July 2006 before undergoing intestinal surgery for an unknown serious ailment. Few observers expect a dramatic change in Cuba upon Fidel Castro's death. However, competing factions in Cuba, including the army, are likely to jockey for power following the death of Raul. The U.S. government has prepared plans for addressing an exodus of Cubans from the island. In 2007, the number of Cubans leaving the island reached its highest level since the most recent mass exodus in 1994, according to U.S. Customs and Border Protection.

The war in Iraq has created 2 million refugees. The United States so far has accepted a few hundred refugees. President Bush has said the United States would resettle about 7,000 refugees by the end of 2008.

Emilio T. Gonzalez, director of Citizenship and Immigration Services for the U.S. Department of Homeland Security and who lived in Washington D.C. while his family resided in the Miami area, resigned, effective April 18, 2008, to live in South Florida with his family.

Hank Slaight, who took over the "Mike's Kids" program after his son Mike passed away, died on October 25, 2003, at seventy-six. On April 11, 2004, Southwest Good Samaritan Ministries renamed the chapel at *Casa Compasión* "Slaight Chapel" in honor of Hank and Mike. On June 3, 2007, Virginia "Jenny" Slaight joined her husband and two sons in heaven. Mike Slaight's children, Mark and Christy, now oversee "Mike's Kids."

Frank C. Mabee, founder of Disciples Rice, died on November 14, 2004, at seventy-nine. In the years before his death, Frank continued to nurture the program he founded, visiting churches to tell them of the need for feeding the refugees, orphans, and others along the Texas-Mexico border. In 1997, Frank became the first director of the Center for Survivors of Torture in Dallas, now the only center dedicated to rehabilitative treatment for torture survivors in the five-state region of Texas, New Mexico, Oklahoma, Arkansas, and Louisiana. In 1999, the Dallas Peace Center recognized him as the 1999 Peacemaker of the Year.

Jacqueline Rosales Wilkinson died on December 18, 2006, after a long and courageous battle with multiple sclerosis. Her children Joel and Ruthie, mother Maria, and Feliberto were at her bedside. Maria, age eighty-seven, lives in Harlingen, Texas, where Joel is a mortgage broker. Ruthie is a public relations account executive in Miami. Feliberto and the three of them who, with Jacqui, arrived together from Cuba in 1969, talk several times each week.

Feliberto's father, Francisco, died on May 17, 2003, at eighty-eight. He was surrounded by his wife of sixty-six years, two sons, and extended family. An evangelist for Christ until his final hours, Francisco led his team of doctors and nurses in a church service from his hospital bed in Cuba just days before his passing. Released to his home to die, Francisco invited members of his church and his family to his bedside and lead them in a final church service. "For as long as I can remember, my father has been a model for my life, and the best one," Feliberto said.

Eldo Pereira remains in Cuba and speaks to his brother by phone monthly. Feliberto's mother, Hermenegilda, age ninety-one, lives in Zaza del Medio and starts each day with a prayer for her son in Texas.

Chapter One Notes:

(1) In a letter to Chris Kelley dated March 25, 2003, when she was eighty-six years old, Feliberto's mother confirmed the day's events. "As for the question you asked me," she wrote, "indeed I can tell you that my son came running for me to tell me that he had felt something very special under the mango tree where he played; that it was a feeling of warmth that covered him. Respectively, I told him that maybe God wants you, my son.

"I give thanks to God because I know that my son was singled out to serve the Lord, and he went on to prepare himself at the evangelical seminary in Placetas, Cuba. I am proud of him. In the middle of trials, God has cared for him and blessed his ministry."

(2) Because of its shape, Cuba is sometimes referred to as the sleeping alligator. The island has the same land area as England. Three mountain ranges provide relief on the island, which is composed mainly of flat or gently rolling plains. Thousands of islands pepper the waters around Cuba, home to about eleven million people. Located in the Caribbean tropics, Central Cuba's temperate conditions sprout carpets of green

landscapes stitched together by an annual average rainfall of 54 inches and an average annual temperature of 77 degrees.

The island was first inhabited by tribes from Central and South America around 1000 BC. The first settlers, the Siboneys, made their homes in caves and were dependent on fishing. When the fiercer Tainos, a tribe of Arawak Indians from the South American mainland arrived, they enslaved the less advanced Siboneys. But even they were ill-equipped to stand up to the arrival of European conquistadors.

Christopher Columbus caught his first glimpse of Cuba on October 27, 1492, declaring that he had "never seen anything so beautiful." In honor of the daughter of Ferdinand V and Isabella I of Spain, he named the island Juana, the first of several names he applied to the island. It eventually became known as Cuba, from its aboriginal name, Cuba-nascan. Columbus' explorers found small villages of thatched huts (on which Cuban peasants still model their homes) and people inhaling the smoke of "certain herbs." This was the Europeans first encounter with tobacco, one of the few legacies left by Cuba's Indians.

(3) Francisco Pereira Sanchez, Feliberto's father, was born on December 17, 1914. Hermenegilda Navarro Gomez, his mother, was born on April 13, 1917. Following the Spanish naming custom of incorporating the family surnames of his father and mother into his name, Francisco Feliberto Pereira Navarro prefers to be called Feliberto or Pereira. The naming system traces back to the nobility classes of sixteenth century Spain and Portugal.

(4) Las Villas was one of Cuba's original six provinces from the nineteenth century. In 1976, Castro's government subdivided the six provinces into fourteen provinces—an act akin to dividing the fifty United States into more than one hundred. Las Villas was splintered into four new provinces. Castro fixed the number of Cuban municipalities at 169. The changes were made in the name of political and administrative efficiency.

(5) Central Cuba is the agricultural heart of the country. The region grows enough sugar to sweeten all the cups of coffee in the world. Cuba's farmers, the *guajiros*, tend the sugar fields and harvest coffee, rice, fruits, and vegetables. Global economic changes today are creating massive

hardships for Cuba's once-thriving sugar industry. In 2002, the Communist government closed seventy-one of the island's 156 sugar mills because they were no longer able to compete in the world market.

(6) The Roman Catholic Church had little influence in Cuba even before Fidel Castro assumed power in 1959. The church is seen by many Cubans as a hangover from Spanish colonial rule—a business run by Spanish priests for the benefit of the social elite. Even today, the Catholic Church remains weaker in Cuba than anywhere else in Latin America, despite a visit by Pope John Paul II in January 1998, aimed at reawakening interest in the church. While the Catholic Church remains Cuba's largest organized religion, only a handful of the country's 4.5 million baptized followers attend Mass regularly. Indeed, one estimate by the Cuban Council of Churches shows that active Protestants (530,000, according to a 2006 report by the U.S. State Department) now outnumber active Catholics. The fastest-growing churches are evangelical Christian congregations, many of them small "house churches."

(7) Translated from the Spanish name, *Alas del Alba*, meaning "Wings of the Dawn." Liduvina Martinez broadcasts were carried by Union Radio only in Cuba. Feliberto later met Mrs. Martinez while at seminary and told her what her radio ministry meant to him as a youngster. "She was very, very moved that I was touched so deeply by her radio ministry. In reality, she prompted my own radio ministry in great part."

(8) Pentecostals are among the fastest-growing segments of the evangelical Christian movement in Cuba. The Assemblies of God, Cuba's largest Protestant denomination, now has more than 100,000 adherents, compared with about 9,000 in 1990. The first Pentecostal missionaries arrived in Cuba in 1899.

(9) Batista came to power by brute force in 1933, when, as a sergeant in the Cuban army, he organized a revolt among noncommissioned officers. His efforts failed, but he nonetheless ended up wielding significant powers behind the scenes. In 1940, he was elected president of Cuba, only to be voted out of office in 1944. He ran for president again in 1952. But three months before the election was to take place, he seized power in a bloodless coup, suspended balloting, and began ruling by decree.

Batista's tactics infuriated twenty-six-year-old Fidel Castro, a lawyer and son of a well-to-do sugar planter. Castro was planning to run for a seat in the Cuban Chamber of Representatives in 1952 when Batista suspended elections. Perhaps naively, Castro began to circulate a petition seeking to depose Batista's government. The effort failed.

With legal means to remove Batista thwarted, Castro turned to violence. In the wee hours of July 26, 1953, he led about 150 young men in an attack on Batista soldiers housed at the Moncada Barracks in Oriente Province. Many of the young rebels were killed. Castro was captured and sentenced to fifteen years in prison. He was released after only two years in an amnesty decree issued by Batista, who was in the habit of making such gestures now and then in an attempt to prove that he was a benevolent ruler.

Shortly after his release, Castro and thirty of his comrades left Cuba for Mexico. There, they began to organize what is now called the July 26 Movement to liberate Cuba from Batista and his U.S.-backed business supporters.

Chapter Two Notes:

(1) On September 25, 1928, Bartholomew Lavastida, better known as B.G. Lavastida, co-founded the Cuba Bible Institute with three other evangelical missionaries, among them American Elmer V. Thompson. The school later became Los Pinos Nuevos Seminary. A Cuban native, Lavastida had left his country to attend college in the United States. While there, word came that his father had been assassinated. Hoping to avenge his father's death, Lavastida returned to Cuba. During the journey home, he began reading a New Testament given to him by a Christian woman. Encountering Christ for the first time, Lavastida said he surrendered his life to God. Rather than seeking his father's killers to settle the score, he instead sought them out to share God's love.

To operate Los Pinos Nuevos, Lavastida and Thompson created the Evangelistic Association of Cuba (Asociacion Evangelica de Cuba). Los Pinos had many U.S. supporters. One was Jessina Park, a Presbyterian from Albany, New York, whom Feliberto later found out was the anonymous donor who paid for his books and tuition at Los Pinos. Today, the association is divided into districts and operates dozens of churches and house churches throughout Cuba. Thompson later founded the West Indies Mission, which is known today as World Team, a mission organization that establishes new churches around the world. Thompson died on October 20, 1998, in Columbia, South Carolina, at ninety-seven. His missionary career spanned more than sixty years, including twenty in Cuba and eighteen as general director of West Indies Mission. Lavastida died in 1994. He was 104.

(2) Fasting is a fundamental tenet of Christian teaching. Fasting allows the Christian to focus on God with all his or her heart. Closely connected to prayer, fasting strengthens virtue, inspires mercy, implores divine assistance, and leads to conversion of the heart. Before beginning his public ministry, Jesus, driven by the Holy Spirit, fasted for forty days as an expression of his trusting abandonment to his Father's saving plan (Matthew 4: 1–4).

Feliberto's statement of faith included five core principles rooted in Scripture as follows:

- Belief in a Trinitarian God (Matthew 3:16, 17).

- Belief that the Bible is the Word of God, verbally inspired and without error as originally written, and the only infallible rule of faith and practice for the Christian (2 Timothy 3:16; 2 Peter 1:21).

- Belief in salvation through Jesus Christ, conceived of the Holy Spirit and born of the Virgin Mary (Luke 1:35), whose death on the cross for the redemption of sinners provided a sufficient and complete atonement for their sin and guilt (1 John 4:10; Ephesians 1:7), and who rose again for the Christian's justification (Romans 4:25), ascended into heaven, and is now seated on the right hand of the Father, interceding for all those who come unto God by Him (Hebrews 7:25). All who believe in and receive the Lord Jesus Christ have eternal life; those who do not will be eternally lost (John 1:12; John 3:36; Romans 10: 9; 1 John 5, 11–12). The Christian waits for the return of the Lord (Titus 2:13) and believes

that all things shall finally be subjected to God through Him
(1 Corinthians 15: 25–28).

- Belief that the true church, the body of Christ (Ephesians 1:23), is
  formed by the work of the Holy Spirit in all those who trust Christ
  as their Savior (Ephesians 2:22; 1 Corinthians 12:13).

- Belief in ministry, in the urgency of every Christian to respond to
  the great commission of Christ (Matthew 28: 19, 20).

(3) Fidel Castro and the eighty-one others who formed the 26th of July
Movement to liberate Cuba returned to the island in December 1956 aboard
a rickety yacht named the Granma. Back in the country only three days,
Castro and his men faced fierce attacks from Batista's army—infantry,
aircraft, and artillery—that forced the rebels to flee in small bands.

Batista's army captured and executed most of the rebels. But Castro, his brother Raul, and two other key rebel leaders, Che Guevara and
Camilo Cienfuegos, escaped to the Sierra Maestras. There, friendly peasants provided them refuge, and over the next weeks and months, Castro
rebuilt his depleted ranks with volunteer recruits eager to overthrow
Batista.

Raul Castro, Fidel's younger brother by five years, has been Cuba's
armed forces minister, and the nation's second-in-command, since the
1959 revolution. A member of the Communist party since 1953, he is first
vice president of the Council of State and Ministers, meaning that under
the Cuban constitution, he is the lawful successor to the presidency. In
July 2006, Raul assumed the presidential duties from his ailing brother,
who announced he was giving up his office temporarily to undergo surgery and recovery from an undisclosed illness. On February 19, 2008,
Raul became his permanent successor after Fidel Castro resigned.

It was Raul Castro who introduced Ernesto "Che" Guevera to Fidel
Castro in Mexico in July 1954. After Fidel and Che, an Argentinean
doctor, talked for ten straight hours through the night, Che joined the
revolution and went on to become an important military leader. He was

very popular among the Cuban people—the word "che" is the familiar diminutive for "you" in Argentina, as in "Hey you!" One month after the revolution, Che was proclaimed a citizen of Cuba "by birth" for his role. He went on to head Cuba's Ministry of Industry from 1959 to 1965 and was president of the national bank. But the restless guerilla—amid rumors of disagreements with Fidel Castro—left Cuba in 1965 and helped lead a revolt in Bolivia. Captured by the Bolivian Army, Guevara was executed on October 9, 1967. He is still revered as a hero in Cuba. In 1997, the Bolivian government allowed his remains to be shipped to Cuba, where he is buried at the site of his greatest revolutionary battle, at Santa Clara, capital of the Villa Clara Province.

In 1958, at the young age of twenty-three, Camilo Cienfuegos commanded a 700-man force of Castro's rebel army, furiously attacking Batista troops. A disciplined captain, he was immensely popular among Cubans. Castro, delivering his victory speech on January 8, 1959, turned to Cienfuegos before a crowd of one million gathered in Havana and asked, "Am I doing all right, Camilo?" Cienfuegos replied to the roar of the crowd, "You are doing all right, Fidel!"—and a new revolutionary slogan was born. Less than a year after the revolution, on October 28, 1959, Camilo's Cessna-310 disappeared over the ocean during a night flight from Camaguey City to Havana. The plane was never found.

(4) Castro recognized early on the importance of winning the support of rural peasants. Under Batista, peasants counted for nothing in Cuban society. Military officials and police robbed them routinely and shot them at the slightest complaint. If wealthy landowners wanted to expand their holdings, they bribed the police or army to evict neighboring peasants from their lands. Castro treated peasants with respect. His guerillas always paid for the food they took, often at twice the market prices. After raiding a wealthy landowner's cattle ranch, guerillas shared their bounty equally with peasants. Between battles with Batista's forces, Castro's rebels organized adult literacy classes and free medical clinics for peasants. In return, the peasant grapevine kept guerillas informed of every move made by Batista's army.

(5) The Cuban revolution had vast support from the people. "A small vanguard of intellectuals did not have to transform the thinking and aspirations of the whole country," according to Lorrin Philipson and Rafael Lierna, authors of *Freedom Flights*. "Rather, Cubans from all social strata—the 26th of July Movement of workers and students, the Directorio Revolucionario members of the middle class, particularly those in the Movimiento Resistencia Civica (Civic Resistance Movement), and peasants who joined the Rebel Army—struggled against Batista."

A 1959 survey, conducted by a respected Cuban pollster during Castro's first few months in office, found that more than 90 percent of the Cuban people favored the new regime, according to the authors. "Their euphoria sprang from the fact that the flagrant greed, corruption, and repression of Batista's dictatorship were over. Most Cubans were unified in their desire for honest government, free elections, an end to police brutality and corruption, agrarian reform to be accomplished by the redistribution of land among small farmers, and guarantees of steady jobs for the many victims of seasonal unemployment caused by Cuba's single crop (sugar cane) economy. Castro himself promised that the new order would bring 'freedom and bread without terror.' The new leaders were going to create a nation free from dependency on the United States or any other country. The Revolution was going to be 'as green as the palm trees,' establishing Cuba for Cubans and realizing the centuries-old dream of freedom embodied by Jose Marti, the famous Cuban poet and patriot, in his struggle against Spanish domination in the 1890s."

(6) From the earliest days of the revolution, Castro went to great lengths to invoke Christ as his role model and Christianity as the philosophical basis of the Cuban revolution. As a child, Castro had attended Catholic primary and high schools. "When Christ's preachings are practiced, it will be possible to say that a revolution is occurring in the world . . ." Castro said in December 1959. "Because I studied in a religious school, I remember many teachings of Christ, and I remember He was implacable with Pharisees. Nobody forgets that Christ was persecuted; and let nobody forget that He was crucified. And that His preachings and ideas were very much fought. And that these preachings did not prosper in high society, but germinated in the heart of the humble of Palestine."

Chapter Three Notes:

(1) Fed up with Castro's government after fifteen tumultuous months, President Dwight D. Eisenhower, on March 17, 1960, approved a covert plan that included a "powerful propaganda campaign" to overthrow Castro. The plan called for elimination of sugar purchases, the end of oil deliveries to Cuba, continuation of the arms embargo in effect since mid-1958, and the organization of a paramilitary force of Cuban exiles to invade the island. The embargo has cost Cuba more than $89 billion, according to a September 2007 report by Cuban Foreign Minister Felipe Perez Roque.

(2) Still active today, the CDRs, the Committees of Revolutionary Defense, were formed by Castro to essentially have neighbors spy on other neighbors. Castro believes CDRs serve as the backbone of his revolution. In his book, *This is Cuba: An Outlaw Culture Survives*, Ben Corbett explains: "Every 300 citizens are organized into a barrio . . . which is presided over by a volunteer president responsible for keeping tabs on everything that goes on in the lives of his or her 300 neighbors. The president looks for anything suspicious, right down to the smallest details of what furniture is bought, who attends what marches, where everyone earns his money, and which neighbors are on leave to other parts. Some CDR Presidents are tough and create a sensation of suspicion and paranoia throughout a neighborhood; others are relaxed and committed more to the individual care of the people rather than to state security. Neighbors often wake up a good CDR President in the middle of the night to discuss a personal problem. If a CDR President is a tyrant, the neighbors try to hide everything from him or her."

Cubans who buck the system are subjected to *actos de repudio* or acts of repudiation by mobs. The government-sanctioned Rapid Response Brigades are designed to marginalize and break the resistance of opponents by whipping up crowds in front of an opponent's house. Stones are thrown and insults and Castroist slogans are spray painted on walls. "Police intervene only when they decide that the 'mass revolutionary action' is becoming physically dangerous for the victims," according to Pascal Fontaine, one of the authors of *The Black Book of Communism*.

(3) Operation Pedro Pan (Peter Pan) involved the transport of 14,048 children ages six to seventeen. The program was created by the Catholic Welfare Bureau (Catholic Charities) of Miami in December 1960 at the request of Cuban parents who wanted to send their children to the United States. The parents wanted their kids to escape radical Communist indoctrination, which Castro was starting to have taught in Cuban schools. When the United States severed diplomatic relations with Cuba on January 3, 1961, the Catholic Welfare Bureau was authorized by the State Department to notify parents in Cuba that visa requirements had been waived for their children. This enabled the children to travel by commercial flights to Miami.

When Castro declared the Cuban revolution to be Socialist in April 1961, just prior to the Bay of Pigs invasion, Operation Pedro Pan moved into high gear. Castro closed the island's public and private schools and forced children to attend new, regime-run schools that acted as centers of ideological indoctrination. No group was more vulnerable to the totalitarianism of Castro's regime than children. By the summer of 1961, a Cuban child between the ages of seven and thirteen was required to join the Union of Rebel Pioneers. Those twelve or older were required to help teach literacy skills to the poor. At thirteen, children were required to join the Association of Rebel Youths. Refusal to participate at any stage resulted in the child's being labeled a counterrevolutionary and isolated as an outcast.

About half the Pedro Pan children were sent to live with relatives in Miami, and the other half elsewhere in the United States. The program ended in October 1962, when the Cuban Missile Crisis saw the termination of all flights to the United States from Cuba. Eventually, about 90 percent of all the children were reunited with their parents through the later "freedom flights." It is believed Castro sanctioned Operation Pedro Pan—the children were issued government exit visas—because he saw it as a way to get rid of domestic opposition, present and future. Meanwhile, some critics have charged that Operation Pedro Pan was nothing more than a U.S. Central Intelligence Agency propaganda ploy aimed at prompting world outrage and possible action to overthrow Castro—a theory that most Cuban exiles living in the United States find offensive.

(4) The Bay of Pigs invading brigades were members of the anti-Castro Cuban National Revolutionary Council. The group had counted not only on U.S. military support during the invasion, which never materialized, but also on an uprising by the Cuban people to overthrow Castro—a costly miscalculation.

In the days after the failed invasion, U.S. press accounts widely reported that the Eisenhower administration had planned the Bay of Pigs attack and that the CIA had been in charge of operations. However, upon taking office in January 1961, President Kennedy decided against supporting a large-scale invasion of Cuba, including any crucial air support. Fearing an international scandal, he was said, instead, to have agreed to provide ships and other equipment to help the Cuban rebels make smaller-scale landings for the purpose of reinforcing anti-Castro rebels already on the island. Nonetheless, one week after the Bay of Pigs, President Kennedy assumed full responsibility for the U.S. role in the botched operation.

Prisoners captured at the Bay of Pigs were interrogated and tried on Cuban television. Negotiations for their release took twenty months. Castro had demanded 500 tractors in exchange for them, a proposition rejected by Kennedy. Finally, on December 23, 1962, all but two prisoners were released in exchange for $53 million in medicines and foods donated by American corporations. The corporations got tax breaks in the United States for agreeing to make the donations.

Surviving members of Brigade 2506 were honored at a ceremony at Orange Bowl Stadium in Miami attended by President and Mrs. Kennedy on December 29, 1962. When he was presented the treasured brigade flag by an invasion force commander who had hidden it away during his incarceration, President Kennedy was overwhelmed by the gesture and discarded his prepared text. "I want to express my great appreciation to the brigade for making the United States the custodian of this flag. I can assure you that this flag will be returned to this brigade in a free Havana." Following Kennedy's death, the brigade flag was sent to the John F. Kennedy Library in Boston for preservation. In 1975, brigade members formally requested return of the flag, now on permanent display at the Bay of Pigs Museum and Library in Miami.

(5) Many have wondered why so many Cubans seemed willing to give up their right to choose their leaders through free elections. In his book, *Fidel Castro: Cuban Revolutionary*, Warren Brown writes: "Castro sensed accurately that most Cubans valued housing, education, health care, and an end to government corruption far more than they valued elections. Accordingly, during the first months after his victory, he ordered rents cut in half for the poorest city dwellers and launched a massive building program in the countryside. New homes, hospitals, and schools sprang up across the island, connected by hundreds of miles of new rural roads." Castro also outlawed prostitution and gambling, which had flourished under Batista. To stop political corruption, Castro made stealing from the government punishable by death. Castro also declared war on illiteracy and dispatched hundreds of young Cubans—known as "alphabetizers"—across the countryside in a massive effort to teach the island's adults how to read.

Mostly, though, Castro knew how to keep hope alive in the midst of hardship and sacrifice. When Hurricane Flora, one of the worst of the century, devastated Cuba (about 1,750 people were killed in Cuba) in early October 1963, Castro was everywhere directing rescue operations, leading and inspiring. ". . . What Castro made his people remember was that they were being educated, fed, housed, protected, and cared for by the revolution as Cubans had never seen before in history," Tad Szulc wrote in his book, *Fidel: A Critical Portrait*. "Therefore, they were in the main loyal to the revolution, grateful to the Commander in Chief, and ready to ferret out counterrevolutionary 'worms,' patrol the cities and the farms at night, and be indoctrinated to the point of numbness in the mysterious phrases of Marxism-Leninism."

(6) The expelled Catholic priests—among them seventy-eight Spaniards, forty-six Cubans, five Canadians, and four Dutchmen, plus three others—represented nearly half of the Catholic clergy remaining in Cuba in 1961. About 300 other priests, mostly non-Cubans who had been jailed following the failed Bay of Pigs invasion, had left after being released. On September 19, 1961, Castro announced that religious processions

would be banned and that Catholic priests who "conspire against the fatherland" would lose their citizenship. The next day, Pope John XXIII accused Castro of persecuting the Roman Catholic Church in Cuba. By year's end, 3,400 priests and nuns would be forced into exile.

Tensions first surfaced between the Catholic Church and Castro shortly after he took power and announced the Agrarian Reform Law, a decree that limited private ownership of land to 1,000 acres. As Castro's Marxist leanings became more evident, many priests publicly criticized the direction of the revolution. As Castro cracked down on political opposition and press freedoms, the Church became a base of opposition to the regime. In the fall of 1960, Cuban bishops issued a series of anti-Castro pastoral letters. They stated that in any conflict between the United States and the Soviet Union over Cuba, the bishops would support America. Written and released when they were—after Castro nationalized U.S.-owned property in June 1960—the letters placed the Catholic Church in clear opposition to the revolution. The situation worsened during the Bay of Pigs, when it was discovered that four priests of Spanish origin participated in the invasion force.

Castro was excommunicated by Pope John XXIII on January 3, 1962. This was consistent with a 1949 decree by Pope Pius XII forbidding Catholics from supporting Communists.

Chapter Four Notes:

(1) After President Kennedy's election, his closest advisors established their own covert structure to eliminate Castro. Code name Operation Mongoose was launched in November 1961, and the initiative called for a six-phase effort by the U.S. government to undermine Castro from the inside. But the operation never came close to attaining its objectives, even though some 400 CIA agents in Washington and Miami were assigned to it.

Operation Mongoose is best known for its plots to assassinate Castro. The CIA first attempted to kill him by working with Mafia figures in 1960. Richard Helms, in 1960 the CIA's deputy director for covert operations, testified before a U.S. Senate committee in 1975 that he had assumed that the "intense" pressure exercised by the Kennedy administration to oust Castro had given the agency authority to kill him. Helms testified: "I believe it was the policy at that time to get rid of Castro and if killing him was one of the things that was to be done in this connection, that was within what was expected." Plots ranged from giving Castro a poisoned cigar to persuading the dictator to use a fountain pen doctored with a hidden needle capable of injecting him with poison. Operation Mongoose was dismantled after the Cuban Missile Crisis.

(2) Cubans have relied on U.S. government broadcasts for news about their country since shortly after Castro came to power. On March 16, 1960, Castro suspended publication of three Havana newspapers, effectively ending freedom of the press in Cuba. The government already controlled seven other Havana newspapers and most small Cuban newspapers. On March 26, 1960, the government took control of Havana's Channel 4, giving Castro control of five of the seven TV stations in the Havana region. Today, all Cuban media is state controlled.

The U.S. government began broadcasting to Cuba via short-wave radio on May 17, 1960, over a CIA-funded station built on Swan Island in the Gulf of Mexico. The number 1 radio station in Cuba for years, Radio Swan was used during the Bay of Pigs invasion to send coded messages to anti-Castro forces throughout Cuba. After the invasion, the station changed its name to Radio Americas and continued to broadcast until May 1968.

In 1981, President Ronald Reagan declared his administration's intention to establish a Radio Free Cuba that would operate like Radio Free Europe. After a series of funding battles and compromises with Congress, his wish became reality. Radio Marti—named for Cuban patriot and writer Jose Marti—signed on the air on May 20, 1985, with 14.5 hours of programming produced under the auspices of Voice of America.

Today, Radio Marti broadcasts seven days a week, twenty-four hours a day, on medium wave (AM) and short-wave radio. Broadcasts include news, music, and a variety of feature and news analysis programs. On March 27, 1990, TV Marti began broadcasting from Florida to Cuba; all radio and television operations were combined into the Office of Cuba

Broadcasting. TV Marti carries news, sports, entertainment, and features on life in the United States and other countries. Voice of America (VOA), which first went on the air on February 24, 1942, broadcasts more than 1,000 hours of programming on radio, satellite television, and via the Internet to 115 million people in forty-five languages.

Today, VOA, the Office of Cuba Broadcasting, and all U.S. government-funded nonmilitary international broadcasting services are overseen by the International Broadcasting Bureau (IBB) and a nine-member, bipartisan Broadcasting Board of Governors (BBG). The IBB and the BBG are independent federal government entities.

(3) To this day, Feliberto believes his Cuban students wanted nothing to do with Castro's dictatorship, despite appearances to the contrary. "They lived in the system but wanted nothing to do with it. They suffer the same insults as the adults. Most instructors try to brainwash the students on the attributes of the system but the students want nothing to do with it."

Chapter Five Notes:

(1) After the Cuban Missile Crisis, Castro dramatically reduced the number of exit visas to the United States. In 1962, about 78,611 Cubans were granted such visas. Between 1962 and September of 1965, the number declined to 15,000. "On the island, more Cubans questioned the course the revolution had taken," wrote Alex Anton and Roger E. Hernandez, authors of *Cubans in America.* "The imposition of a totalitarian state that deprived the people of fundamental human rights, along with the rapidly deteriorating economy, brewed discontent. As an escape valve to release the pressure," the authors contend, Castro made the September 28, 1965, announcement, signaling a new wave of Cuban emigration to the United States.

(2) The Immigration and Nationality Act of 1965 (also known as the Hart-Celler Act) abolished national-origin quotas that had been in place since 1882. Spawned by the civil rights movement, the 1965 amendment established a system based on reunification of families and needed skills and professions. In the case of Cuba, the Johnson administration and Castro's government agreed on November 6, 1965, that Cubans who had close

relatives in the United States should be given the first priority to leave.

"The future holds little hope for any government where the present holds no hope for the people. And so we Americans will welcome these Cuban people," Johnson said in signing the Hart-Celler Act. "For the tides of history run strong, and in another day they can return to their homeland to find it cleansed of terror and free from fear."

On December 1, 1965, the first flight under the U.S.-Cuban airlift agreement departed the airport about eighty-five miles east of Havana. Aboard the U.S.-supplied DC-3 were seventy-five Cuban refugees who landed at Miami. In its first year, the airlift—which expanded to twice-daily flights—brought more than 45,000 refugees to the United States.

The overwhelming number of Cubans desiring to flee prompted President Johnson on November 2, 1966, to sign into law the Cuban Adjustment Act, which exempted Cuban immigrants from general U.S. immigration laws. The result was that any Cuban who had reached U.S. territory since January 1, 1959, was eligible for permanent residency after two years. Approximately 123,000 Cubans immediately applied for permanent status.

The last freedom flight took place on April 6, 1973, when Eastern Airlines Flight 8894 landed at Miami at 11:55 a.m. carrying eighty-four Cuban passengers.

Figures vary on the total number of Cubans who arrived on the flights. In her book, *Havana USA*, Maria Cristina Garcia reports that 3,049 flights brought 297,318 Cubans to the United States between 1965 and 1973. Lorrin Philipson and Rafael Llerena, authors of *Freedom Flights*, cite the figure of 260,651. Alejandro Portes and Alex Stepick, in their book, *City on the Edge: The Transformation of Miami*, place the number at 340,000. At the time the flights ended in 1973, the Cuban Refugee Center of Miami estimated that 1.3 million Cubans were waiting to get seats on the flights.

(3) Jacqui's uncle and aunt, Miguel and Lolita Dominguez, lived in Brooklyn—a place that could hardly be more different from Cuba. The family had come from Cuba in the late 1940s and had subsequently helped more than a dozen family members settle in the United States. Under the November 6, 1965, "Memo of Understanding" between Cuba

and the United States, relatives of Cubans living in the United States were given first priority to rejoin their families. Included were parents whose children were younger than twenty-one; children under twenty-one whose parents were in the States; brothers and sisters under twenty-one, and husbands and wives. Persons not in these categories but who could be included were non-relatives or distant relatives who lived in the same household with the qualified emigrants and whose eligibility could be established on humanitarian grounds. This is the category into which Feliberto and his family fit.

Formal sponsorship requirements in 1965 were relatively simple: an application noting the names of emigrating family members and the circumstances surrounding the decision to emigrate. Having "sponsoring" relatives in the United States was a critical requirement because the U.S. government did not want arriving immigrants to seek welfare.

To assist in the sponsorship of the Pereiras, the Dominguezes (with the support of their congregation) turned to Church World Service's immigration and refugees program. The ecumenical agency was formed in the aftermath of World War II when U.S. churches came together to respond to the needs of war refugees from Europe and Asia. A cooperative ministry of thirty-five Protestant, Orthodox, and Anglican denominations, Church World Service has helped resettle more than 450,000 refugees since its founding—a projected 8,000 in 2007. It operates in eighty countries.

(4) In 1961, Fidel Castro ended Christmas as a national holiday. He reinstated the holiday in 1998, following Pope John Paul's visit to the island. Today, all Cubans get December 25 off from their forty-eight-hour workweek.

(5) Since 1959, Castro has imprisoned hundreds of thousands of men and women from all walks of life. His agents intrude on privacy, intimidate Cubans into absolute acceptance of state policy, and smother dissent of any kind. During the repressions of the 1960s, between 7,000 and 10,000 Cubans were killed and 30,000 imprisoned for political reasons, according to *The Black Book of Communism*. The Seguridad del Estado (G-2 or State Security), the brutal agency charged with enforcing Castro's

totalitarian regime, is to blame for much of the bloodshed.

Feliberto recounted Castro's reign of terror during a 1973 speech to a Rio Grande Valley church: "The jails were so small for so many thousands of people. Death was the order of the day, and the death of a person insignificant. It was as common as drinking a glass of water. Along with this came a cruel and horrible system of investigations. Everyone was watched every hour of the day everywhere they would go. Spies were everywhere and even the spies were spied on. You could not react to the injustice. . . . Regardless of your feelings in any matter, you had to live and talk as if you agreed with everything. No longer existed the freedom of enterprise because the state is the owner of all. Every human being now became a true slave."

For years, human rights organizations have documented cases of Cubans imprisoned for political views in opposition to Castro. Political prisoners are intimidated and tortured during interrogation, denied legal counsel, detained secretly, and never brought to trial. Inmates of Cuba's overcrowded prisons are often forced to eat, sleep, and defecate in the same confined space. They receive inadequate or inedible food, resulting in severe malnutrition and other illnesses. They are denied medical assistance and must endure the presence of rats, lice, bedbugs, and other insects. Many are kept in solitary confinement for extended periods in cells that are totally dark, without ventilation or insulation. Some are subjected to electroshock. Some are confined in cells known as *gavetas* (drawers) where they are packed so closely they have to remain standing.

In the mid- to late 1960s, the *granjas* held tens of thousands of clergymen, homosexuals, and others labeled by the government as social parasites. In July 1968, after international condemnation of the prison camps, Castro announced that he was abolishing them; he reportedly shredded all the paperwork associated with the sites. The camps underwent some cosmetic changes. Their names were changed to "Military Units," and they largely held young men dissatisfied with Castro's Communist revolution. Because the men in the camps received a small salary for long and harsh working hours, Castro did not acknowledge that they were prison camps—even though confinement there was forced. Feliberto described his experience at the camps—regardless of what Castro called them—as a "slice of hell."

In March 2003, the Castro government carried out one of its most brutal crackdowns when it arrested on various charges seventy-five human rights activists, independent journalists, and opposition figures. Reporter Tracey Eaton, formerly of *The Dallas Morning News*, in a June 24, 2003, dispatch from Havana, wrote of Cuba's prisons: "Their names sound like something out of the Magic Kingdom: Happy Camp and Friendship, Green Sea and Dark Woods, Taco Taco and Pork Fat Beach. But they're anything but enchanted."

(6) The events of June 14, 1966, remain a mystery. Feliberto had not met the two pastors before that day, knowing them only by reputation. Following his release, Feliberto never had a chance to speak to them to determine what really happened that day. He does not know how the two men knew where he was, how they persuaded the commander to release him, or why they intervened on his behalf.

One of the pastors, the man who flashed the identification badge, died in a car accident shortly after the event. Feliberto later found out that the man had served side-by-side with Castro in the late 1950s. Feliberto speculates that Castro had arranged for the man to have a special identification badge. The other pastor moved from Camaguey Province, and Feliberto has not been able to locate him. "I feel like those two men were angels," he said.

Feliberto would later confirm one aspect of the day's events: The men loaded onto the trucks at the city hall were, in fact, taken to the concentration camp outside Nuevitas. He does not know why he was the only one spared. He has come to believe what his mother does about the episode: That what happened that day was a miracle, a marvel like that recorded in Acts Chapter 12, where Peter's escape from prison is recorded.

Feliberto still celebrates June 14 as a day of thanksgiving in recognition of the two ministers. On June 14, 1985, upon moving into a new home in the Rio Grande Valley, he planted two palm trees in his backyard in honor of the "two angels."

Chapter Six Notes:

(1) Torture was the rule of law in Castro's prison camps, especially for evangelical Christians. Feliberto said: "A friend of mine was stood naked against the wall with his hands in the air for ninety-six hours while cold water was poured over his head. He was told to repeat that there was no God, but all he would say was, 'I do believe in God.' This was done until he collapsed from a lack of nourishment. Others were tied naked in the hot sun and made to stay all day and night when temperatures cooled off. Mosquitoes attacked them at night and they were unable to help themselves. Others were forced to stand in dung pits for hours with only their heads showing.

"I also know of a man who was committed to a refrigerated room where he was terribly over exposed. Then, he was taken to an overheated room. After that, they took him to a third room and strapped him to a chair with a 500-watt bulb shining directly in front of his face. Even if he would shut his eyes, the light was so intense that he suffered great effects. He was not able to move his head to the side, and consequently he was driven temporarily insane."

(2) During the eighteen months when he was confined to forced-labor camps, Feliberto was allowed to return home ten times for weekend visits. He would arrive home Saturday morning and return to the camp Sunday night. He was given no advance notice of when he would get a weekend pass. "If or when I could go depended on the moods of the camp lieutenant," he said. "One time, we got a lieutenant to let us out (for a weekend) in exchange for buying him a bottle of rum." Many men in the labor camps were never given furloughs.

(3) Risking severe punishment, the men in Feliberto's prison camp would sometimes secretly listen to Christian broadcasts from Florida and Latin America over small transistor radios they had smuggled in. "The radio programs would be spiritual food for us," Feliberto said. "Even non-Christians received comfort from these programs." He added that the programs he heard in prison helped inspire his decision to start a radio ministry in the United States.

(4) For Feliberto, strength to endure the forced labor camps came

from daily Bible readings. "Only God could give me the peace to face those months of separation from my family," he said. "The reason that I love God and will give my life for Him is because I live because of His miraculous intervention." He relied on the Bible's many promises. Among the most meaningful to him:

Psalm 46:1: *God is our refuge and strength, an ever-present help in trouble.*

Psalm 91:1–3: *He who dwells in the shelter of the Most High will rest in the shadow of the Almighty. I will say of the Lord, "He is my refuge and my fortress; My God, in whom I trust." Surely He shall deliver you from the fowler's snare and from the deadly pestilence.*

Psalm 124:6–8: *Praise be to the Lord, who has not let us be torn by their teeth. We have escaped like a bird out of the fowler's snare; the snare has been broken, and we have escaped. Our help is in the name of the Lord, the Maker of heaven and earth.*

Romans 8:28: *And we know that in all things God works for the good of those who love him, who have been called, according to his purpose.*

Matthew 28:20b: *. . . and surely I am with you always, to the very end of the age.*

Chapter Seven Notes:

(1) Beginning in elementary school a "cumulative academic record" is kept on every Cuban child. The file measures "revolutionary integration." Not only is the student assessed in revolutionary indoctrination, but his family is, as well. Although Feliberto never had to actually complete the paperwork as a teacher, he had firsthand knowledge of the system—part of Castro's repressive and secretive attempts to control the population.

The "academic" record documents whether or not the child and his or her family participated in mass demonstrations or belong to a church or religious group. The dossier accompanies the child for life and is continually updated. It is a powerful weapon of intimidation that hangs over the student and his or her family. Any blot on the cumulative record means the student is guilty of political misconduct and could be refused entrance to college or university and denied many career possibilities. Privileged careers, those with "social impact," are reserved for the "integrated."

A major goal of the Cuban school system is to indoctrinate children— *pioneros*, the national pioneers of Cuba's socialist future—for membership in the Communist party.

Children enter first grade at age six and wear uniforms of Cuba's national colors, red and white. At eleven, they graduate from the sixth grade and enter secondary school, where the uniforms are white and gold. All students over twelve, at some juncture, are required to do "voluntary" farm work at "schools in the countryside." At fifteen, students are tested, and the results determine their future classification. At sixteen, students enter Cuba's *beca* system, the pre-university high school that preps students either for higher education or a working trade. Competition is keen for university slots, and only the top 5 percent of Cuban students are eligible to compete for them.

Armando Valladares, U.S. ambassador to the U.N. Human Rights Commission from 1986 to 1990, said in an essay published in 2000: "From his elementary school days on, (a student) will hear that God does not exist, and that religion is 'the opium of the masses.' If any student speaks about God, his parents will be called to school, warned that they are 'confusing' the child and threatened. The Code for Children, Youth and Family provides for a three-year prison sentence for any parent who teaches a child ideas contrary to Communism. The code is very clear: No Cuban parent has the right to 'deform' the ideology of his children, and the state is the true 'father.' Article 8 of the same code reads, 'Society and state work for the efficient protection of youth against all influences contrary to their Communist formation.' "

And the "protection" doesn't stop after adulthood is reached. To control the overall population, the Castro government created an agency within the Interior Ministry to recruit thousands of *chivatos* (informers), according to Pascal Fontaine's report in *The Black Book of Communism*. "The agency keeps a file on every Cuban citizen, monitors public opinion, and keeps an eye on the church and its various congregations through infiltration."

(2) New Jersey and South Florida are the two chief centers for Cuban exiles in the United States. Of the 1.2 million Cubans in America, according to the 2000 Census, about 833,120 live in Florida and about 77,300 in New Jersey. By comparison, about 72,000 live in California and about 63,000 in New York.

The U.S. Cuban population has grown rapidly. In 1960, for example, the Hispanic population of Dade County, Florida, was only 5 percent. As successive waves of Cuban immigrants arrived, they became the dominant group among Hispanics. Little Havana, as the Cubans' central area of Miami is called, became their cultural center. By the year 2000, Hispanics accounted for 57 percent of Dade's population of 2.3 million. Of the Hispanics, about 60 percent are Cuban-Americans.

As for delivering the message to the camp lieutenant's sister, Feliberto said he did so within a few weeks of arriving in the United States. He doesn't know if the lieutenant made it out of Cuba.

(3) Today, the airport at Varadero is one of Cuba's busiest. Once the departing point for tens of thousands of Cubans seeking to flee, Varadero now is the gateway for millions of tourists flocking to some of the world's most spectacular beaches and world-class resorts. Most who visit Varadero, the tourist capital of Cuba, are from Europe or Canada. Tourism has replaced sugar exports as the growth engine of the Cuban economy. U.S. citizens are banned from traveling to Cuba except under special circumstances. The U.S. government believes tourism supports Castro's regime.

The Varadero peninsula features about twelve miles of white sandy beaches—a slice of heaven for sun worshippers. While tourists first started coming to Varadero in 1872, international development didn't begin until the 1930s, when U.S. chemical millionaire Irene Dupont Nemours built a large estate on the peninsula. Al Capone also used to holiday in Varadero. His stone beachfront house is a popular tourist destination today.

(4) Since 1959, nearly 2 million Cubans have gone into exile. The refugees hail from all areas of the island and represent all races and socioeconomic groups. It has been a painful exodus that has, tragically, divided many Cuban families.

Four major waves of emigration have occurred since 1959. The first, from 1959 to 1962, consisted of professionals and others who could not tolerate Castro's Communist-leaning "reforms." The nationalization of businesses and schools and the confiscation of private property prompted about 125,000 people to leave, primarily for the United States. Operation Peter Pan was part of this first wave.

The second wave, from 1965 to 1973, was prompted by Castro's offer to let Cubans join relatives in the United States. The wave started first with a boatlift from Camarioca and continued with freedom flights from Varadero to Miami. All of the émigrés, Feliberto among them, were granted political asylum.

The third wave, from 1979 to 1984, started as a trickle but eventually turned into a torrent. The rush came after Castro announced that everyone who wanted to emigrate could do so without a visa. The port of Mariel, designated to receive boats from the United States, launched 125,000 immigrants. The Mariel boatlift of 1980 was a crisis that overwhelmed U.S. immigration officials. It led to a migration agreement between the United States and Cuba in 1984.

The fourth wave, from 1990 to 1994, was prompted by the U.S. government's granting of only about 2,500 exit visas per year, rather than the 20,000 per year that the 1984 accord established. The pent-up demand for freedom led about 29,000 émigrés to leave the island on rafts or hijacked boats. A new migration accord was reached in 1994. Under it, the United States pledged to accept a minimum of 20,000 émigrés per year and to grant visas to 19,000 Cubans on a waiting list.

Today, the United States offers only two legal means of immigration for Cubans. Those who have been persecuted or who fear persecution on the basis of race, religion, nationality, membership in a particular social group, or political opinion may apply for an exit visa through the U.S. Interests section of the Embassy of Switzerland in Havana. About 3,000 to 4,000 refugees are admitted to the United States through this program per year.

In addition, any adult Cuban may emigrate to the United States through the Special Cuban Migration Program, or "Cuban Lottery," known as El

Bombo. The program is intended to bring the total number of Cuban immigrants up to the 20,000 total that the United States agreed to accept in 1994. Applications are held and drawn from a two-year period. In the 1998 lottery, 541,500 Cubans—or 5 percent of the Cuban population— applied for El Bombo. In July 1998, Feliberto's nephew Aziel, son of his brother Eldo, applied for El Bombo. On June 20, 2003, he was notified that he had won the lottery. He, his wife, and two daughters now live in Miami.

Meanwhile, illegal immigration from Cuba remains a great concern. The 1999 case of six-year-old Elian Gonzalez attracted international attention. The boy, whose mother and stepfather drowned when their U.S.-bound boat capsized off the coast of Florida, was taken from relatives in Florida by U.S. agents in a raid and returned to his biological father in Cuba. That case, combined with an incident in June 1999, known as the case of the "Surfside Six"—in which the U.S. Coast Guard was videotaped using fire hoses and pepper spray to stop six Cuban rafters from reaching shore—has focused attention on the "wet-foot/dry-foot" policy of the U.S. government.

Under this policy, Cubans intercepted at sea are returned to Cuba; those who actually reach U.S. soil can apply for permanent residency after one year. The distinction remains a source of controversy.

(5) Seven commercial airlines provided chartered planes for the freedom flights, officially known as "family reunification flights." The planes carried refugees from Varadero, the Cuban port of departure, to Miami 190 miles away. Two flights departed and arrived daily, except on weekends and holidays. One of the most commonly used airplanes was the DC-7, which had seats for eighty-two passengers, although many parents carried small children on their laps. The flights, which ended in 1973, cost the U.S. government more than $50 million.

Chapter Eight Notes:

(1) Little is known about "Freedom Gate" at Miami International Airport. It was a special terminal operated by the U.S. Immigration Service, and it housed representatives of agencies, such as Church World

Service, that assisted Cuban refugees. According to U.S. Census figures, 41 percent of Cubans who emigrated to the United States after the Castro revolution came during the years of the freedom flights. Feliberto was one of 49,415 Cuban refugees processed at Freedom Gate in 1969.

(2) The exodus from Cuba prompted the U.S. government, for the first time, to establish an emergency refugee program that made America a country of first asylum for a mass population of refugees. During the first two years of Castro's rule, 50,000 Cubans fled to the United States. President Eisenhower responded by establishing the Cuban Refugee Emergency Center in Miami in 1959.

Revolutions in Latin America at that time were often temporary phenomena, and Castro's takeover of Cuba was considered no different. As a result, Cuban refugees were permitted to be "free-livers" in the United States, meaning they faced no restrictions as to movement, residence, or employment. As far as U.S. law was concerned, they were temporary guests who would be returning to their homeland once Castro faded from the scene. Indeed, at first, Cubans did not consider themselves refugees but, rather, temporary exiles from their homeland.

By the end of 1960, though, the Cuban government was confiscating real estate and personal property of its residents. This meant the refugees arriving in Miami were usually destitute, placing a huge financial burden on local social service agencies. As more poor Cubans poured into Miami, President Kennedy directed that a formal Cuban Refugee Program be established. Its goal was to help Cubans resettle in other parts of the United States until Castro's government failed and the exiles could return to Cuba. On June 28, 1962, Congress passed the Migration and Relief Assistance Act, which allocated funds for the program. The Cuban Refugee Program, administered at the Cuban Refugee Center at the Freedom Tower near downtown Miami, was unique at the time in that it was developed using the services of existing agencies to as great an extent as possible, although overall responsibility for the program rested with the U.S. Department of Health, Education, and Welfare.

Church World Service was one of four private service agencies that helped resettle Cuban refugees, among them Feliberto and his family. The others were the Catholic Relief Services, the United Hebrew Immigrant and Aid Society, and the nonsectarian International Rescue Committee.

By the early 1960s, 1,500 Cuban refugees were pouring into Florida every week. To help ease the burden on Miami, the Kennedy administration urged Americans elsewhere to offer all possible assistance to the refugees. "The quest for human dignity unites East Germans in Berlin, Chinese in Hong Kong, and Cubans in Miami," President Kennedy said. "We must identify ourselves with this cause." Still, many refugees chose to stay in Miami. They were close to home, the climate was familiar, Spanish was widely spoken, and there were politically active groups there, formed to oppose Castro.

To encourage Americans to help resettle the refugees, the government and social service agencies embarked on a marketing campaign. One brochure on the Cuban Refugee Program appealed to American generosity and patriotism with the headline, "Sponsor Cuban Refugees. Fulfill their faith in Freedom." Helping the refugees, the brochure said, was "what you as a free American can do to help those who have fled the tyranny of Communist Cuba."

It continued: "When you sponsor refugees, you may be sure that they have been passed by the U.S. Immigration Service and checked by the U.S. Public Health Service. The Cubans who fled to freedom are grateful guests. Many have held responsible positions. No matter what their backgrounds, they have risked the deprivations of drastically altered lives. They are appreciative of any opportunities here to work in the freedom for which they have sacrificed heavily. Cubans are the first refugees from political oppression to come to the United States as the country of first asylum. With the Communist menace now close to our shores you and your community face a new challenge to show the Cubans who flee from it the heart in our way of life."

As a result of the resettlement program, there are sizeable Cuban communities throughout the United States—in New York City and Northern New Jersey, Chicago, New Orleans, and Los Angeles.

In 1966, President Lyndon B. Johnson signed the Cuban Adjustment Act, which exempted Cubans from general U.S. immigration laws. It permitted Cubans to apply for permanent residency after one year. The act enabled Cuban professionals to take state licensing tests in various occupations and elderly Cubans to qualify for benefits normally available only to permanent residents or American citizens.

(3) For Miami exiles, awaiting freedom flight reunions with loved ones was nerve-wracking. Many anxiously listened to daily broadcasts on Spanish language radio stations, during which the names of the day's expected arrivals were read from an official list. When possible, the Cuban Refugee Program alerted relatives in America when people were cleared to leave Cuba. Still, sometimes, relatives showed up in Miami with no warning.

Under the memorandum of understanding between Cuba and the United States, the two countries exchanged lists of prospective freedom flight passengers. The American lists contained the names of Cubans claimed by relatives in the United States whom the U.S. government considered eligible for entry.

The Cuban lists contained the names of Cubans that Havana considered eligible for exit permits. Names that appeared on both lists formed the basis for what were called joint consolidated lists—lists of persons both governments had approved for passage on the freedom flights.

(4) In the early years of the Cuban Refugee Program, refugees were taken to a U.S. immigration center at Opa-Locka, a former Navy airfield, about eleven miles from the Miami airport, for background checks and medical and job aptitude tests. During the years of the freedom flights, Cuban families were taken to apartments or barracks, nicknamed *Casas de la Libertad*, "Houses of Liberty," where they stayed until they could be resettled with relatives. Feliberto's family was taken to "Freedom House," an apartment complex near the airport

(5) Miami and Dade County were transformed by the Cuban revolution from a sleepy, southern tourist destination into one of the most vibrant international cities in the Western Hemisphere. Today, Miami-Dade has a population of nearly 2.4 million, about 55 percent of which is Hispanic. Half of the nation's Cubans live in Miami-Dade, according to the Census Bureau.

Little Havana, a ten-block area of Miami, is the cultural and political heart of the Cuban exile community. Eighth Street, *Calle Ocho*, is its main artery. Each year, on the last Friday of March, more than a million people descend on Little Havana for the Calle Ocho Festival, the country's largest Hispanic street party.

Another Miami icon for Cubans is Freedom Tower. Built in 1925 as the headquarters of the now defunct *Miami News & Metropolis* newspaper, and modeled after the Giralda bell tower on the cathedral of Seville, Spain, Freedom Tower earned its name after serving as the processing center for thousands of Cubans between 1962 and 1975. When the freedom flights ended, the building was closed. It fell into disrepair and passed through several owners until it was donated to Miami-Dade College, which has plans to use it as a monument to the Cuban community.

(6) The Christian Church (Disciples of Christ) is a Protestant denomination with about 800,000 members in the United States and Canada. The Disciples of Christ declare only one essential tenet of the faith: belief in Jesus Christ as Lord and Savior. Those who wish to join are not required to affirm any statements of belief other than this: That Jesus is the son of God and that He offers saving grace to all, as all are God's children.

Almost all Disciple churches share several common practices:

- Open Communion. No one who attends a worship service is ever refused Communion.

- Baptism by immersion. However, Disciples honor other baptism traditions in converts.

- The unity of the church. Disciples believe that all Christians are called to be the "Body of Christ." They don't claim that any denomination (including their own) is the "one true Church." Disciples seek opportunities for common witness and service with other denominations. Early Disciples leader Barton Stone declared, "Unity is our polar star."

- Common ministry: Disciples ministers are ordained by their respective regional church, based on criteria established by the

general church. Ministerial candidates must be sponsored by at
least one local congregation, and normally the ordination service
is hosted by that congregation. An ordained Disciples minister
normally holds a Master of Divinity degree from a theological
seminary. Laypersons often lead Disciple worship services, and lay
elders and deacons preside at Communion.

The roots of the Disciples of Christ lie in the Restoration Movement
of the early 1800s, with a focus on Christian unity and a lack of strict
denominationalism. This focus came from a study of the New Testament
by the movement's founders, Thomas Campbell and Alexander Campbell
of Pennsylvania and Barton W. Stone of Kentucky. Both families were
originally Presbyterians.

Prominent members of the church include James Garfield; Lyndon
Baines Johnson; Ronald Reagan (baptized into the Disciples as a youth,
but a member of Bel Air Presbyterian Church in his later years); J. William Fulbright, a U.S. senator from Arkansas; and Oscar-winning actress
Frances McDormand.

The insignia of the church is a red chalice with a white St. Andrew's
cross in the upper left corner. Texas Christian University in Fort Worth,
Texas, is loosely affiliated with, but not governed by, the Disciples of
Christ.

(7) Brooklyn is New York's most populous borough, with 2.5 million
residents. If it were an independent city, Brooklyn would rank as the third
most populous in the country, behind Los Angeles and Chicago. Iglesia
Cristiana Sinai, founded in 1951, is in the Bushwick neighborhood. The
church's vision, as expressed on its Web site: "To make Sinai a church
of high effectiveness in the proclamation of the gospel of Jesus Christ
through the implementation of a school of Leaders; a strategy for the
development of evangelistic cells and the implementation of a structured
leadership that will allow the development and growth of new leaders in
our congregation; to have a church involved in a program of educational
Christian foundation in the sacred scriptures."

(8) Nightmares are among the common symptoms of post-traumatic

stress disorder. Severe PTSD is often seen among victims of torture, including not just those who were tortured, but also those who have witnessed torture, discovered tortured bodies, were forced to engage in torture, had friends or loved ones who were tortured, or lived in an environment where torture was a real danger. By this broad definition, an estimated 500,000 torture victims from other countries now live in the United States.

Treatment options for torture survivors vary, depending on the survivors' experience, said Sharmin DeMoss, assistant director of the Center for Survivors of Torture in Dallas, the only center in the five-state region of Texas, New Mexico, Oklahoma, Arkansas, and Louisiana dedicated to the rehabilitation of torture survivors. "Counselors help clients find safe, appropriate ways to express their anger," she said. "Survivors don't get a chance to talk back at the time of their torture. Those who did were killed." Those who experienced severe torture require long-term care, she said. "I had a client of severe torture who said he would end his life if his family ever found out what had been done to him," Ms. DeMoss said. He told her that the resulting shame would be too great to bear. "I can't scream," the client told her. "How can you scream loud enough and long enough for how bad it was?" In cases like this one, she said, "You just help clients let off the steam from the pressure cooker, hoping that over time healing occurs."

In addition to his nightmares, Feliberto suffered from acute digestive illness brought on by the poisoned water he was forced to drink at the prison camps. It wasn't until 1972—nearly three years after he left the camps—that his digestive tract was cleared, through treatment by a Cuban doctor in Brownsville.

(9) Before accepting the factory job at the stove manufacturing plant, Feliberto interviewed for several different positions. At JFK Airport, he interviewed for a baggage handler's position, but his lack of English skills disqualified him.

Another opportunity was promising and paid good money, but Feliberto had no interest in the job: embalming bodies at a funeral home. "You will earn $500 per corpse," the funeral home director told Feliberto. "No, thank you," Feliberto replied. "I prefer to die of hunger first. I saw too much crying and death in Cuba. I don't want to deal with dead bodies."

Feliberto did take another part-time job, in addition to his church and factory jobs. For a few months, he sold audio tapes door-to-door in the heavily Spanish-speaking neighborhood of Corona, Queens. "They were tapes that taught Spanish speakers how to speak English. Here I was the one person who knew no English selling English tapes. I was a pretty good salesman. And the tapes were very helpful to me."

(10) With a population of 2.2 million, second only to that of Brooklyn, Queens is home to a diverse immigrant population. In the 2000 Census, immigrants made up 46 percent of the borough's residents. The Corona neighborhood is home to about 84,000 people, three-quarters of whom are Hispanic.

(11) Feliberto's name was first floated as a possible minister for the Second Christian Church of San Benito (Segunda Iglesia Cristiana) by Miguel Angel Morales, the pastor of Sinai Christian Church, the church attended by Lolita and Miguel Dominguez. The San Benito opportunity came to his attention through the founder of Sinai Christian Church, Eliseo Rodriguez, who in 1969 was pastor of a large Hispanic congregation in Brownsville. Eliseo Rodriguez, Lolita's brother, had recently begun trying to revive the San Benito church, which closed in 1966. Aware of the need in San Benito and a strong candidate to fill it, Domingo Rodriguez (no relation to Eliseo), at the time head of the Christian Church (Disciples of Christ) Hispanic convention in Indianapolis, flew to New York to meet Feliberto. In a memoir he wrote at the end of his career, Domingo Rodriguez said of Feliberto: "I was greatly impressed by his youth, by the manner of his expression, and his desire to work at whatever had to be done in the ministry. I persuaded him to move from New York to San Benito to start his new mission. He accepted."

Chapter Nine Notes:

(1) The Rio Grande Valley, in the southernmost tip of Texas, got its name from early settlers from Mexico, who considered the term "valley" more appealing to tourists and potential investors from the North than the

term "delta." Many current residents, 80 percent of whom are Hispanic, simply refer to the place as "*El Valle.*"

The four counties that make up the region—Starr, Hildalgo, Willacy, and Cameron—are among the poorest in the United States. Despite the poverty, the Valley is a popular tourist destination during the winters, mostly for retirees from the Midwest and Canada. The average annual temperature is about 74 degrees and average annual rainfall is about 26 inches. South Padre Island in Cameron County is a top spring break destination for college students. The island, home to dozens of species of exotic birds, also attracts birders from around the world.

San Benito, a city of 25,000 that marked its centennial on April 3, 2007, is best known as the home of musician Freddy Fender, who died in October 2006.

(2) Eliseo Rodriguez, a Cuban before emigrating to the United States, was pastor of Bella Vista Christian Church in Brownsville, one of the nation's largest Hispanic churches of the Christian Church. The San Benito congregation that he worked diligently to revive was founded in 1935, the third Hispanic congregation of the Christian Church in Texas (after churches in San Antonio and Robstown). Eliseo, who founded Sinai Christian Church in Brooklyn in 1951, continued his theological studies in Oregon before accepting the pulpit in Brownsville.

Hispanics are the fastest-growing segment of the Christian Church (Disciples of Christ)—as they are in several denominations. Major challenges confront Hispanic ministry, according to a 2003 report by the Duke University Divinity School and the Center for the Study of Latino Religion at the University of Notre Dame. The most pressing needs include:

- Better opportunities for formal theological education

- Training for laity to assume leadership responsibilities

- Increased cultivation of second-and third-generation Latino youth

- Initiatives that would help church leaders to advocate for the social needs of their communities

- Programs to provide lay leaders and clergy with practical administrative skills

- A permanent national dialogue on Hispanic pastoral leadership

(3) The Rio Grande Valley is one of the fastest-growing regions in the United States. Between 1990 and 2000, the four counties of the region saw their population increase nearly 40 percent. Unemployment hovers around 12 percent, well above the Texas rate of 6.2 percent. Per capita income in the Rio Grande Valley is $9,337, less than half the state average of $19,617. With high unemployment and low income, it is not surprising the poverty rate is 35.7 percent, more than double the state rate of 15.4 percent.

(4) Feliberto's energy and enthusiasm were jaw-dropping to those who worked alongside him at the San Benito church. Raquel Garcia was San Benito's city secretary when she joined the congregation in 1974. "The little church was already full on Sunday, even though we had no heat in the winter or air conditioning in the summer. His dedication to calling on people built the attendance. They would come and stay and tell their friends. There was no advertising at all. The Holy Spirit was jumping to us."

Rush Barnett, the retired minister of the First Christian Church of San Benito, said Feliberto's "work with Christ has opened all the doors he has ever needed. A man who takes Christ seriously realizes that the gifts he is given are not his. He can't develop them on his own because they aren't his. Feliberto's commitment to Christ has been the center of his life from the beginning. If a person is in trouble, he is going to put on his spurs and ride to the rescue no matter what time the day or night. He changed the entire climate between the brotherhood in the Valley, between Hispanics and Anglos. Feliberto is one of the greatest pastors I have every known. If he asked me to jump off a cliff with him, I would follow him."

(5) First begun in 1969 as a program aimed at encouraging listeners to attend the Christian Churches (Disciples of Christ) in the area, *The Christian Hour* was funded by an anonymous donor. After two years, the program had not achieved the desired results, and a church committee

decided to end it. But seeing the program as an opportunity for spreading the Good News, Feliberto volunteered to take over its production. The donor agreed.

Feliberto's first broadcast aired on Sunday, September 5, 1971, at 9 p.m. on KGBT (1530 AM), a 50,000-watt station in Harlingen that can be heard throughout the Rio Grande Valley and Northern Mexico. In 1976, the program was picked up by HCJB World Radio (now HCJB Global), an evangelical short-wave radio station based in Quito, Ecuador, that reached millions of listeners in Latin America and the Caribbean; and by Trans World Radio, the most far-reaching radio network in the world, transmitting from Bonaire, an island in the Netherlands Antilles near Venezuela.

Two men were instrumental in helping Feliberto with the radio ministry: Clinton Looney and Banner Shay. Clinton, a minister of the Independent Christian Church with an active missionary program in Mexico, placed the program on Mexican radio stations and oversaw day-to-day operations of *La Hora*, including fund-raising. Banner, a retired printer, donated the use of an old offset printer in Harlingen to produce Bible correspondence courses for listeners.

The program emphasized two main points. The first was a message aimed at people who did not know Christ. One set of booklets taught listeners how to receive Christ as their personal Lord and Savior. The second message was devoted to encouraging listeners to follow Jesus, to be a true witness in all circumstances. A second set of booklets dealt with the topic of the active Christian's life and challenges. All of the courses were designed to impart a broad knowledge of the Bible and emphasized the need of each listener to be a personal evangelist.

The program was a labor of love for Feliberto. He received no pay to prepare the radio sermons, which took five to six hours each to prepare. After a full day of church duties, he would be writing his radio sermons out in the wee hours, then, stopwatch in hand, time them until they were exactly eight minutes long. Each broadcast was fifteen minutes, but that included seven minutes of introductions, announcements, and hymns.

The program brought thousands of letters from grateful listeners. One seventeen-year-old girl, Erica from Chile, said the program saved her life. Filled with bitterness and grief over the death of her only brother, she wrote, she was "determined to commit suicide. I started from a room to the kitchen, where I planned to take my life. I do not know why, but as I passed by the radio, I turned it on and your program was on the air. At the end of your preaching, I wanted to have this Christ that you preached in my heart. I am writing because I wanted to tell you that I did not kill myself."

Following the death of key program contributors, Feliberto and Clinton made the decision in 1995 to record no new programs and offer only repeats of previous messages. As the costs of airing the program skyrocketed—time slots that once cost $100 a month were $5,000 by 2000—they decided to end *The Christian Hour* on August 31, 2004, after thirty-three years.

(6) The year 1979 was bittersweet for Feliberto. For nearly ten years, he had prayed that he would be allowed to return to Cuba to visit his aging parents—and then return to Texas. In May, the opportunity arose for him and Joel, fifteen at the time, to make the trip on a seven-day visa. "When we left Cuba in 1969, we were told we would never have permission to return. But with God, everything is possible." Travel to and from Cuba each took a full day. "In the five days we were visiting, we hardly slept. My relatives and friends came day and night to visit Joel and me. The trip was full of stress. We were watched by the government all the time we were there, and we could not talk openly. My very close niece whispered to me about how for the past years she had wanted to write me letters, but did not dare to because the Castro government had brainwashed the Cuban people to believe that anyone in Cuba who had family in the U.S. were from the CIA."

But the trip to Cuba had its amusing moments, Feliberto said. "I told Joel that it was customary for boys his age to kiss the cheeks of relatives upon greeting them for the first time. He embraced everybody who came to the house—no matter who it was. He was not distinguishing between who was family or a friend of mine. People were telling me, 'Your son is very friendly.' " Since the first trip to Cuba, Feliberto has made seven additional trips—in 1989, 1990, 1994, 1998, 1999, 2003, and 2008.

Chapter Ten Notes:

(1) The recent strife in Central America can be traced to the 1960s when several countries in the region attempted to industrialize their economies. However, the region's long-standing class struggles made industrialization difficult, triggering revolutionary and counterrevolutionary insurgency and counterinsurgency movements. The ensuing warfare not only killed thousands and displaced hundreds of thousands, it also institutionalized a migration pattern that previously had been very minor: emigration to the north.

Civil strife and widespread human rights abuses forced nearly two million residents of Nicaragua, El Salvador, and Guatemala to leave their homes. The poor and displaced were among the first to leave for the United States, followed by a huge influx of the middle-class. A conservative estimate, derived from the 1990 U.S. Census, is that more than one million Central Americans fled their homelands and sought safe haven in the United States during the tumultuous decade of the 1980s.

The United States sided with reactionary dictators in El Salvador and Guatemala, investing billions of dollars to fight "Communists." This put Washington in a difficult position politically when hundreds of thousands of Salvadorans and Guatemalans began fleeing to seek asylum in the United States. To accept their tales of torture, rape, forced recruitment, and other crimes would have been to acknowledge the moral failings of the U.S. government's policies.

These policies, opposed by many liberal Americans, gave rise to what became known as the American Sanctuary Movement. It originated in border churches in Arizona but quickly spread to other parts of the country. More than 500 congregations began sheltering Central American refugees from U.S. immigration authorities. Various faiths were involved, including Jews, Muslims, Catholics, Presbyterians, Methodists, Baptists, Quakers, and Mennonites.

The U.S. Justice Department prosecuted dozens of activists in the movement. The defendants claimed their actions were justifiable to save the lives of people who would have been killed if the U.S. government had sent them home.

Feliberto never participated in the early Sanctuary Movement because he considered its activities to be illegal. All refugee assistance he provided was authorized by U.S. immigration authorities.

By the mid-1980s, nearly all sides in the various conflicts in Central America had grown weary of the violence and were beginning to seek political solutions.

In May 2007, an interfaith organization, Clergy and Laity United for Economic Justice, announced the creation of the "New Sanctuary Movement" involving more than fifty U.S. churches. The organization will provide sanctuary to undocumented immigrants who face deportation. "We're launching now because we're fed up with detentions, deportations, and raids," Dr. Donna Schaper, senior minister of Judson Memorial Church in Greenwich Village, told *The New York Times*. "We felt it was not morally possible to remain silent."

(2) Casa Romero was a popular sanctuary for arriving refugees. Named for Oscar Romero, the martyred archbishop from El Salvador, it sheltered more than 130,000 refugees from Central America, serving more than 2.5 million meals while it was open as a "safe house" from 1982 to 1986. It was financed and overseen by Bishop John J. Fitzpatrick of the Catholic Diocese of Brownsville.

The authors visited Casa Romero on several different occasions, serving beans and rice to families who sought shelter there. Feliberto and Bishop Fitzpatrick developed a close working relationship. Casa Romero was closed in 1986 after the city of San Benito asked the diocese to move the shelter because of conflicts between residents and neighbors. The shelter was reopened at another location but was used only sporadically after U.S. immigration authorities began raiding the compound for what it said were illegal Mexican immigrants living there. Bishop Fitzpatrick died in July 2006, at eighty-seven.

(3) A study by an immigrant advocacy group, the Center for the Promotion of Border Studies and Human Rights, found that 1,034 bodies were pulled from the Rio Grande between 1980 and 1992. Of that number, 959 were males. The study showed that 144 of the victims had been shot, stabbed, or beaten to death.

(4) Like many newlyweds, the Pereiras faced their share of struggles. Feliberto's ministry to refugees posed the most extreme and immediate challenge for them. "Feliberto's first love is the church, and while I knew that was so, it was still very hard for me at first," said Mica. "I was jealous. Sometimes, he would bring refugees home because, literally, there was no other place for them to stay. We would have our problems."

However, the arrival of daughter Sarah brought the couple great joy. "I thank the Lord for Sarita. She keeps me busy. Together, she and I have forced Feliberto to slow down and take two weeks of vacation in July and give us more attention overall. I told Feliberto a story I heard one time about a minister who passed away. Everybody was saying good things about that man—he was such a good pastor, a good minister. His son then got up and spoke. 'Now, I know why my father didn't spend much time with me.' That's Feliberto. People love him, and he loves people."

(5) While many of Feliberto's friends, most of whom were ministerial colleagues, were surprised by his decision to seek Mica's hand, two of his closest friends said they believed God ordained the marriage.

David Vargas, an executive of the Christian Church (Disciples of Christ), said: "I would not have participated in the marriage ceremony, and I know the six other ministers who also participated would not have either, if we didn't believe this was God's will."

Rene Hidalgo, a retired minister of the Disciples, stood by his longtime friend through his divorce and his decision to remarry. "Pereira was destroyed by his divorce from Jacqui," he said. "I was with him as he cried in agony over Jacqui's decision to leave the marriage." He said Feliberto's decision to marry again after several years of healing "was a good surprise. I was very happy, very happy for him. I had been telling him that he needed a companion. He could have married any number of women, but the Lord had the best wife for him—Mica."

(6) The first recorded refugee family settled by a Disciples of Christ congregation was a Jewish family of four sponsored by First Christian Church of Eureka, Illinois, in 1941. They arrived from Nazi Germany through the American Friends Service Committee. The minister of the Eureka church wrote: "It is and has been my conviction that this was one

of the most important things that has happened in my entire ministry."

In 1949, the Disciples began resettling refugees from Europe in cooperation with Church World Service. The plan was to end the resettlement effort once it was no longer needed. However, the world continues to produce refugees, and the Refugee and Immigration Ministries, part of the Disciples Home Missions, continues a rich tradition of service nearly sixty years later.

In July 2006, in Amherst, New York, the Disciples of Christ resettled its 30,000th refugee, a member of a family of eight Liberians who had been living in a refugee camp since fleeing their homeland in 1996.

The Refugee and Immigration Ministries (RIM) has helped people from Africa, the Middle East, Central America, and Southwest Asia. Southwest Good Samaritan Ministries is the largest ministry in the RIM program.

(7) After his service to Southwest Good Samaritan Ministries, Robin Hoover moved to Tucson to become minister of First Christian Church (Disciples of Christ). In the spring of 2000, he founded Humane Borders Inc., an interfaith group that established a network of watering stations in the southern Arizona desert, where, since 1998, more than 3,250 people have died trying to cross into the United States. Humane Borders now has sixty-three drivers and about 8,000 volunteers to service eighty-four water stations on both sides of the border. Its pump trucks make about 750 trips a year to fill water tanks—recycled Coca-Cola syrup drums, painted to keep algae from blooming. In 2006 Humane Borders began distributing maps in Mexico and Central America showing the location of the water stations and of U.S. border patrol emergency beacons, as well as the spots where earlier travelers had died. "I want to tell them the information they need to save their lives," Robin told *The Christian Science Monitor*. "Not to do so is abuse."

In December 2006, Robin was awarded *Reconocimiento Cum Laude*, highest honorary recognition, by the Human Rights Commission of Mexico—the first American so honored. The gold medal was presented by Mexican President Felipe Calderon Hinojosa at the presidential residence. In a May 2005 column for *Desert Fountain*, the Human Borders newsletter, Robin paid tribute to Feliberto. "Good Sam (Samaritan Ministries) is run by my very dear friend, the Rev. Feliberto Pereira... A rabid anti-Communist, he has helped many, many thousands of refugees."

(8) Feliberto says Southwest Good Samaritan Ministries would not have thrived—and might not have survived—without Raquel Garcia. As the ministry's assistant director, she is Feliberto's keeper. Jennifer Riggs, director of the Disciples' Refugee and Immigration Ministries program, said of Raquel: "She bosses him around very well and keeps him in line."

To many who work closely with Feliberto and Raquel, it's a match made by heaven. Feliberto tends to be disorganized and pay scant attention to administrative details, preferring to focus on the ministry's big picture and the daily needs of refugees; Raquel, on the other hand, is hyper focused, efficient, and detail-oriented.

The two have known one another nearly from the time of Feliberto's arrival in the Rio Grande Valley in 1973. Raquel's nephew began telling her about a young, dynamic Cuban minister who was reviving a small Christian Church in San Benito—the church her nephew began attending. Raquel's family had been cradle-to-grave Presbyterians, whose worship styles, she said, were conservative and rigid. At her nephew's invitation, she began attending Feliberto's church and soon joined the choir. "I would leave the Presbyterian services and run over to Emmanuel Christian Church to sing with my nephew," she said. Soon, she became an active member of Feliberto's church.

"They were beautiful years," she said. "The church would be packed every Sunday morning and on Sunday nights. On Saturday nights, we would get 100 people at a prayer meeting." Almost all of them were poor. "There were maybe four of us in professional occupations." But it didn't matter. Church members tithed faithfully, building new facilities and breaking attendance records Feliberto preached on the importance of stewardship, she said, "but he never—not once—asked for money from members of the church."

She jokes that she has Feliberto trained to follow her organizational directives. "It is not easy to work with Feliberto," she said. "It's hard for him to stay focused, and he carries the information I need written down only in his head. He does not like desk work, and he loses things. . . . I can never seem to finish a conversation with him because the phone will ring or someone will come in." The biggest challenge, she said, is that "he never says no. It doesn't matter who a person is, what religion or race. He will be there for any human being at any time of the day."

At seventy-three, she has no plans to retire. "I love to work. I am slowing down some, but I will go to the point when I can't any longer. Feliberto will probably go longer than I. As long as I find someone to keep him focused, he'll be just fine until the Lord calls him home."

(9) Larry Cox is executive director of Juntos Servimos (Together We Serve), a nonprofit organization dedicated to serving the poor near Matamoros, in northern Mexico. A country of 756,000 square miles (slightly less than three times the size of Texas) of deserts, forests, and seashores and populated by 109 million people, Mexico is classified as a developing nation. In 2006, per capita income was $10,700 compared to $44,000 in the U.S. In Mexico, 40 percent of the population is below the poverty line, according to a 2003 estimate, while in the U.S., 12 percent are below the poverty line (2004 estimates). In Mexico, 26 percent of the population lives on less than $2 per day, according to the United Nations High Commissioner for Refugees.

Juntos Servimos operates three medical clinics in the Matamoros colonias of Derechos Humanos (Human Rights), Cinco de Marzo, and Santa Maria. It built a community kitchen and a water purification system and constructed or improved more than sixty homes at Derechos Humanos, a shantytown of plywood and cardboard shelters that sits atop a former garbage dump.

In February 1992, Larry left a six-figure income executive job with an internationally known health and beauty products firm to fulfill a calling to serve in ministry along the Texas-Mexico border. As a volunteer in the United Methodist Church, he worked with Feliberto in the late 1990s on many projects in Mexico—notably the Casa Bethel orphanage—before focusing his ministry on the colonias of Matamoros in 2001.

The Juntos Servimos clinics provide medical and dental services to thousands of people who would otherwise go without health care. The organization also provides health services to outlying homes and villages in the Matamoros area, in fishing villages southeast of Matamoros, and in the Mexican state of San Luis Potosi. The clinics are overseen by Dr. Nancy Rodriguez, Medical Director of Juntos Servimos and Larry's wife.

(10) Jennifer Riggs, director of the Disciples' refugee and immigration ministries, is one of the givers. Feliberto credits Jennifer as a co-founder of Southwest Good Samaritan Ministries. "Jennifer is a partner in our ministry who has been very supportive of our work with refugees from the beginning. Her advice and friendship through some very challenging times has been so valuable. I could not do my ministry without her."

Johnny Wray, director of the Week of Compassion ministry—the relief, refugee and development ministry fund of the Christian Church (Disciples of Christ)—is a generous and faithful provider to Southwest Good Samaritan Ministries. In 2004, he arranged for Southwest Good Samaritan Ministries to receive a new Toyota van, desperately needed to transport refugees.

There are many other examples of unexpected generosity in behalf of refugees:

- One Sunday morning, the pastor of a Christian church in The Woodlands, Texas, asked from the pulpit, "What if, for once, we really did what God wants us to do? What if we really made the least of these our brothers and sisters? What would happen?" Then, he surprised everyone in the pews and pledged the entire morning's offering to the Southwest Good Samaritan Ministries.

- Similarly, a middle-aged couple from a Christian Church in Dallas decided one Sunday morning in July 2007 to visit every Sunday school class at their Dallas church. During their brief visits, they spoke of Southwest Good Samaritan Ministries and passed a small basket. By the end of the Sunday School hour, the couple had collected $600.

- A group of management consultants in Fort Worth, Texas, contributed more than $10,000 to equip Casa Bethel orphanage with computers and Internet access.

- At churches throughout the United States, more pancakes than can be counted have been sold at "Pancake Breakfasts" to support Feliberto's ministry.

- Members of the Christian Women's Fellowship have contributed thousands of health kits for refugees.

- In Austin, Texas, Shepherd of the Hills Christian Church provided the means for a Mexican child with a hearing defect to have hearing aids implanted. The church also provided the money to purchase the property for *Casa Compasión*.

- In Pampa, Texas, two men from the First Christian Church, Johnny Harper and senior minister Barry Loving, organize an annual "Ride for the Refugee" motorcycle trip. Riders go from Liberal, Kansas, to Los Fresnos, Texas, collecting funds and needed items from churches along the route.

- Jimmie Muckleroy and Nathan Higginbotham, two volunteers in men's ministry in Texas, oversaw construction of the *Casa Compasión* campus in February 2000. They raised money for a new building to house refugees and brought in twenty-nine men to build it.

- John Callison, a minister of the Bluebonnet/Lower Rio Grande Valley Area of the Christian Church, helps oversee the finances of Feliberto's ministry and otherwise has been a faithful supporter and friend.

"I am deeply moved when such acts of generosity are prompted by God's movement and promises—grace of which I'm completely unaware until a check arrives in the mail or a phone message is left," Feliberto said.

Chapter Eleven Notes:

(1) At 347 acres, the 900-bed Port Isabel Service Processing Center is one of the largest detention centers operated by U.S. Immigration and Customs Enforcement. It is three miles northeast of Southwest Good Samaritan Ministries' *Casa Compasión*. A former U.S. Naval Air Station, the center is called El Corralon (The Coral) by detainees. It is adjacent to the Laguna Atascosa Wildlife Refuge, a 45,000-acre preserve that is world famous for the variety of its birds and other wildlife.

Immigration and Customs Enforcement is one of three branches of the old Immigration and Naturalization Service, which was reorganized as part of the new Department of Homeland Security, created on March 1, 2003. The other two immigration-related branches are Customs and Border Protection, which enforces immigration laws at borders and airports, and the Citizenship and Immigration Services, which processes applications for permanent residence, asylum, and naturalization.

On a typical day, Customs and Border Protection manages 326 ports of entry, processes 1.1 million travelers annually, and patrols 95,000 miles of shoreline. Each day, Citizenship and Immigration Service conducts 135,000 national security background checks, adjudicates 30,000 applications for immigration benefits, issues 20,000 green cards, takes 50,000 calls at four customer service centers, sees 25,000 visitors at 92 district offices, takes 8,000 set of fingerprints at 130 application support centers, welcomes 3,000 newly naturalized citizens, greets 100 arriving refugees, and helps American parents adopt 100 foreign children.

The government spends more than $1 billion a year to detain more than 27,500 undocumented immigrants monthly at seven processing centers, nine contract detention facilities, and hundreds of local jails and private prisons across the United States at an average cost of $95 per day per person. Plans are under way to expand detention capacity to 31,000 by the end of 2008. By September 30, 2008, an additional 3,000 border patrol agents are to be hired and trained, bringing the total to 17,800, under legislation already approved by Congress.

The country's largest detention center, in Raymondville, Texas, about forty-five miles from Southwest Good Samaritan Ministries'

Bayview facility, is temporary home to 2,000 immigrants living in ten giant, futuristic tents ringed by barbed wire. The $65 million tent city, in Willacy County, was built hastily in the summer of 2006 to detain captured undocumented non-Mexican nationals until they are processed and deported. (Once detained, Mexican nationals are given the opportunity to leave the U.S. immediately). Previously, most detainees were released in the United States pending their deportation hearings—and most of them disappeared. Critics derisively called that system "catch and release." The new detention policy has served as a deterrent. After quadrupling over four years, the number of non-Mexicans apprehended within 100 miles of the border fell 35 percent in 2006, *The Washington Post* reported in February 2007.

Civil liberties groups and immigrant advocates said that the Raymondville facility confines detainees twenty-three hours a day in its windowless tents, which are constantly flooded by lights, making sleep difficult. Detainees have insufficient food, clothing, medical care, and access to telephones, according to the groups. Immigration violators have no right to appointed lawyers. Under federal guidelines, they are supposed to be given access to law libraries, telephones, and the phone numbers for legal aid organizations.

ICE officials maintain that the Raymondville facility is modern, clean, humanely administered, and in compliance with federal standards. (ICE has thirty-eight detention standards for the care and treatment of immigration detainees that they are required to follow.)

"With roughly 1.6 million illegal immigrants in some stage of immigration proceedings," The Post reported, "ICE holds more inmates a night than Clarion Hotels have guests, operates nearly as many vehicles as Greyhound has buses, and flies more people each day than do many small U.S. airlines."

U.S. officials want to add another 1,000 beds at Raymondville, at a cost of $45 million, by the summer of 2008.

(2) To help provide housing, legal services, and spiritual care for refugees released to its custody, Southwest Good Samaritan Ministries relies on partner organizations, among them La Posada Providencia

("The Inn of God") in San Benito, Texas. The organization is part of the Sisters of Divine Providence, a Catholic order founded in Germany in 1851. Led by Sister Margaret Mertens, La Posada has operated since 1989, providing a safe and welcoming home for more than 4,000 refugees. Sister Margaret and her colleagues provide services ranging from food and shelter to spiritual counseling, from medical care to language assistance. A full-time coordinator of legal services ensures that every refugee is assisted with asylum claims and the residency process.

Southwest Good Samaritan also works closely with the two major nonprofit legal aid services in the Rio Grande Valley: the South Texas Pro Bono Asylum Representation Project (ProBAR) and Proyecto Libertad. ("Project Liberty").

Few refugees can afford to hire lawyers or post the substantial immigration bonds required for release. Studies by various organizations have concluded that asylum seekers who have legal representation are more likely to obtain refugee status and be freed from detention. One such study, done in 2005 by the U.S. Commission on International Religious Freedom, showed that one in four asylum seekers with legal representation were granted asylum, compared with one in forty for asylum seekers who had no representation.

Founded in 1989, ProBAR recruits and trains volunteer attorneys, law students, and legal assistants. ProBAR is a joint project of the American Bar Association, the State Bar of Texas, and the American Immigration Lawyers Association.

Without ProBAR's pro bono legal services, Feliberto believes, thousands of refugees would have been deported to their home countries, where they would have faced persecution or even death. "ProBAR saves lives," he said.

Casa de Proyecto Libertad was founded in 1981 to provide free legal services to Central American immigrants. It has evolved into a multifaceted, community-based organization assisting immigrant families in a variety of ways.

(3) U.S. border agents apprehended 1.1 million immigrants in 2006, mostly Mexicans who were promptly sent back to Mexico. However,

another 500,000 people entered illegally or overstayed their visas or evaded capture, according to government statistics. An additional 630,000 are at large, ignoring deportation orders, and 300,000 more who entered state and local prisons for committing crimes are to be deported but will probably slip through the cracks after completing their sentences, *The Washington Post* reported in February 2007.

In an attempt to stem illegal migration from Mexico, Congress has approved, and President George W. Bush has signed, legislation authorizing construction of a fence along 700 miles of the 1,951-mile border. Mexico and twenty-seven other members of the Organization of American States opposed the measure, which was approved in October 2006. Its $2.2 billion estimated cost remains unfunded. About 125 miles of fence currently exists.

Feliberto opposes the fence, calling it a new "Berlin Wall."

"I know the border cannot be open to all people," he said. "We are in fear of terrorism, though you don't hear of many Hispanic terrorists. Certainly, there are drugs and gangs, but they exist in all cultures everywhere. The Mexicans I know love Americans. The border should bring us together, not separate us."

He says of the border region, "This place is difficult for people to understand. All of this was once one nation. We cannot forget history. Mexicans that were born here two or three generations ago, their aunts and uncles and cousins are on the other side. Sometimes, you have one brother here and another brother there. One is American and one is Mexican. What divides the family? A river. A wall is not going to stop them."

After the defeat of immigration reform legislation in the Senate in August 2007, the White House announced seventeen administrative initiatives to further curb illegal immigration. One is a proposed rule that would require employers to fire workers who don't have legitimate Social Security numbers. Employers who failed to comply could face criminal fines and sanctions. Million of undocumented workers are likely to lose their jobs under the program, which has been challenged in U.S. federal court.

Meanwhile, state and local governments, frustrated by the failure of Congress to overhaul immigration laws, have enacted their own legislation.

In 2007, every state debated immigration issues, and forty-one adopted new laws, according to the National Conference of State Legislatures. About 100 U.S. municipalities have approved strict ordinances against illegal immigration since 2006—although most of the ordinances have been successfully challenged by civil rights groups.

(4) The U. N. High Commissioner for Refugee's 2006 Global Trends report shows a 14 percent increase in the worldwide refugee population, to almost 10 million, since 2005. The war in Iraq, which has created 2.2 million refugees, was largely responsible for the increase, according to the report.

(5) An imam is an Islamic leader, often the leader of a mosque, akin to a priest in Christianity. When the six men left Feliberto's care after being issued a travel permit, they gave him their copy of the Quran as a gift. Knowing it was their only copy, Feliberto at first refused the gift. But the men insisted that he take it.

(6) In a seminal academic paper on the refugee experience, Barry N. Stein, a political science professor at Michigan State University, wrote: "In the language of migration theory, it is common to think of the immigrant as pulled to his new land—attracted by opportunity and a new life. The refugee is not pulled out; he is pushed out. Given the choice, he would stay. Most refugees are not poor people. They have not failed within their homeland; almost all were functional and independent; a great many were successful, prominent, well-integrated individuals who flee because of persecution.

"There is a tendency to dwell on refugee success stories, which are not representative of the experiences of the group. Such stories set a standard of expectations that are not representative of the experiences of the group. In reality, lives torn apart are not easily repaired. The refugee pays a high price for flight. Remember, though, that the refugee fled for safety and freedom, not for economic or social values and opportunities."

Chapter Twelve Notes:

(1) The nature of the asylum process, in which the applicant is subjected to multiple security checks and interviewed in depth, is effective,

experts say, in weeding out individuals and stories that are not credible. U.S. asylum officers and immigration judges only grant asylum in about a third of the cases that cross their desks.

"The perception persists that asylum provides a convenient cover for terrorists and their sympathizers," according to the United Nations High Commissioner for Refugees 2006 World Report on Refugees. "Asylum systems are not immune to abuse, and it would be naïve to believe that terrorists have ignored the opportunity to consider how the systems might be exploited. At the same time, the security threat posed by the movement and presence of asylum seekers must be put into perspective. Asylum seekers are, for example, amongst the most closely scrutinized of all foreign nationals; they are routinely fingerprinted and checked against national and international databases. Those who arouse any suspicion are liable to be detained and to be monitored upon their release. If a terrorist wishes to enter and remain in a country undetected, submitting an application for asylum would not appear to be the most promising means of achieving that objective."

Since its establishment in 1995, the U.S. Asylum Corps has not been sufficiently staffed. Asylum officers have limited access to investigative support services, locally and internationally, to help verify events, locations, and people referred to in asylum applications. The result is that many asylum claims are not evaluated expeditiously. Applicants may face backlogs ranging from six months to three years. (See the Appendices for more information.)

Two high-profile criminal cases in 1993 raised serious questions about how the U.S. government conducts background checks on asylum applicants and helped prompt needed reform of the asylum system. Ramzi Ahmed Yousef, one of the planners of the 1993 World Trade Center bombing, claimed political asylum in November 1992 and was given a hearing date without being detained because immigration detention centers in the New York area were full. He made up a story about being a Pakistani brought up in Kuwait who had lost his passport—claims that were never investigated. Captured in 1995 and tried in New York for terrorist acts, Yousef was sentenced to life in prison without parole.

Mir Aimal Kansi, a Pakistani citizen who was allowed to remain in the United States while his asylum application was pending, spent four years on the FBI's Ten Most Wanted list after he shot five people with an AK-47, killing two, as they drove toward the entrance to the CIA headquarters in Langley, Virginia, in January 1993. He was captured in Pakistan four years later, returned to Virginia to face trial, and convicted of murder. He was executed by lethal injection in 2002.

(2) In 2005, about 191 million people worldwide lived outside of their country of birth, according to the United Nations.

In the United States, about 11.1 percent of the population is foreign-born—the highest percentage since the 1950s. Historically, however, when America was evolving as a "nation of immigrants," the percentage was higher: 13.3 percent in 1880, 13.6 percent in 1900, and 11.6 percent in 1930.

The immigrant population in the United States increased by 57.4 percent between 1990 and 2000.

The rapid modern rates of immigration can be traced to the 1965 passage of the Hart-Celler Act, which ended 1920s-era quotas and provided for the family reunification program. For over a decade, family reunification has accounted for more than 200,000 newcomers annually—63 percent of all legal immigration in 2001.

Approximately 12 million of the foreign-born individuals living in the United States are unauthorized migrants, including those who entered illegally and those who entered legally but overstayed their visas.

In 2007, legal and undocumented immigrants accounted for about 13 percent of the U.S. workforce, the highest percentage since the 1930s. By some estimates, immigrants hold about one of every three unskilled jobs in America. These are low-paying jobs that Americans aren't filling. On the other end of the scale, foreign-born workers account for about 25 percent of scientists and engineers, half of those receiving doctoral degrees in computer science and math, and 60 percent of those with doctoral engineering degrees. These are jobs U.S. employers say they can't find enough Americans to fill—a claim some dispute.

Immigrants accounted for nearly 50 percent of the total labor force increase between 1996 and 2000 and as much as 60 percent of the increase between 2000 and 2004, according to the 2007 World Population Data Sheet of the Population Reference Bureau (PRB). New immigrants and their children, assuming net immigration of 1 million per year, will account for all of the growth in the U.S. labor force between 2010 and 2030, according to the PRB.

In an editorial published on Labor Day 2007, *The Dallas Morning News* said the United States is harming its economic future by not adequately addressing the nation's needs for foreign workers. "When Congress nixed a proposed guest-worker program (as part of immigration reform legislation)—and with it the prospect that more than 12 million illegal immigrants could leave the underground economy—it also killed an increase in H-1B visas designed to increase the pool of foreign-born high-tech talent available to U.S. companies," *The News* editorial said. "Congress' decision could well lead to critical worker shortages at both ends of the wage and skill scales. Low-wage illegal immigrants probably will go deeper into the shadows, while the scarcity of certain high-tech skills will further encourage businesses to outsource that work overseas. Whether they cut lawns, build homes, or work in America's high-tech professions, immigrants are vital to America's economic well-being. And that's a Labor Day message worth remembering."

(3) Writing in the May 2007 newsletter of the U.S. Citizenship and Immigration Services, Emelio T. Gonzalez, himself a Cuban immigrant, said: "The USCIS mission is a delicate balance of precaution and compassion. We have a dual responsibility to the American people to maintain the integrity of our national immigration system while ensuring that we remain true to our historic tradition as a welcoming nation, one that was founded by and sustained through successive generations of immigrants from every corner of the globe. ...Citizenship programs that promote a common civic unity and collective American identity within immigrant populations are just as important as the background checks and identity screens we employ at USCIS."

In an annual report to Congress in June 2007, the ombudsman for Citizenship and Immigration Services recommended that the asylum application be redrafted to make it is less complicated and more understandable. The ombudsman also recommended that asylum officers be provided timely access to investigative services, to help them corroborate claims made by asylum seekers.

(4) Lawsuits by the American Civil Liberties Union on behalf of ten immigrant children, ages three to sixteen, alleged that by operating the Hutto facility, ICE is violating its duty to comply with a 1997 settlement agreement that calls for the prompt release of children to family members, or when that's not possible, for detention in the least restrictive settings available. ICE defends Hutto and a similar facility in Leesport, Pennsylvania, saying the facilities "provide an effective and humane alternative to maintain the unity of alien families as they await the outcome of their immigration hearings or the return to their home countries."

In August 2007, the ACLU and ICE announced a landmark settlement of the lawsuits, which resulted in the release of dozens of families from Hutto and improved conditions for those remaining. Under the settlement, children no longer will be required to wear prison uniforms. They are allowed much more time outdoors. Educational programming has been expanded, and guards have been instructed not to discipline children by threatening to separate them from their parents. Other changes include installing privacy curtains around toilets and adding a full-time pediatrician to the facility. Finally, it provides for periodic review of conditions at Hutto by a federal magistrate.

"The Hutto facility is, realistically, what's available. Hutto is not ideal," U.S. District Judge Sam Sparks of Austin said in announcing the settlement. "It is a former prison. It is, and will remain, constructed in a manner designed to house adult inmates."

The settlement covers Hutto only, not other existing or future facilities. And it does not address the policy of detaining families. "We remain concerned that the detention of families is inappropriate and urge Congress to ensure that ICE pursues alternatives to detention which are infinitely more appropriate for families with children," said Michelle Brane of the Women's Commission for Refugee Women and Children.

(5) Shining Path is a rebel movement in Peru that, in its heyday in the

1980s, waged a brutal insurgent war against the government for control of large areas of the countryside. Inspired by Mao's Cultural Revolution in China, the movement seeks to establish a Communist state and ruthlessly rules the rural areas it seizes, killing villagers and those who minister to them if they are suspected of siding with the government. Shining Path members view evangelical Christianity as a threat to their power base. With the 1992 arrest of Shining Path leader Abimael Guzman, the movement has weakened significantly and is largely confined to jungle areas.

(6) Mexico grants only a few hundred cases of asylum each year—a tiny number, given that more than 300,000 undocumented and poverty-stricken immigrants cross into the country from its southern border annually. Mexico City, a mega city of 19.2 million people, expands daily, its population fed by a steady stream of migrants who pour in, hoping against all odds to find better jobs and more comfortable lives. In neighboring Honduras, 53 percent of the population lives below the poverty line and 27 percent are illiterate. In Guatemala, 80 percent of the population lives below the poverty line; in El Salvador, 48 percent are below the poverty line; and in Nicaragua 47 percent.

(7) "Coyotes," those who make their living illegally by smuggling undocumented immigrants across the border, derive the name from the desert animal's traits of inventiveness, mischievousness, and evasiveness. Feliberto said, "They don't have a conscience. I have known them to rape and steal. It is very difficult to find a coyote who has a good heart." Furthermore, by resorting to the use of a smuggler, an asylum seeker compromises his or her claim in the eyes of many asylum-granting governments.

(8) Katherine Guerrero said Feliberto's intervention was an answer to her family's constant prayer.

"After we registered our asylum case with U.S. immigration and were paroled to his custody, Brother Pereira took us to *Casa Compasión* at Bayview. The camping trailer we were living in was too small for the five of us. At Bayview, he gave us rice and beans, health kits and fresh clothing—all the clothing we needed. And, he gave us games to play. He took us to the HEB Grocery store and bought us some other things we needed. We felt so safe. On Sunday, Brother Pereira took us to church and the entire church prayed for us. We attend there now.

"We are proof for what God does. We had no clothes, and now we have clothing. We had no food, and now we are hungry no more. We needed a place to stay, and God provided shelter for us. It is all from God.

"We are going to make it in this country. I came to the U.S. knowing not one word of English. I started reading books in English, and now I've become a very good reader and speaker. I started with Dr. Seuss and graduated to reading English pages on the Internet. God gave me wisdom to pick up English pretty easily. In college, I want to study history and, perhaps, become a history professor. My brother learned English and started in college on a scholarship. He is extremely intelligent. He is studying mechanical engineering at the University of Texas at Brownsville and will transfer to Texas Christian University for the spring 2008 semester. My sister speaks very good English, too. My parents want to learn English, but it is harder for them, and they rely on us to translate. My mom speaks one phrase in English, which she tells only to English speakers: 'God Bless You!' My dad now has a work permit. He works very hard every day in produce warehouse. It is good to see my dad at peace again.

"I believe God is going to see to it that our political asylum request is granted. . . .I believe God wants us to stay in this country."

Chapter Thirteen Notes:

(1) As a member institution of the Southwest Region of the Christian Church (Disciples of Christ), Southwest Good Samaritan Ministries supports three active programs of ministry in Mexico and accommodates many other humanitarian needs there on a case-by-case basis. Feliberto is a popular worship service speaker in northern Mexico and regularly visits hospitals there to minister to patients. Dani Loving Cartwright, the denomination's southwest regional minister, said of Feliberto: "He's our missionary to Mexico. That should be his title, in addition to what he

does at Good Samaritan."

(2) Those who visit Southwest Good Samaritan Ministries on mission or fact-finding trips seem to come away from the experience enlightened if not changed. "When the Anglo groups come here, what they discover is that the church is still worth something," said David Vargas, co-executive director of Global Ministries of the Christian Church (Disciples of Christ). "A lot of groups come from petrified cultures where all the answers are in the bulletin and where the testimonies are those of the traditional saints of the church. When they come here, they see the basics… that the true church lives. In the petrified church, they have heard a lot about Matthew 25, but they have never seen it. Here, it is real and church members move from theory to reality."

(3) Monika Hellwig, a Catholic author, suggests that the poor have some "spiritual advantages" over us who are not:

- The poor know they are in urgent need of redemption.

- The poor know not only their dependence on God and on powerful people but also their interdependence with one another.

- The poor rest their security not on things but on people.

- The poor have no exaggerated sense of their own importance, and no exaggerated need of privacy.

- The poor expect little from competition and much from cooperation.

- The poor can distinguish between necessities and luxuries.

- The poor can wait, because they have acquired a kind of dogged patience born of acknowledged dependence.

- The fears of the poor are more realistic and less exaggerated, because they already know that one can survive great suffering and want.

- When the poor have the Gospel preached to them, it sounds like good news and not like a threat or a scolding.

- The poor can respond to the call of the Gospel with a certain abandonment and uncomplicated totality because they have so little to lose and are ready for anything.

Author Philip Yancey, reflecting on what Monika Hellwig has written, said: "In summary, through no choice of their own—they may urgently wish otherwise—poor people find themselves in a posture that befits the grace of God. In their state of neediness, dependence, and dissatisfaction with life, they may welcome God's free gift of love."

(4) Born April 27, 1925, in rural Iowa, Frank Mabee eventually landed in the big city as pastor of Midway Hills Christian Church (Disciples of Christ) in Dallas from 1968 to 1980. With all his heart, Frank is convinced that one of the primary missions of Christians is to be socially and politically active in correcting injustices and helping those in need. "Social action always has to be a result of conversion and Christian faith," Frank said. "It has to come from one's understanding of the Gospel."

Frank's understanding of the Gospel meant he often cut against the grain of popular culture, taking controversial stands in support of farm workers, minorities, prisoners, refugees, and others who are poor or downtrodden. There is never a doubt where Frank stands on an issue, and he has paid a price for this candor. He says he was officially censured by more than one church board when he served as Coastal Plains area minister for the Disciples until his retirement in 1990. "It's when I'm in the doghouse . . . those are the moments I feel the most alive."

(5) Ernie Williams of Amarillo, Texas, is a founder of the "Disciples Beans" program. "Remembering the miracle of the loaves and fishes, we thought that by all of the churches (in the High Plains area) contributing something, each small amount could grow into something large and significant," he said. "Sure enough, sufficient money and beans were contributed at our area assembly that fall to enable us to send fifteen tons of beans in the winter of 1992. In subsequent years, we have focused on the giving of money so that we could purchase the beans in the Valley,

saving the immense shipping costs incurred in our first two years. We now have a broker, knowing the source of the money and who the beans are for, who does not charge us a commission." Over the years, churches, especially those in small towns, have established "bean stalks" and "bean jars" to collect pocket change, which is contributed to bean purchases.

(6) The "Mike's Kids" program continued under Mike Slaight's father Hank for more than a decade. Today, the program is overseen by Mike's children, Mark Slaight and Christina Gill, a longtime family friend, Marvin Carter, and his wife, Treena. With the help of hundreds of volunteers from many denominations who collect and pack thousands of items of clothing and toys, the program has grown. The Christmas bounty no longer fits in a van. It's transported in a tractor-trailer.

(7) In 1997, Casa Bethel initiated a new program: a year-long Bible institute for young evangelists, some of whom were raised at the orphanage. "When Lorena and I saw that these young people we raised were learning very well, we decided that we had to put these young people to work." said orphanage founder Ismael Sifuentes. "They said, 'We want to open missions.' I said, 'If you are interested, then let us do it.' And that was the beginning."

Ismael and Lorena named the program "the Ebenezer Movement," in honor of Feliberto's Ebenezer Christian Church in Los Fresnos. More than 140 student evangelists have gone through the program. Through youth rallies and worship services in Mexico, they have exposed more than 55,000 people to the Gospel. The movement has spread to eleven states of Mexico, resulting in fifty-two new congregations.

(8) Volunteers are the life-blood of Southwest Good Samaritan Ministries. In 2000, Caroline Herbert joined the organization, serving in many roles for many years without salary. "Caroline is a true Disciple of Christ, a person who after a full career as an environmental engineer, retired and completed seminary at Brite Divinity School at Texas Christian University," Feliberto said. "Soon, she sold most of her belongings and, followed the calling God placed on her heart, and came to Southwest Good Samaritan Ministries to serve refugees, orphans, and the volunteer work groups. She is a very, very hard worker for the Lord."

Said Caroline: "We all have a certain number of minutes in life, and we ought to be productive. If it weren't for Feliberto, many of us would be sitting on the curb stone throwing rocks into a pot."

Feliberto credits Les and Connie Hodson of McKinney, Texas, for tackling key long-range planning and operational assignments for Southwest Good Samaritan Ministries. For seventeen of the ministry's twenty-five years, Les and Connie—who spent many of those years holding down full-time jobs 600 miles away in North Texas—have faithfully served the "least of these." Les is responsible for designing the refugee facilities at Ebenezer Christian Church. He also arranged for work crews to build them. He secured the land for *Casa Compasión*, designed the campus facilities, and arranged for their construction.

Les and Connie met at a Disciples of Christ youth camp in Abilene, Kansas, while both were in college. She was eighteen, he was twenty. They married two years later in 1968. The parents of two children, now grown, both had successful careers, she as an educator, he as an engineer. Les's first trip to Southwest Good Samaritan Ministries came in 1992, when he and other adults took seventeen teens from First Christian Church of McKinney on a mission trip to the Valley over spring break. "Like so many others, I entered this ministry to refugees very skeptically," Les said. "But once you walk the path (with refugees), you walk away knowing that you're forever touched." Every year since, Southwest has hosted a spring break work group from First Christian Church of McKinney.

"I've seen so many kids' lives changed by what they experience during a mission trip," Les said. He named three teens who, after trips to the Valley, decided to pursue careers in medicine and education, so they could help those in need. "There are blessings that happen that are almost miraculous. They meet refugees and others who literally do not own any possessions. Not being able to speak each others' languages, the kids and the refugees are left to develop a relationship based on their hearts and God's love for them."

Taking earlier retirement from their respective careers, Les and Connie in 2006 started spending half of each year in the Valley, living at *Casa*

Compasión, where Les is the unpaid director of strategic planning.

In the summer of 2007, in conjunction with the Disciples' Week of Compassion and Disciple Volunteers in Mission, Les initiated "the Casita Project" to provide small prefabricated houses to those left homeless by hurricanes and poverty in northern Mexico. Minimal construction skills are needed to build the homes, because the materials are pre-cut and assembly is relatively simple, following a step-by-step guide.

At *Casa Compasión*, plans are being drafted for an education building to provide training, development, and continuing education opportunities for church members, ministers, and seminary students. Discussions are under way with two seminaries about the possibility of a remote education and training program for seminarians who wish to specialize in working with refugees and impoverished populations.

Why do they work up to twelve hours a day for no salary in a place far from home? "Matthew 25 is why we do it," Les said. "We do it because we want to do it and because we feel it is a necessity. We've been so surprised by God's hand taking over."

Said Connie: "God wants us here. I'm not sure exactly why, but I know he wants us here now."

Feliberto remains an inspiring figure for all who work with him, Les said. "There is an aura around individuals who walk with God on a real-time basis and when you feel that or see it, you want to be a part of it," he said. "The sacrifices Feliberto has made in his life go beyond any level you can recognize personally or understand. Working with that sort of person is life changing."

Les said Feliberto will never retire from Southwest Good Samaritan Ministries. "He will die in service to God."

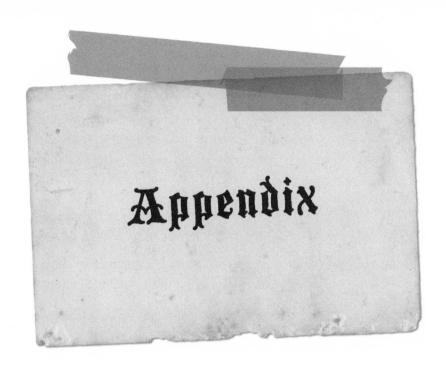

Appendix A

A Glossary of Immigration Terms

Alien: The term used by some governments, including the U.S. government, to describe any person who is not a citizen (born in a country) or a national (a person who has pledged allegiance to a certain country.) Aliens have many forms of lawful status—for example, as foreign students, tourists, or temporary workers. The terms immigrant, newcomer, and migrant are used interchangeably with alien.

Asylum: Protection offered to a refugee by a state.

Deportation: The removal of an alien for violation of immigration laws. Deportation is ordered by an immigration judge

Green card: The popular name for an Alien Registration Receipt Card, a photo ID given to individuals who successfully become legal permanent residents of the United States. At one time, the card was actually green; now, it is pink.

I-94 card: A green or white card issued to "nonimmigrants," those who enter the United States temporarily for some particular purpose but do not plan to remain permanently—typically, students, temporary workers, and visitors. The I-94 card is stamped with a date indicating how long the nonimmigrant may stay.

Immigrant visa: A document that allows a noncitizen to enter the United States, take up permanent residence, and seek a green card.

Lawful permanent resident: A noncitizen with a **green card**. They can apply for naturalization after five years (three if married to a citizen.)

Naturalization: The process of conferring citizenship on a person after birth.

Nonimmigrant visas: Various documents issued to people planning on staying only temporarily—such as students. Each type is identified by a letter and number. Student visas, for example, are F-1; those for investors are E-2. The duration of nonimmigrant visas varies. For example, a visitor's visa is good for only six months.

Parole: The status of people allowed to enter the country on humanitarian grounds.

Petitioner: A U.S. citizen or business that makes a formal request for legal status in behalf of a non-citizen. The petitioner is typically a relative of the applicant or an employer. Often, the petitioner is referred to as a sponsor.

Preference categories: Groups of people who are given priority to obtain green cards under an annual quota. The preferences are broken into two broad groups: family preferences (aimed at reuniting family members) and employment preferences (aimed at allowing U.S. employers to hire needed skilled labor.) Because of the quotas, it can often take years to get a green card.

Refugees: People outside their own countries who are unwilling or unable to return because of persecution or a well-founded fear of persecution based on race, religion, nationality, social group membership, or political opinion. The term is often used to include a larger group of individuals who are in need of safe haven but who may not technically qualify as refugees under the strict legal definition.

Removal: The expulsion of a noncitizen. This expulsion may be based on grounds of inadmissibility or deportability. The Illegal Immigration Reform and Immigrant Responsibility Act of 1996 authorized the INS to quickly remove certain inadmissible aliens—for example, those with no entry documents or falsified entry documents—through a procedure known as expedited removal.

Special interest aliens: Immigrants from forty-three so-called "countries of interest" in the Middle East, South Asia, and North Africa. These countries—including Iraq, Iran, Syria, Afghanistan, Somalia, and the Philippines—are singled out because terrorist groups operate there. Immigrants from these countries are automatically detained in U.S. immigration facilities, often for months, and subjected to extra screening, including FBI interrogation.

Temporary protected status: A classification that the U.S. attorney general may bestow on people from a foreign country where conditions pose a danger to personal safety because of armed conflict or an environmental disaster.

Undocumented immigrants: Foreigners residing in the United States without permission. These may be people who entered the country illegally or who violated the terms of a visa—such as its expiration date—after entering legally.

Visa: A government document that allows the bearer to apply for entry to the United States under certain conditions. A visa does not guarantee that the application will be approved.

Voluntary departure: A process under which an alien is given the opportunity to leave the United States voluntarily or face detention, fines, and the inability to re-enter the United States legally for many years.

Appendix B

Political Asylum in the United States: A Timeline

1948

The Unites States was one of the original signatories of the December 1948 Universal Declaration of Human Rights, which gave considerable weight to the concept of asylum. Eleanor Roosevelt chaired the U. N. committee that drafted the document, which declared that "everyone has the right to seek and to enjoy in other countries asylum from persecution." The U.S. Displaced Persons Act allowed 100,000 people displaced in World War II to enter the United States. (Later, the number was increased to 400,000.) But national origin quotas and other restrictions kept out many people who had been victims of the Nazis.

1950

A legal provision is adopted to allow people at risk of persecution to remain in the country, a precursor of today's asylum provisions.

1951

The United Nations Convention relating to the Status of Refugees provides the international community with a definition of a refugee: "a person outside his/her country of nationality who, owing to well-founded fear of persecution for reasons of race, nationality, membership in a particular social group, or political opinion is unable or unwilling to return."

The convention also outlines certain obligations of signatory states regarding the treatment and processing of refugees. Those states may not penalize refugees and asylum seekers who "enter or are present in their territory without authorization, provided that they present themselves without delay to the authorities and show good cause for their illegal entry or presence."

1952

The Immigration and Nationality Act, also known as the McCarran-

Walter Act, becomes the first statute governing U.S. immigration policy. The act abolishes racial restrictions, but continues the policy of restricting the numbers of immigrants from certain countries. Eventually, the act establishes a preference system, under which certain ethnic groups and certain labor qualifications are deemed desirable over others.

1953

The Refugee Relief Act overrides national origin quotas for refugees from Communist countries. Admitted under this policy will be 340,000 Cubans and 90,000 Soviet Jews.

1965

The U.S. Immigration Act, also known as the Hart-Celler Act, ends national origin quotas that had been in place since 1924 and replaces them with ceilings for the Eastern and Western hemispheres. Priority is given to those with special skills and those who already have family in America. The act is amended in 1978 to provide a single, worldwide ceiling.

1968

The United States signs the *1967 Protocol relating to the Status of Refugees*, agreeing to abide by the asylum obligations outlined in 1951 by the U.N. convention on refugees. (However, the United States won't come into compliance with the 1967 protocol until after passage of the U.S. Refugee Act of 1980, the U.S. government's first comprehensive approach to dealing with refugees.) The protocol provides a broad context for asylum: "Any alien who is physically present in the United States or who arrives in the United States irrespective of such alien's status may apply for asylum...."

1976

In the aftermath of the Vietnam War, thousands of refugees from Southeast Asia are accepted. An estimated 1.3 million will arrive by 1998.

1980

The Refugee Act of 1980 creates the Federal Refugee Resettlement Program to provide for the effective resettlement of refugees and to assist them in achieving economic self-sufficiency as quickly as possible. Prior to the act, government policies related to refugees, such as those from Indochina in the 1970s, were considered on an ad-hoc basis. Congress' intent was to establish a politically and geographically neutral adjudication standard for both asylum status and refugee status, a standard to be applied equally to all applicants regardless of country of origin.

The act also distinguishes between "political refugees," who are eligible for asylum and "economic refugees," who are not.

It takes effect just as Central America explodes in political violence, sending tens of thousands of refugees northward to the United States. While it is clear that the refugee act is saving the lives of tens of thousands of people, the influx of asylum-seekers overwhelms the capacity of U.S. immigration operations. From 1968 to 1975, the United States averages about 200 asylum applications a year. Now, the country admits 125,000 Cuban refugees alone, as part of the Mariel Boatlift Operation.

1990

The U.S. Immigration Act increases the number of legal immigrants allowed into the country each year. It also gives "temporary protected status" (eighteen months without deportation) to individuals fleeing emergency situations, such as earthquakes and floods.

The Immigration and Naturalization Service creates the Asylum Corps, officers specially trained in human rights issues to review political asylum cases, which takes responsibility for asylum cases away from INS district offices. A resource information center is established to keep asylum officers informed of human rights conditions around the world. (Seven asylum offices will became operational in 1991, followed by an eighth in 1994).

1992

Asylum applications reach 103,000 per year, with a backlog of more than 300,000. The overtaxed system becomes more vulnerable to fraud and abuse. While bogus asylum seekers take advantage of the situation, legitimate refugees are deprived of expeditious hearings because of the huge backlog.

1993

President Bill Clinton orders the Department of Justice to fix the asylum process—to speed up decisions, eliminate the backlog, and discourage abuse. (Reform regulations are implemented January 4, 1995.) As a result of the reforms, not only did the backlog fall dramatically, but so did the number of new asylum applications, as fewer individuals filed frivolous claims. (New cases declined from more than 147,000 in 1995 to 46,000 new cases filed in 2003).

1996

Additional reforms are authorized. The Antiterrorism and Effective Death Penalty Act allows the government to designate groups as "foreign terrorist organizations." People involved in these organizations are ineligible for asylum.

The Illegal Immigration Reform and Immigrant Responsibility Act (finally implemented at the end of 2000) requires people entering the United States without proper documentation to demonstrate "credible fear" of persecution before they may apply for asylum. Those who cannot do so face an expedited removal. The act also redefines refugees to include people who have been persecuted for resisting coercive national population-control programs.

It also requires a thorough identity check before asylum may be granted and adds a penalty for filing a bogus application.

2001

In late October, President George W. Bush signs the USA Patriot Act of 2001 (Uniting and Strengthening America by Providing Appropriate

Tools Required to Intercept and Obstruct Terrorism.) This is in response to the September 11, 2001, terrorist attacks.

The act expands the grounds for refusing to admit immigrants suspected of involvement with terrorist organizations. It also broadens the definitions of "terrorist activity" and "terrorist organization." Its provisions are made retroactive, applying regardless of when an alien filed his or her asylum application.

2002

President Bush signs the Enhanced Border Security and Visa Entry Reform Act. It requires the INS to issue employment authorization documents containing at least a fingerprint and photograph to anyone granted asylum.

The president also signs the Child Status Protection Act, which says that a child of asylum seekers who turns twenty-one after his or her parent's application is filed but before a decision is made will continue to be classified as a child, eligible for derivative asylum status.

2005

In May, President Bush signs the Real ID Act. Among its many provisions affecting asylum seekers are:

- Eliminating a cap of 10,000 per year on the number of people who can obtain permanent residence.

- Eliminating a cap of 1,000 per year on the number of people granted asylum for resisting coercive population control methods, such as involuntary sterilization.

- Barring from asylum anyone who has provided "material support" to "terrorist organizations." Strict interpretation of these provisions hinders more than 1,000 applications for asylum or refugee status.

- Allowing immigration judges and asylum officers to deny claims based on inconsistencies in testimony, even if they are incidental to the asylum claim—for example, inconsistencies on dates of school attendance or inconsistencies between an airport interview and subsequent testimony before an asylum officer. Claims may also be denied because of an applicant's "demeanor"—for example, a lack of the expected emotion or a refusal to look an immigration judge in the eye. Finally, an application can be denied if a judge doubts its "inherent plausibility."

Appendix C

Frequently Asked Questions About Political Asylum

What is political asylum?

Political asylum is legal permission to remain in a country, extended by that country's government to people born elsewhere who have fled persecution or danger in their home countries. People who must flee their countries quickly or who for some other reason are unable to request refugee resettlement services become asylum seekers.

What's the difference between asylum seekers and refugees?

Like refugees, asylum seekers are fleeing persecution, but they have not yet been classified by an approved legal authority as meeting the legal definition of a refugee. Usually, they are forced to flee without proper documentation, such as a passport or visa, and often arrive in very poor physical, emotional, mental, and spiritual condition following long and dangerous journeys to safety. Once they arrive in the United States, they must apply for asylum.

Where did the concept of asylum come from?

Asylum is an ancient concept, but its modern foundations are rooted in international law developed in the aftermath of World War II atrocities. The idea of granting protection to those fleeing persecution gained strength from the widespread agreement that what had happened to Jews under the Nazis should never be allowed to happen again to anybody, anywhere, although such atrocities continue.

Who seeks asylum?

Every year, hundreds of thousands of people around the globe find themselves in need of protection because they have been persecuted or fear
they will be persecuted on account of their race, religion, nationality,
membership in a particular social group, or political opinion. Many of
them come to the United States. If granted asylum by the U.S. government, a refugee is allowed to remain in the country, pursue citizenship,
and enjoy freedom from harm.

Generally speaking, how does the U.S. asylum program work?

The U.S. asylum program provides protection to qualified refugees who
are already in the United States or are seeking entry. The asylum program
is different from the U.S. refugee program, which provides protection to
refugees by bringing them to the United States for resettlement. People
may seek asylum regardless of their country of origin. There are no quotas on how many individuals may be granted asylum each year.

A lengthier list of asylum questions and answers can be found at the U.S.
Customs and Immigration Services Web site at www.uscis.gov.

Who is eligible to apply for asylum in the United States?

Asylum may be granted to people who are arriving in, or already physically present in, the country. Asylum is requested at a port-of-entry (airport, seaport, or border crossing), or by filing Form I-589, *Application
for Asylum and for Withholding of Removal*, (available on the CIS Web
site and at a U.S. Customs and Immigration service center) within a year
of arrival. Asylum may be sought regardless of immigration status. The
government confirms receipt of a completed application in writing.

How are asylum claims processed?

Asylum seekers in the United States apply for asylum in one of two
ways. An "affirmative" application is submitted directly to one of the
eight asylum offices in the United States. An interview with a specially
trained asylum officer follows. A "defensive" application is submitted
when an asylum seeker has already been identified for removal from

the United States. In defensive cases, an immigration judge decides the application.

Are asylum seekers subject to immediate deportation?

In some cases, yes. Asylum seekers with false or no documents must establish a fear of persecution at an on-the-spot interview before an immigration officer or face immediate deportation. Such "expedited removal" hearings do not allow an asylum seeker to consult legal counsel or present their claims before an immigration judge. However, if an asylum seeker subject to immediate deportation raises a claim for asylum—or expresses fear of removal—he or she will be given the opportunity to explain his or her fears to an asylum officer at a detention center where the seeker is being held. If the asylum seeker meets the credible fear test, his or her case is heard by an immigration judge. Immigration authorities have the discretion to release an asylum applicant from detention.

Is there a fee to apply for asylum?

No.

Are asylum seekers held in detention?

Yes, most are. Consistent detention of asylum seekers became standard practice following 9/11. Those detained are placed in federal immigration detention centers or local jails. There is no limit on the length of time that asylum seekers can be detained while their proceedings are progressing. Typically applicants are detained until FBI background checks (including fingerprinting) are completed, which can take several weeks to several months. Asylum seekers may request their release, but release policies vary widely across the country. There is no process for appealing a decision to initially detain an asylum seeker, nor a subsequent decision to deny release, to a court or another independent judicial authority. The U.S. Commission on International Religious Freedom has criticized these practices. By international convention, to which the United States is a signatory, detention of asylum seekers should normally be avoided when an individual can establish that he or she is likely to appear for all hearings and other immigration matters and that he or she poses no danger to the community.

How is asylum eligibility determined?

Information on the application and offered during an interview with an asylum officer or at a hearing before an immigration judge is used to determine whether an asylum seeker meets the definition of a refugee. The legal definition of a refugee is "someone who is unable or unwilling to return to and avail himself or herself of the protection of his or her home country or, if stateless, country of last habitual residence because of persecution or a well-founded fear of persecution on account of race, religion, nationality, membership in a particular social group, or political opinion."

A person will be barred from asylum if he or she has engaged in any terrorist activity, threatened to engage or incite such activity, or has ever been involved with a group associated with terrorist activity. A person will also be barred if he or she:

- Ordered, incited, assisted, or otherwise participated in the persecution of any person on account of race, religion, nationality, membership in a particular social group, or political opinion.

- Were convicted of a particularly serious crime (including aggravated felonies).

- Committed a serious non-political crime outside the United States.

- Pose a danger to the security of the United States.

- Firmly resettled in another country prior to arriving in the United States.

How long does the asylum process take?

The initial interview on asylum applications should take place within forty-five days after the date the application is filed. A decision should be made within 180 days, unless there are exceptional circumstances. Decisions are not final until a mandated FBI background check is completed. In late 2007, the FBI faced a background check backlog of more than 329,000 cases, meaning waits of well over a year for most applicants.

Are asylum applicants provided a lawyer or an interpreter?

No. However, an applicant may provide for his or her own legal representation at an asylum interview and during immigration proceedings before the immigration court. A list of free or reduced price immigration lawyers is available on the Customs and Immigration Services Web site. An applicant must bring an interpreter (eighteen or older) if he or she does not speak English fluently.

What happens at an asylum interview?

Asylum interviews are administered by an asylum officer at a Customs and Immigration Services office. Interviews are confidential. After taking an oath, applicants are asked basic biographical questions and the reasons they are seeking asylum.

An applicant must demonstrate that he or she has suffered badly enough to have endured severe persecution in the past or that he or she has a very good reason to believe "a well-founded fear" that such persecution will happen in the future. The persecution must have been on account of something about the applicant that he or she is either unable or completely unwilling to change: race, religion, nationality, political opinion, or membership in a particular social group. An applicant does not have to prove that he or she is likely to be singled out for persecution from the members of a generally persecuted group. The applicant needs only show a pattern or practice, where groups of persons who are similar are being persecuted. Applicants must show that he or she either belong to or would be identified with the persecuted group.

In evaluating an application for asylum, an asylum officer will answer to his or her satisfaction such questions as:

1. Is the applicant credible?

2. Do I believe this person's story?

3. Is there a well-founded fear of or past persecution?

4. Is the harm serious enough to rise to the level of persecution?

5. Is fear based on one of the five eligible grounds to claim asylum?

6. Is there a "nexus" of the five grounds?

No decision on asylum is made at the hearing. Asylum officers will evaluate the credibility of the claim, examine evidence presented by the applicant, and decide whether the situation in the applicant's home country, the "country conditions," have changed so much since the time he or she left that there is no longer any danger. An applicant returns to the service center to receive the decision on asylum.

What happens after asylum is granted? Can asylum be taken away?

Once asylum is granted, the applicant receives an I-94 *Arrival and Departure* record documenting that he or she is able to remain indefinitely in the United States as an asylee. The applicant is authorized to work in the United States for as long as he or she remains in asylee status. And, the applicant can file needed paperwork to bring his or her spouse and/or children to the United States or allow them to remain in the United States. Asylee status may be terminated if it is determined that the applicant no longer has a well-founded fear of persecution because of a fundamental change in circumstances, has obtained protection from another country, or has committed certain crimes or engaged in other activity that makes the applicant ineligible to retain asylum status in the United States. An asylee may apply for lawful permanent resident status after he or she has been physically present in the United States for a period of one year after the date asylum was granted.

What happens if asylum is denied?

An applicant will automatically be placed in "removal proceedings" in an immigration court. An immigration judge will make a final decision on removal from the United States.

Can those granted asylum become U.S. citizens?

Yes. The process of becoming a U.S. citizen is called "naturalization." An asylee may apply for naturalization if over the age of eighteen and if he or she meets the following requirements:

- Lives in the United States for at least five years as a permanent resident (or three years if married and living with a U.S. citizen).

- Has been present in the United States for at least thirty months out of the past five years (eighteen months out of the past three years if married and living with a U.S. citizen).

- Lives within a state or district for at least three months before application is made.

- Is functionally fluent in spoken and written English, able to pass a test showing basic understanding of U.S. history and the U.S. system of government.

- Possesses "good moral character."

- Is willing to take an oath of allegiance to the United States. The oath includes being willing to bear arms on behalf of the United States if the law were to require it.

Some applicants may obtain their citizenship without meeting all these requirements, such as persons who served in the U.S. military in active duty status during certain periods of war.

Notes on Sources

In preparing this book, we have undertaken careful and conscientious research. Some documents and interviews were translated from Spanish to English, and careful attention was paid to ensure the accuracy of translations. We have been careful to give proper credit to quoted material. It is possible, however, that we have not been able to identify every single instance. Any mistakes are solely ours.

Chapter One

Braun, Theodore A. *Perspectives on Cuba and its People*. New York: Friendship Press, National Council of Churches, 1999.

Coe, Andrew. *Cuba*. Hong Kong, China: Odyssey Publications, Ltd., 1999.

Hatchwell, Emily, and Calder, Simon. *Cuba In Focus: A Guide to the People, Politics and Culture*. New York: Monthly Review Press, 1995.

Knight, Kevin. General Background on Catholics. http://www.NewAdvent.org (accessed March 26, 2001).

Levi, Vicki Gold, and Heller, Steven. *Cuba Style: Graphics from the Golden Age of Design.* New York: Princeton Architectural Press, 2002.

Mawer, Fred. *Fodor's Exploring Cuba.* New York: Fodor's Travel Publications Inc., 1998.

Mira, Ramon. General background on Cuba. http://www.CubaFacts.com (accessed December 14, 2004).

Sale, Richard. *Cuba, Automobile Association.* Lincolnwood, Illinois: NTC/Contemporary Publishing Group, Inc, 1998.

Associated Press, "Timeline on the History of the U.S. Naval Air Base at Guantanamo Bay," http:www.cbsnews.com (accessed August 24, 2004).

Chapter Two

Cox, Harvey. *Fidel and Religion.* New York: Simon and Schuster, 1987

Microsoft Encarta Encyclopedia on CD-Rom. Entry on Camaguey, Cuba. Microsoft: Redmond, Washington, 2003.

New Life Community Church, Stafford Va., "Biblical Fasting: What It Is and How To Do It," http://www.new-life.net/fasting (accessed August 21, 2003).

Philipson, Lorrin, and Lierena, Rafael. *Freedom Flights.* New York: Random House, Inc., 1980.

United Bible Society. *Havana Rally Marks Close of Cuban Evangelical Celebration.* World Report No. 343, September 1999.

Vail, John J. *Fidel Castro.* New York: Chelsea House Publishers, 1986.

General background on Christian Fasting, http://www.vatican.va (accessed August 22, 2003).

Chapter Three

Brown, Warren. *Fidel Castro: Cuban Revolutionary*. Minneapolis, Minnesota: Millbrook Press, 1994.

Conde, Yvonne. *Operation Pedro Pan: the Untold Exodus of 14,048 Cuban Children*. New York: Routledge, 1999

Corbett, Ben. *This is Cuba: An Outlaw Culture Survives*. Cambridge, Massachusetts: Westview Press, 2002.

Fontaine, Pascal. *Black Book of Communism: Communism in Latin America*. Cambridge, Massachusetts: Harvard University Press, 1999.

Geyer, Georgie Anne. *Guerilla Prince: The Untold Story of Fidel Castro*. New York: Little Brown and Company, 1991.

"Latin America entries from 1958-1964," *Facts on File*. New York: Facts on File, Inc., 2007.

Moore, Don, "Revolution! Clandestine Radio and the Rise of Fidel Castro," *Monitoring Times*, April 1993, pgs 1-17.

Operation Pedro Pan Group, Inc. http://www.PedroPan.org, (accessed September 23, 2003).

Sierra, J.A., General background on Cuba, http://www.HistoryofCuba.com. (accessed August 21, 2003).

Szulc, Tad. *Fidel: A Critical Portrait*. New York: William Morrow and Company, Inc., 1986.

Associated Press, "Castro Rules Out Further Elections." *The Dallas Morning News*, May 2, 1961.

Associated Press, "Cuba: Embargo's Toll $89 Billion," *The Dallas Morning News*, September 19, 2007.

Weber, David, Mexico City Correspondent, "Castro's Spies Are Thick: Watch What You Say," *The Dallas Morning News*, August 4, 1960.

Chapter Four

Bethell, Leslie. *Cuba, A Short History*. Melbourne, Australia: Cambridge University Press, 1993.

The Sixth Floor Museum at Dealey Plaza, "Unfinished Business: Kennedy & Cuba (Operation Mongoose)," http://www.jfk.org/cuba/mongoose_Plots.htm (accessed November 7, 2000).

Chapter Five

Blazquez, Agustin and Sutton, Jaums, *UMAP: Castro's Genocide Plan*. Silver Spring, Maryland: AB Independent Productions, 1999.

Castro, Fidel. Speech at ceremonies marking fifth anniversary of the CDR at Havana Plaza de La Revolucion, September 29, 1965, Latin America Information Network, Castro Speech Database, University of Texas at Austin.

Clark, Juan, "Religious Repression in Cuba," Florida International University, 1998. http://www.fiu.edu/~fcf/clark12298.html (accessed September 13, 2003).

Eaton, Tracey, "For Cuban Prisoners, 'Hell' Does Exist," *The Dallas Morning News*, June 24, 2003.

Garcia, Maria Cristina. *Havana USA*. Berkeley, California: University of California Press, 1996.

Johnson, Lyndon B, Remarks at the signing of the Immigration Bill, Liberty Island, New York, October 3, 1965, Archives of the Lyndon Baines Johnson Library and Museum, Austin, Texas.

Organization of American States, Inter-American Commission on Human Rights. "The Situation of Human Rights in Cuba: Seventh Report (Right to Religious Freedom and Worship)," October 1983.

Portes, Alejandro, and Stepick, Alex. *City on the Edge: The Transformation of Miami*. Berkeley, California: University of California Press, 1993

U.S. Department of State, Bureau of Democracy, Human Rights and Labor, "International Religious Freedom Report on Cuba." Washington, D.C., 2003.

Chapter Six

Clark, Juan. *Cuba: Exodus, Living Conditions and Human Rights*. Florida International University, 1997. http://www.fiu.edu/~fcf/juanclark.cuba/clark97.humrtscond.html (accessed June 19, 2001).

Chapter Seven

Anton, Alex, and Hernandez, Roger. *Cubans in America*. New York: Kensington Publishing Corp., 2002.

Clark, Juan, "The Cuban Exodus: Background, Evolution and Impact in USA," Union of Cubans in Exile, 1977. http://balaseros.miami.edu/occassionalpapers.htm (accessed June 19, 2001).

Contreras, Joseph, and Evan Thomas, "The Fight for Elian Gonzalez," *Newsweek*, April 17, 2000.

Pedraza, Silvia. *Cuba's Refugees: Manifold Migrations, In Origins and Destinies: Immigration, Race, and Ethnicity in America*. Edited by Silvia Pedraza and Rubén G. Rumbaut Belmont, California: Wadsworth, 1996.

U.S. Census Bureau. *Population Estimates Program*. http://www.census.gov (accessed September 24, 2003).

Valladares, Armando, "A Firsthand Account of Child Abuse, Castro Style," *The Wall Street Journal*, May 5, 2000.

Chapter Eight

Christian Church (Disciples of Christ). "Discover the Disciples." http://www.disciples.org/discover

Church World Service, et al. *Flights In Freedom: A Cuban Refugee Resettlement Program*. Brochure, 1965.

Figueroa, Domingo Rodriguez. *Vivencias Y Memorias De Un Pastor* (Experiences and Memories of a Pastor). self-published, 1998.

George, Paul S., "Miami: One Hundred Years of History, Historical Museum of Southern Florida," *South Florida History Magazine*, Summer 1996.

Metcalfe, Luke, *Online Statistical Encyclopedia*, entry on Brooklyn, New York. http://www.nationmaster.com (accessed September 6, 2004).

Department of Veteran Affairs. *National Center for Post Traumatic Stress Disorder: Fact Sheet on PTSD U.S.* http://www.ncptsd.va.gov (accessed September 5, 2004).

The New York Times. "Online Real Estate Database." http://www.realestate.nytimes.com (accessed September 5, 2004).

Old Farmer's Almanac. *Online Weather History Database*. http://www.almanac.com (accessed February 7, 2007).

Quigg, H.D., "Cuban Refugees Superimpose Culture and Customs," United Press International dispatch from Miami, April 14, 1966.

Sonneborn, Elizabeth. *The Cuban Americans*. Farmington Hills, Michigan: Lucent Books, Inc., 2002.

Thomas, John F., "Cuban Refugees in The United States," *The International Migration Review*, Spring 1967.

Tucker, William E., and McAllister, Lester G. *Journey in Faith: A History of the Christian Church (Disciples of Christ)*. St. Louis: The Bethany Press, 1975.

Chapter Nine

Coffey, Carole, "A Ministry to Millions," *The Disciple*, Christian Board of Publication for Christian Church (Disciples of Christ), May 1985.

F. Feliberto Pereira, "The Church Expanding," *The Disciple*, Christian Board of Publication for Christian Church (Disciples of Christ), April 17, 1983.

Hays, Richard B. *Moral Vision of The New Testament.* New York: HarperOne, 1996.

Hernandez, Edwin I, et al. *Strengthening Hispanic Ministry Across Denominations: A Call to Action*, Duke Divinity School Pulpit & Pew Research Reports and Center for Study of Latino Religion at the University of Notre Dame, 2003.

Office of the State Climatologist, *Texas Climatic Bulletin*, Texas A&M University. http://www.met.tamu.edu/osc/ (accessed October 18, 2007)

Suggs, James C., "Rebirth in San Benito," *World Call*, Christian Board of Publication, Christian Church (Disciples of Christ), June 1973.

U.S. Census Bureau, *Income Statistics for Rio Grande Valley Communities and Texas.* http://www.census.gov (accessed February 27, 2007)

Chapter Ten

Barron, James, "Churches to Offer Sanctuary," *The New York Times*, May 9, 2007.

Catholic News Service, Bishop Fitzpatrick obituary, July 15, 2006.

Chaddock, Gail Russell, "Backstory: The Canteen Man of the U.S.-Mexico Border," *The Christian Science Monitor*, January 22, 2007.

Disciples Home Missions, "Disciples Resettle 30,000th Refugee," *Disciples World*, July 1, 2006.

Eckholm, Erik, "Inside a Jumble of Poverty, Texans Build a Future," *The New York Times*, August 27, 2007.

Garcia, James E., "Thousands Die Crossing River to U.S.," Cox News Service, *Wisconsin State Journal*, May 23, 1993.

Gordon, David F., *Growing Global Migration and Its Implications for the United States*, National Intelligence Council, March 2001. http://www.dmi.gov/nic/PDF_GIF_otherprod/migration.pdf (accessed February 27, 2007).

Patterson, James, "Southwest Good Samaritan Ministries Gives Hope to Many," *Disciple News Service*, February 2006.

Organization of American States, "The Open Society Institute Forced Migration Projects for the Conference on Regional Responses to Forced Migration Emergencies in Central America and the Caribbean," White Paper, 1997.

Tomsho, Robert. *The American Sanctuary Movement*. Austin: Texas Monthly Press, Inc., 1987.

Welch, William M., "Border-Crossing Deaths on Rise," *USA Today*, August 1, 2007.

Robertson, Shari, and Camerini, Michael, *Well-Founded Fear*, The Epidavros Project, Inc., 2004. Film.

Chapter Eleven

Bowden, Charles, "Our Wall," *National Geographic*, May 2007.

Caldern, Sara Ins, "No More Catch and Release," *The Brownsville Herald*, August 25, 2006.

Caldern, Sara Ins, "Life an Orderly Affair at Port Isabel Detention Center," *The Brownsville Herald*, November 27, 2005.

Elizondo, Virgilio P. *The Future is Mestizo: Life Where Cultures Meet.*

Boulder: University Press of Colorado, 2000.

Lazarus, Emma, *New Colussus* tablet, Liberty State Park, Division of Parks and Forestry, New Jersey Department of Environmental Protection. http://www.libertystatepark.com/emma.htm (accessed January 2, 2007).

Mills, Nicolaus, ed., *Arguing Immigration: The Debate Over the Changing Face of America*. New York: Touchstone Books, 1994.

McCullough, John L., "Comprehensive Immigration Reform." Presentation for the Church World Service, May 10, 2007.

Muller, Thomas, *Immigrants and the American City*. New York: New York University Press, 1993.

Priestner, Kevin, "TYLA Partners with ProBAR to Represent Unaccompanied Children," *Texas Bar Journal*, October 2006.

Preston, Julia, "Surge in Immigration Laws Around U.S.," *The New York Times*, August 6, 2007.

Presidential Determination No. 2008-1, Memorandum for the Secretary of State, 2008 Refugee Admissions Numbers. http:www.state.gov/p/af/rls/93213.htm (accessed October 18, 2007).

Pomfret, John, "Despite Security and Dangers, Border Crossers Find Way North," *The Washington Post*, May 18, 2006.

Skerry, Peter, "How Not to Build a Fence," *Foreign Policy*, September/October 2006. http:www.foreignpolicy.cover/story/cms.php?story_id=3557&print=1 (accessed October 18, 2006).

Stein, Barry N., "Refugee Experience: Defining the Parameters of a Field of Study," *International Migration Review*, 1981.

Associated Press, "U.S Seeks to Curb Illegal Immigration," *The New York Times*, August 10, 2006.

U.S. Immigration and Customs Enforcement, Fact Sheets, May 2007.

http://www.ice.gov (accessed August 6, 2007).

Valle, Fernando Del, "Shelter Begins American Dream," *Valley Morning Star*, February 6, 2005.

Valle, Fernando Del, "Federal Detention Center in Willacy County Set to Expand," *Valley Morning Star*, July 25, 2007.

Chapter Twelve

Aizenmen, N.C., "Young Migrants Risk All to Reach U.S." *The Washington Post*, August 28, 2006.

Alcala, Maria Jose, *A Passage to Hope: State of the World Population 2006*. New York: United Nations Population Fund, 2006

Brané, Michelle, "Hutto Settlement a Good First Step; Lack of National Family Standards and Alternatives to Detention Remain a Concern," statement to the press, Women's Commission, August 28, 2007. http://womenscommission.org/newsroom/press_releases/082007/ (accessed September 9, 2007).

Brezosky, Lynn, "Foster Program for Immigrants Criticized," Associated Press, *The Washington Post*, July 21, 2007.

Caparros, Martin, et al. *Moving Young: State of the World Population 2006*. New York: United Nations Population Fund, 2006

Caruavele, Ellen, *2007 World Population Data Sheet*. Washington, D.C.: Population Reference Bureau, 2007.

Council on Foreign Relations, Background Briefing Paper on Shining Path (Sendero Luminoso), November, 2005. http://www.cfr.org/publications/9276 (accessed October 18, 2007)

Dallas Morning News Editorial Staff, "The Labor Equation," *The Dallas Morning News*, September 3, 2007.

Durham, Ron, "Ministry to Immigrants Symbolized by Beanstalk," *San*

Angelo Standard Times, November 23, 1996.

Ewing and Johnson, "Asylum Essentials: The U.S. Program Needs More Resources, Not Restrictions," Immigration Policy Brief, February 2005.

Fears, Darryl, "Policy on Asylum Seekers Faulted," *The Washington Post*, February 10, 2007.

Gamboa, Suzanne, "Panel Pushes to Expedite Asylum Reforms," *The Washington Post*, February 8, 2007.

González, Emilio T., "Message from USCIS Director," *USCIS Monthly*, May 2007.

Hsu, Spencer S, "Backlog at Borders, Cracks in the System," *The Washington Post*, May 14, 2006.

Hsu, Spencer S, and Moreno, Sylvia, "Border Policy's Success Strains Resources," *The Washington Post*, February 2, 2007.

Humans Rights First, Background Briefing Note, *The Detention of Asylum Seekers in the United States: Arbitrary under the ICCPR, 2005*. http://www.humanrightsfirst.org (accessed February 21, 2007).

Johnson, Kirk, "Anxiety in the Land of the Anti-Immigration Crusader," *The New York Times*, June 24, 2007.

Martine, George, *Unleashing the Potential of Urban Growth, State of the World Population 2007*. New York: United Nations Population Fund, 2007

Merheb, Nada, et al. *State of the World's Refugees 2006, United Nations High Commissioner for Refugees*. New York: Oxford University Press, 2006.

Parfit, Michael, "Mexico: Bright with Promise, Tangled in the Past," *National Geographic*, August, 1996

Preston, Julia, "Big Disparities in Judging Asylum Cases," *The New York Times*, May 31, 2007.

Associated Press, "Judge OKs Settlement in Suit Over Immigration Facility," *The Dallas Morning News*, August 31, 2007.

United Nations High Commissioner for Refugees, *Country Operations Plan for Mexico, UNHCR, 2006.*
http://www.unhcr.org/home/PROTECTION/432540332.pdf
(accessed August 21, 2007)

Report on Asylum Seekers in Expedited Removal, Volume II: Expert Reports. United States Commission on International Religious Freedom, 2005.

Wucker, Michele, *Lockout: Why America Keeps Getting Immigration Wrong When Our Prosperity Depends On It.* New York: Perseus Books Group, 2006.

Chapter Thirteen

Finley, James, *Merton's Palace of Nowhere*, rev. ed. Notre Dame, Indiana: Ave Maria Press, 2003.

International Religious Freedom Report-2006, Peru. U.S. Department of State, Washington, D.C., 2006.

National Immigration Project, 2006 Daniel Levy Memorial Award description of Casa de Proyecto Libertad, September 25, 2006.

Simnacher, Joe, "Frank C. Mabee: Christian Church Pastor devoted Life to justice for All," *The Dallas Morning News*, November 16, 2004.

Vera, Richard, "Christians Urged to Fight Social Injustice," *Houston Post*, January 16, 1988.

Yancey, Philip, *Where is God When It Hurts*. Grand Rapids, Michigan: Zondervan, 2002 (anniversary edition)

Epilogue

Boadle, Anthony, "Illegal flow of Cubans to U.S. on the rise," http://www.Reuters.com (accessed October 1, 2007).

Church World Service, press statement on the resettlement of displaced Iraqis, Church World Service, August 20, 2007. http://www.churchworldservice.org/immigration/archives/2007/08/174.htm (accessed August 23, 2007).

Los Angeles Times Editorial Staff, "Shunning Iraq's Refugees," *The Los Angeles Times*, January 19, 2007.

Winik, Lyric Wallwork, "What's Next For Cuba?" *Parade*, September 9, 2007.

Appendices

Bensman, Todd, "Breaching America: The Dangers of Illegal Immigration from Islamic Countries," *San Antonio News Express*, four-part series beginning May 20, 2007.

Jefferys, Kelly, *Refugees and Asylees, Homeland Security: Annual Flow Report.* U.S. Department of Homeland Security. Washington, D.C., May, 2007.

U.S. Committee for Refugees and Immigrants, *World Refugee Survey 2006*, 2007. http://www.refugees.org (accessed April 29, 2007).

U.S. Citizenship and Immigration Services, Office of Citizenship, Welcome to the United States: A Guide for New Immigrants. U.S. Department of Homeland Security. Washington, D.C., 2007.

United Nations High Commissioner for Refugees, *2006 Global Trends Report on Asylum-seekers*. New York: United Nations, 2006.

Acknowledgments

We are indebted to our family, friends, and colleagues for their sustained prayers of support and interest in *I Was a Stranger.*

From Feliberto:

I am forever indebted to my fellow Americans—and Presidents Lyndon Baines Johnson and Richard M. Nixon and the U.S. Congress—who inaugurated the series of daily flights between Cuba and Miami to rescue those of us oppressed and persecuted by Fidel Castro.

To my fellow Christians who suffered persecution under Castro, I dedicate this book to you.

To the thousands of volunteers who have supported Southwest Good Samaritan Ministries, thank you from the bottom of my heart.

To my children and to Mica, thank you for your love and support.

To Sara and Harold Edwards of Whitney, Texas, I owe a deep debt of gratitude for their love and support. Sara also brought Chris Kelley into my life.

Finally, to my father, mother, brother, and family in Cuba, I love you, and I know we will share eternity together.

I welcome your prayers. Feel free to contact me at:
Southwest Good Samaritan Ministries
P.O. Box 273
Los Fresnos, Texas 78566

From Chris Kelley:

Words don't adequately capture my gratitude to the dozens of family members, friends, and colleagues who have supported Feliberto and me, as we worked together to tell his story.

I am particularly grateful to my colleagues at *The Dallas Morning News* and A.H. Belo and Belo for their friendship and support for twenty-seven years. I shall always be part of the team. My colleagues from the Associated Press Managing Editors remain a source of inspiration.

To Doug and Mary Lynn Skinner and my extended family at Northway Christian Church, notably my Crossroads Sunday School class. I am forever grateful.

No undertaking like a book is done without the support of a personal village. To my Lake Highlands family and friends, Kelley Group clients, Levenson & Hill and Levenson & Brinker clan, Nancy Barry, and others too numerous to name here (you know who you are!), thanks for all your support.

I am indebted to Feliberto's family, his "army" of staff and volunteers—Raquel Garcia, Larry Cox, Les and Connie Hodson, Danny Cruz, Caroline Herbert, and the more than thirty others who consented to interviews over many years. I am particularly grateful to Jennifer Riggs, director of the Refugee and Immigration Ministry of the Christian Church (Disciples of Christ), who provided extremely helpful information and research on the plight of the world's refugees. Frank Mabee and Hank Slaight, who both died during the preparation of the book, were enormous sources of information and inspiration.

Because the first language of Feliberto's story is in Spanish, I owe a real debt to those who helped me with key translations: Elaine Kellam, who generously jump-started my research by seeing to it that two of Feliberto's sermons from *La Hora Cristiana* were transcribed into English; Valerie B. Maldonado, a professional transcriber; Richard Jones, a friend who is bilingual; and friend and bilingual brother Judd Austin Jr., a Dallas lawyer raised in Mexico City, who along with his wife, Kathy, gave generously of their time.

Richard, Jack Arrington, Paula Hughes, Sheila Martinez, Stephen Reeves, and Doug Skinner offered many helpful comments on the final draft of the book. My long-time friend and gifted colleague, Bruce Tomaso, edited the book and improved it greatly. Another long-time colleague, Juan Garcia, provided much of the photography for the book, and we had a wonderful time together collecting the shots. Thank you is inadequate.

I shall always be grateful to friends Ken and Bev Hawari, Alan Frol, and Mary and Raymond Anderson for their support.

Finally, this book would not have happened without the love and support of my family: Mike and Lynn Betka, my nephew Jason Cox, and my other Arizona- and Kansas-based relatives, and my brother- and sister-in law from New Mexico, Carter and Michele Edwards and their kids, nephew Pearce and niece Annie.

My son, Curran, and daughter, Siobhan, sacrificed countless hours of dad time while I pursued this book when not at the office.

Both kids let me read early chapters to them and provided valuable feedback. I can't imagine a father more blessed than I.

Although my parents are no longer living, I am privileged beyond measure with Sheryl's parents, Harold and Sara Edwards, whom I call my own. Harold may well be my biggest fan. Sara first introduced me to Feliberto. This book would not have been possible without her vision, love, and support. From the bottom of my heart, I thank her.

Next to my decision in March of 1973 to personally know God, the best day of my life was the day Sheryl Edwards said yes when I asked her in 1987 to become my wife. She is the source of my earthly inspiration and being.

About the Authors

Feliberto Pereira is pastor of Ebenezer Christian Church (Disciples of Christ) and executive director of Southwest Good Samaritan Ministries, both of Los Fresnos, Texas. Founded in 1985 to assist asylum seekers from Central America and elsewhere, the organization has helped thousands of asylum seekers request refugee status from the U.S. government. Pereira became a U.S. citizen on July 4, 1984. Learn more at www.swgsm.org .

In his twenty-seven-year career at *The Dallas Morning News*, Chris Kelley won many national reporting awards—among them the 1996 Sidney Hillman Foundation Award for social justice reporting. Former long-time editor of DallasNews.com, Web site of *The Dallas Morning News*, Kelley and his colleagues received more than twenty regional and national interactive journalism awards. He lives in Dallas with his wife and two children.

Learn more at www.iwasastranger.org.